ROUGH STUFF CYCLING
in the Alps

Compiled by Fred Wright

CONTENTS

Cycling and walking have several advantages over motorised methods of getting around the Alps; they are quiet and non-polluting and they let you go at your own speed, stop where you like and get to more parts of the region. Each has its own advantages. The walker (including the rock-climber) can get to some places with less difficulty than the cyclist, but because of his (this word, as usual, covers both sexes) slowness he is restricted in the ground he can cover. The cyclist, setting out from an airport or railway station, can cover a large area of the Alps, but in doing so he will sometimes find himself on unpleasantly busy roads.

The aim of this guide is to narrow the gap between the cyclist and the walker, and to show the former how he can enjoy some of the benefits he may have thought to be available only to the latter – access to remote areas, peace and solitude. A cyclist will often look at a map, see a road running up into the mountains and ending there, and say to himself, 'If I go up there, it's a long climb and I shall have to turn round and come back, and end up where I started; so what's the point?' This guide will show him that often he need not be discouraged like this, and that with the right equipment (see Appendix II) and a variable amount of effort he can go up the valley and over into another valley, then get back on his bike and go on his way.

This, the second edition of the guide (see publisher's note, below), includes several new reports and updates. It is mainly addressed to cycle-tourists doing tours of, say, two weeks or more, but it may be found useful for day trips on certain routes. There is, it is hoped, something for all tastes, from the very easy (Montbovon–Aigle **G08**: a few km on a path along the edge of a lake) to the very difficult (Col Collon **E49**: glaciers and a ladder).

Each route in the guide has a three-digit number of the form **A12**. Routes which are thought likely to be more popular have been described fairly fully, others are listed in their proper place with only a short description.

This edition contains some photos. One or two of these, showing a loaded bike or its rider, are included to make it clear that the routes in the guide, even those marked **VS** (very severe), can be, or at least have been, done with a quite heavy load.

Publisher's note: Rough Stuff Cycling in the Alps as published by Fred Wright incorporated material from six Alpine rough stuff guides created by Mr E. D. 'Clem' Clements which were privately circulated in the late 1980s and early 1990s. Fred refers to his Ibex Press edition as the 'second', but it was the first that was publicly available.

As in the first edition, an attempt has been made to indicate the difficulty of a route by assigning to it a letter, as follows:

E   Easy. Typically, a route which is largely or wholly feasible for jeeps or such vehicles, but also some easy and not-too-steep paths

M   Moderate. Some hard work, possibly occasional lifting

D   Difficult. Often hard work, some carrying

S   Severe. Much carrying, some double carrying (bike, then luggage)

VS   Very severe – like severe but more so

As in the first edition, again, an attempt has been made to show the scenic quality and interest of a route by giving it from one to five + signs. This ranking, like that of the difficulty, is at best approximate and subjective, and it is not expected that everyone will agree with it.

To show that Alpine rough stuff is not only for the young and athletic, and to encourage readers to have a go, the grade of difficulty assigned to a route is sometimes followed by a number in brackets, which represents the age of the oldest cyclist who is known to have done that route. Thus D (55) means that the route is graded Difficult but at least one cyclist aged 55 is known to have done it.

It has been thought useful, as in the first edition, to give a rough idea of the time necessary to do a route, but again this is a subjective and approximate matter. The time you take will depend on such things as your age, whether you have a mountain bike or a touring bike, and how much luggage you have. Times given in the guide do not include time for stops. They are often based on very little experience.

In giving directions, the right/left bank of a river, or side of a valley, is right/left looking downstream.

In the sketch maps, a double line indicates a surfaced road, a thick black line indicates a rough-stuff route.

Beginners are advised to look at Appendices I and II before planning a tour.

Fred Wright
September 2001

Whether we called it that or not at the time, 'rough stuff' is an aspect of cycling that many of us will have experienced: carrying early ATBs both up and down hills in the '80s, or those interesting days out when the road turns into a track and you continue regardless… that's rough stuff. If your bikes and your reasons for riding have always been about exploring, then rough stuff is often a fair result. Even if that means being forced to – or willingly – walking some of the tricky sections.

My interest in wide-ranging bikes and seeking out varied riding terrain led me to ride longer distances, touring and then bikepacking. With that came an increasing appreciation of those who had gone before me – the Rough Stuff Fellowship, the Crane cousins, the Cyclos Montagnards, the Moe brothers, and so on – who had explored, or looked to go further, on varied terrain for the challenge and the sake of the journey. It's easier to relate to them than a Grand Tour winner, and their achievements are more valued in many ways.

In among these riders and their rides was Fred Wright's book of routes in the Alps. It featured both areas I knew well and areas I wanted to know better, and I found Fred's attitude to riding inspiring. He also had a refreshing approach: his self-published books were available only by cheque, his maps were drawn by hand and his descriptions typed out. Surely, this care and attention must be a better quality filter than anything created simply by hitting the upload button! A friend, Paul Errington, owed me a miscellaneous tenner so he ordered two copies, to save sending separate cheques and it arrived with a hand-written note from Fred. Cross-referencing Fred's book with inked IGN maps from past tours, and with a 3D relief map on my wall and Google Earth, became a rainy-day pastime. (Any of my reservations about global monopolies and the march of technology can be shot down by my love of Google Earth.) I built a dot-to-dot puzzle: yellow pins in a Google Earth map, that resulted in a week or more's riding. In a similar vein as those ongoing 'to-be-perfected' local riding loops, the perfect solution could only be found by testing early drafts. In 2015, another friend, Andy Purkis, and I explored a number of these high routes between Turin and Nice, carrying our bikes in Fred's footsteps and finding our own links between tracks and cols in the Alps. That ride evolved into the Torino-Nice Rally event, which has helped many others to experience the results of the various route-finding processes that both Fred and I have enjoyed so much.

Fred's explorations years ago would no doubt have been assisted by the information we have now at our fingertips and on our screens, but his timeless attitude to exploring won't be surpassed by technology. To truly follow Fred and other contributors to his book, one must accept leaving something to the unknown. In doing that, little has changed over the decades – over the century, perhaps – that rough stuff touring has been practised.

Perhaps that, right there, is the challenge to us all. New technology, information and mapping are valued, but maybe our challenge is to use these resources well – sparingly but sufficiently – so that we do not forget that much of the value of the experience is found in the unknowns: in discovery rather than in the certainty of the outcome.

For that experience in cycling, Fred's book is just the ticket.

James Olsen, @torinonicerally
May 2018

HOW TO USE THIS GUIDE IN THE 21ST CENTURY
A PUBLISHER'S NOTE ON THE SECOND EDITION

The oldest of the rides in this book date back to the mid 1950s, and a lot has happened since then. A lot has happened even since 2002, when Fred Wright's guide was first published – GPS and Google being the most startling – but equally a lot of things have remained the same.

We'll deal with both here. But first the things that Fred and other pioneers would have recognised, which are constant from one generation to the next: the mountains and the hazards therein. In the high peaks even in high summer the weather can turn without warning; and roads, tracks and trails that one year were passable may the next year be covered by avalanche or rockfall (equally, those that had been obliterated may be cleared). We would never advocate anyone heading out into the mountains unprepared. Rough-stuff riding by definition takes you to the more remote and isolated corners of the Alps – that is its appeal – and this demands more from the rider. Know where you are going, and not only via a line on a screen, so that if a storm blows clouds in, or your devices die, you won't be stuck. Know where the towns and villages are, and the refuges and mountain restaurants. Know you have tools and food, and enough water and clothes if it gets boiling hot or starts to snow, and always know your Plan B. Use common sense and stay safe.

That may seem elementary to many, but it is worth restating and it would be irresponsible not to do so here. A guidebook is no substitute for good planning, and this reissued guide is intended to be a springboard, the first step on an adventure whose next step is plenty more research.

Which brings us to the changes in technology: since Fred's day there has been a proliferation of information about mountain routes. Once you have some route ideas in mind, take advantage of all of them. Streetview can show you where you might leave the road; Google Earth will give clues to paths up valleys; hiking forum discussions might give you some ideas of the state of the trail, French mountain bikers an idea of whether you'll make it without pushing and German overland motorbike videos on YouTube an incredible preview of what you might see. Use all of them, and then you'll be as confident as you can be, when you've annotated your maps, written your route notes and created your GPX, that you'll succeed.

There are a few more things to say. Fred's route designations need a little explaining. The first part is simple: the letter denotes the area and the relevant map, but the numbers are chosen simply so there is room to add more routes to the maps. For example, where **F04** is the Fenêtre de Champorcher in the Val d'Aosta and **R30** is the Passo Tognola in the Dolomites, the **04** and the **30** are more or less arbitrary – but they mean that our additions to the new edition (there are around 20 new routes) can fit in without having to renumber everything else. Thus, the new Col de Sollières **C06** route squeezes between the Col du Petit Mont Cenis **C04** and Mont Malamot **C08** without disturbing anything.

Anything we have added to existing route descriptions is in italics.

There is more to say about paper maps, too: Fred painstakingly listed many different companies' maps covering the Alps at a useful scale. Many of these editions have changed, or are no longer available. We have retained the references – for people who own the old maps or want to buy them second hand – while also trying to indicate what is currently on the shelves. Please see Appendix III for more information.

Finally, a note on languages. Mostly we have kept col names in the native language, and they have been cross-referenced to maps (paper and Google) to check they are in the most comprehensible form. Where cols hit the border and the two sides' names differ significantly both are sometimes given: thus Timmelsjoch/Passo del Rombo; Col de Larche/Colle della Maddalena etc. In Switzerland and the Südtirol in particular, where several languages are used, life is a little more difficult and readers should exercise caution. The original guide is not always consistent when naming towns – Brunico and Bruneck are both used, for example – and passes, are sometimes given in their English form: Simplon Pass rather than Simplonpass, and Great St Bernard rather than Grand St Bernard or Gran San Bernardo. And huts (German: *Hütte*) and valleys (*Tal*) appear several ways: Martal Tal and Zillertal and Inn Valley; Braunschweiger Hütte, Hagelhütte and Anhalter hut. Since it seemed difficult to choose a universally clearer and more consistent way of naming them, where it has not impeded comprehension they have been left.

Happy adventuring!

ABBREVIATIONS

1:100K, ETC.	1:100,000, ETC.
N, S, ETC.	points of the compass
+, ++, +++, ++++, +++++	scenic quality and interest
CC	*Cycloclimbing* (magazine of the U.K. section of the Ordre des Cols Durs)
D&R	Didier & Richard
E, M, D, S, VS	grades of difficulty, sometimes followed by numbers in brackets (see Introduction) (E may mean East in another context)
F&B	map by Freytag & Berndt (1:50,000 series)
GR	Grande Randonnée
IGC	Istituto Geografico Centrale, Turin
IGN	Institut Géographique National, Paris
KM	kilometre
L, R	left, right
LK	Landeskarten der Schweiz
M	metre
M C7, ETC.	Michelin map NO. 926 (Austria, 1:400,000)
M216, ETC.	Michelin map NO. 216 (1:200,000 SERIES)
MAIR	map by Mair (1:200,000 SERIES)
ÖK	Österreichische Karten
r/s	roughstuff
RSJ	*Rough-Stuff Journal* (journal of the Rough-Stuff Fellowship)
TCI	Touring Club Italiano

ACKNOWLEDGEMENTS

FIRST EDITION. IBEX PRESS. 2002

This guide has been compiled from reports by many cyclists, many but not all of them members of the Rough-Stuff Fellowship or the UK section of the Ordre des Cols Durs, whose names are sometimes given under the appropriate route. The subject is not exhausted, and conditions are always changing; therefore new reports (if possible with exact dates), suggestions, corrections, and updates will always be welcomed, as will photographs (originals will be returned to owners).

One book, in particular, has been the inspiration for many of the descriptions in the guide, and it contains many routes, easy by our standards (rough roads, not footpaths), which do not yet appear in the guide. This is Eduard Denzel, *Grosser Alpenstrassenführer* (Denzel-Verlag, Innsbruck). Mr Walther G. Stoll of Basel, Switzerland, has supplied literature on several Swiss passes. The sketch map of the Val d'Aosta (map E) is due to Mr Ivor Robards. Appendix III (maps), all the map references and many suggestions based on the maps are due to Mr E. D. Clements. The photograph of the Parpaillon was provided by Mrs E. Wagstaff; that of the Pas de Chèvres ladder by the late Signor Antonio Gasparini of Agno, Switzerland, and the others by Mr F. Wright.

Other sources of information are mentioned at the appropriate places. The staff of Ashford Library have provided valuable help with the word processing.

SECOND EDITION. ISOLA PRESS. 2018

Our biggest thanks must of course go to Fred Wright, the indefatigable explorer and compiler of the Ibex Press first edition. Without his years of hard work – and his giving permission to reprint – the information on the journeys recorded here would neither have been first set down nor now made available to a new audience.

Thanks also to Rod Dalitz of the Ordre des Cols Durs for the files, and to John Haigh for helping Fred with several inquiries. Also instrumental in the making of this book were James Olsen, organiser of the Torino-Nice Rally and Stefan Amato of Pannier.cc. Without James we would not have had our original hard copy to work from, nor an email address for Fred; without Stefan, no enthusiastic early backing or amazing illustration.

To Will Davies (Cycling-challenge.com), Chris White, Ludwig Brunagel and Igor Tavella, thank you for the routes added herein.

Thanks to the staff of Stanfords book shop in Covent Garden, London, for their patience and help in checking maps.

Finally, our thanks must also go to every single backer of our Kickstarter: it is their support that has made this re-edition possible.

BIBLIOGRAPHY AND WEBSITES

Denzel's book has already been mentioned on p.10, and www.amazon.de gives some titles:

Geser, Rudolf — *Die schönsten Alpentouren mit dem Mountainbike* (40 routes, which seem to be all or mostly rough roads, not footpaths).

Stanciu, Ulrich — *Traumtouren Transalp: die schönsten Alpenüberquerungen mit dem Mountainbike* (the emphasis seems to be on day trips).

Hammerle, Claudia — *171 Mountainbiketouren Nord- und Osttirol* (some mountain bike tours in the Tyrol).

As for websites, here are some starting points; the reader can make use of links to other sites where they are offered.

AUSTRIA:
www.abacho.at, then type 'Mountainbike Touren'.

FRANCE:
www.centcols.org, the site of the Club des Cent Cols – the section 'libre service' contains some route descriptions (the club also publishes guides in book form called TOPOs, which contain descriptions, with detailed route maps, of numerous French routes); also www.vtt.org.

ITALY:
www.arianna.it, then type 'mountainbike'.

SWITZERLAND:
www.swissgeo.ch (thanks to Mr Jerry Nilson for this one) publishes online maps of any part of Switzerland you choose, at any scale you want (within the scales provided by Landeskarten der Schweiz). Another good site is www.trail.ch. Or try www.search.ch, then type 'Mountainbike Touren'.

UK
The site of the Ordre des Cols Durs is www.ocd.org.uk [*note: now subsumed into the Audax UK site, www.aukweb.net/ocd*]; that of the Rough-Stuff Fellowship is www.rsf.org.uk.

OTHER:
www.dcf.dk is a Danish site. The Trento Bike Pages at www.trentobike.org contain a list of (mostly European) countries, with a section 'trail descriptions' for each, which is about off-road routes.

If any reader knows of a particularly good book or site not included above, we shall be grateful for news of it and shall acknowledge the help if we list it here.

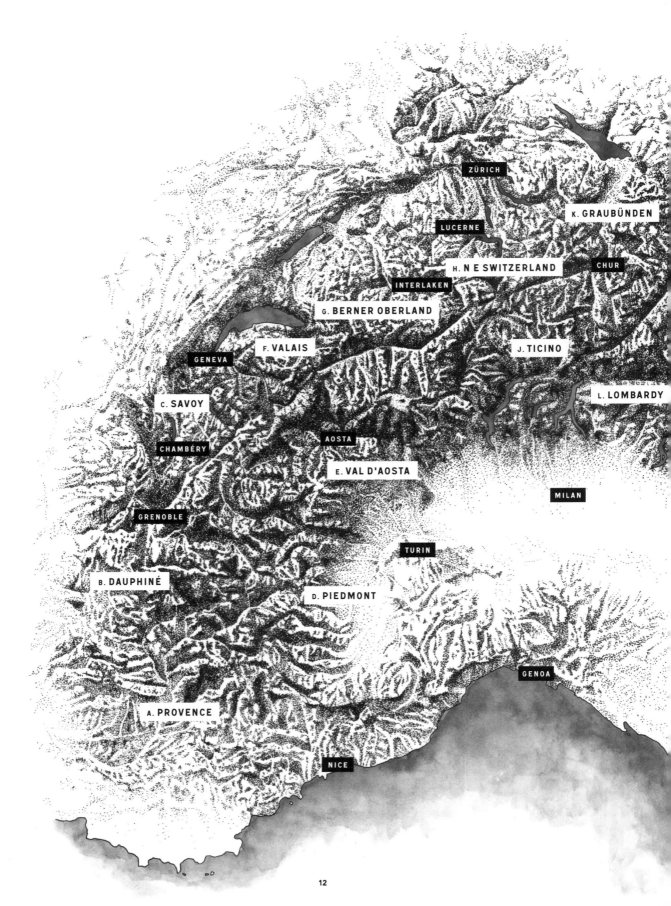

ZÜRICH

K. GRAUBÜNDEN

LUCERNE

H. N E SWITZERLAND

CHUR

INTERLAKEN

G. BERNER OBERLAND

F. VALAIS

J. TICINO

GENEVA

L. LOMBARDY

C. SAVOY

AOSTA

CHAMBÉRY

E. VAL D'AOSTA

MILAN

GRENOBLE

TURIN

B. DAUPHINÉ

D. PIEDMONT

GENOA

A. PROVENCE

NICE

MUNICH

VIENNA

SALZBURG

P. SALZBURGERLAND

INNSBRUCK

M. TIROL

N. ALTO ADIGE

Q. OSTTIROL

KLAGENFURT

R. DOLOMITES

BOLZANO

LJUBLJANA

TRENTO

TRIESTE

VENICE

VERONA

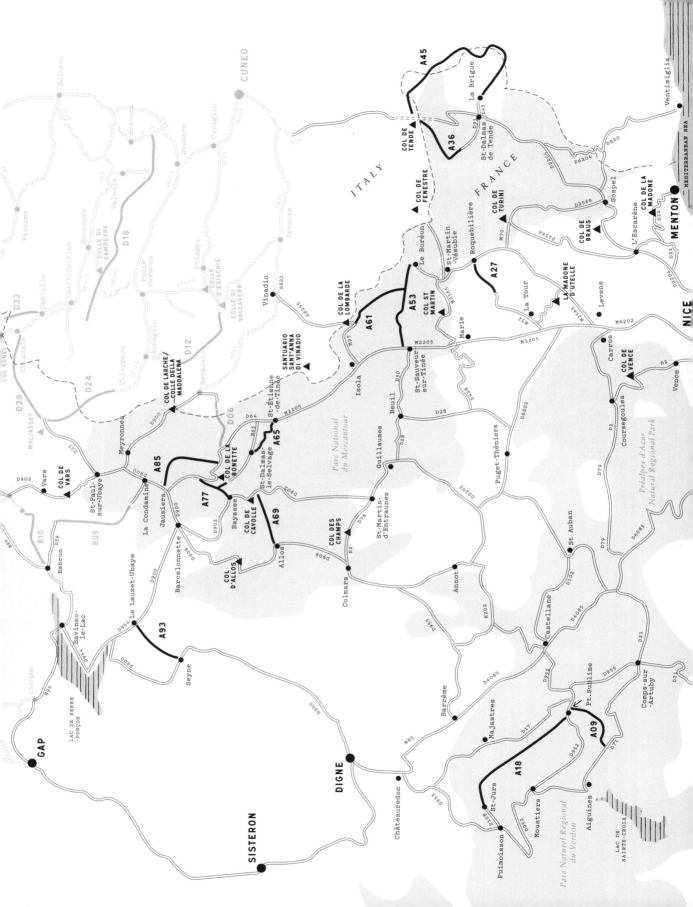

A. PROVENCE

This is perhaps the sunniest and driest part of the Alps. For restrictions on taking bikes into the Parc National du Mercantour, see Appendix II. This applies to **A53**, **A61**, **A69**, **A77** and **A85**.

A09   GRAND CANYON DU VERDON   S ++

M527 or M334; IGN 1:100K map 61 & 1:25K map 3442 west sheet (M245 folds 35 & 34 or M81 fold 17)

From the Belvédère Couloir Samson (apparently on the L (E) bank, just S of Point Sublime at the upper end of the gorge) to La Maline (on the L bank, about 10 km from the Lac de Ste Croix). There is some doubt about the start – Michelin shows the path going through a tunnel on the R (W) side of the gorge, the D&R 1:50K map shows the path switching to the L (E) side here. Mainly level walking along a steep hillside, with a few awkward places, including crossing a scree slope and negotiating about 40m of rung ladders.

A18   COL DE ST JURS   1318M
                                  E? +

M527 or M334; IGN 1:100K map 165 & 1:25K map 3442 west sheet (M245 folds 35 & 34 or M81 fold 17; IGN 1:100K map 61)

From St-Jurs (6km N of Moustiers, just N of the Lac de Ste Croix) to the D952 near Point Sublime (at E end of Canyon du Verdon). Shown as a road over the col, soon becoming a rough road down to Les Louches (note to fork L just before col, because rough road to R is a dead end). There is also a rough road (**D17**) from Majastres, linking up to this road, with a high point of about 1400m at its junction with the rough road up Chiran (1905m).

A27   COL D'ANDRION   1681M
                                  E +

M527 or M341; IGN 1:100K map 165 & 1:25K map 3741 west sheet (M245 fold 25 or M84 fold 19; IGN 1:100K map 61 fold 8C)

The W side, starting in the Tinée valley 4 km N of where the Tinée joins the Var, is a surfaced road, quiet with pleasant views, to Granges de la Brasque (1687m) (road summit at 1750m). This is [or was] a children's summer camp, but out of season, at least, there are no signs of food or accommodation. The E side, down to Roquebillière in the Vésubie valley, is unsurfaced but easily ridden in reasonable conditions.

(J. Haigh, 1989, written up in CC 50, 1989, p. 13)

A36   BAISSE DE PEYREFIQUE   2028M
                                        E ++++

M527 or M341; IGN 1:100K map 165 & 1:25k map 3841 west sheet; IGC 1:50k map 8 (M245 fold 26 or M84 fold 10, inset; IGN 1:100k map 61 fold 10b)

From St-Dalmas-de-Tende, in the Roya valley, to the Col de Tende. The route starts with a surfaced road up the Minière valley, which has a collection of prehistoric carvings on the rocks and a wealth of superb wild flowers. Once on the r/s it takes about 3 hours to get to the summit. Bear R round head of main valley at 1750m. Views are superb.

A45   LA BRIGUE TO COL DE TENDE   E   +++

M527 or M341; IGN 1:100K map 165 & 1:25K map 3841 west sheet; IGC 1:50K map 8 (M245 fold 26; IGN 1:100K map 61 fold 11B)

From La Brigue, just E of St-Dalmas-de-Tende, to the Col de Tende, at least 55km rough road. There is not much running water, because you are mostly high up on a ridge; therefore several water bottles are recommended. From La Brigue you can go either to Val-del-Prat or to Notre-Dame-des-Fontaines; the latter is probably preferable. There is a rough road which becomes tarmac for the last kilometre before the Col Linaire, 1430m. From here take the road (rough) marked 'Baisse de Sanson, frontière, 4 km'. The road is rough from here on, rideable only in short stretches. From the Baisse de Sanson, 1694m, the surface is better and the road is level or gently downhill for perhaps 1 km. Fork L at a rough track which after a short climb reaches the top of the ridge, then descends to the Pas de Collardente, 1599m. Then the road climbs again and comes above the trees. The next pass is the Pas du Tanarel, 2045m, after which the road, now on the Italian side of the ridge, descends gently for about 3 km. After a short stretch of concrete the road continues, fairly level, for about 10 km, and then climbs to the Col de la Vieille Celle, 2099m. The climb continues to a height of a bit over 2200m; then there is a descent to the Col des Seigneurs, 2111m, from which a track leads down into Italy. The road, still above the trees and now among rocks, recrosses into France. There is a pass (called, according to Denzel, the Colle Malaberghe) about 4 km before the next pass, the Col de la Boaïre, 2102m, which is 10 km from the Col de Tende. From the Col de la Boaïre the road climbs to about 2200m and then is level for a short way before dropping steeply in zigzags to pass a station for a ski lift. Another climb, level stretch and descent bring you to the Col de Tende, 1871m.

This route is probably ideally suited to mountain bikes. Otherwise, assuming that for much of the way you can't ride, allow 12 hours.

(F. Wright, 17.7.86)

Much of the high ridge road is now also known as the **VIA DEL SALE**. *A good hostel, the Rifugio Don Barbera, is at the Col des Seigneurs.*

(M. Leonard, 9.8.2017)

A53 COL DE SALÈSE   2031M

W SIDE M, E SIDE E ++

M527 or M341; IGN 1:100K map 165 & 1:25K map 3641 east sheet (M245 folds 24 & 25 or M81 fold 10; IGN 1:100K map 61 fold 8B)

From the Tinée valley, 4km N of St-Sauveur-sur-Tinée, to Le Boréon. See the remark at the beginning of this section. The village of Mollières, destroyed during the Second World War and almost abandoned since then, and with no shops, has no downhill link with the Tinée valley except by a rough path, up which it is possible but not always easy to push the bike. The only road from the village goes over the Col de Salèse; it is rough and unrideable (uphill), till it meets tarmac about 3km before Le Boréon.

(F. Wright, 15.7.86)

Our understanding is that the track from Le Boréon to the Col de Salèse, and all the way up to Mollières is permitted, but not the path into the Tinée (even pushing a bike). Information found at: bit.ly/MercantourBike.

(M. Leonard and J. Olsen, correspondence, 2016)

A61 COL MERCIÈRE   2342M

E ++

M527 or M341; IGN 1:100K map 165 & 1:25K map 3641 east sheet (M245 folds 24 & 25 or M81 fold 10; IGN 1:100K map 61 folds 7 and 8B)

From the Col de Salèse A53 to the Col de la Lombarde. See the remark at the beginning of this section. Mostly old and very rough military roads. Long, but not difficult.

Our understanding is that this track is permitted. Information found at: bit.ly/MercantourBike.

(M. Leonard and J. Olsen, correspondence, 2016)

A65 COL D'ANELLE   1739M

E ++

M527 or M341; IGN 1:100K map 165; 1:25K map 3639; IGC 1:50K map 7

From St-Étienne-de-Tinée to St-Dalmas-le-Selvage, at least 8km r/s. Take the road behind College Jean Franco in St-Étienne, which quickly turns into an easy 4×4 track and climbs steeply (double digits) through chalets and cabins for around 6km. After a flatter 2km the Col d'Anelle is reached; from there, an easy descent 3km to St-Dalmas, where the track rejoins tarmac via the bridge across the Torrent de Jalorgues, under the church. Probably better views taken in reverse.

(M. Leonard, 29.9.17)

A69 COL DE LA PETITE CAYOLLE   2639M

W SIDE M, E SIDE D +++

M527 or M341; IGN 1:100K 165 & 1:25K map 3540 west sheet fold 3F (M245 fold 23 top, or M81 fold 8; IGN 1:100K map 61 folds 4A and B)

From the Col de la Cayolle (16 km SE of Barcelonnette) to the Lac d'Allos and Allos, 6km r/s. In June 1995 there

were notices on the W side saying bikes were banned in the Parc National du Mercantour (see Appendix II). The same report mentions a lot of snow on the path. It is easier and safer to do the route from E to W. The path starts on a bend just N of the refuge (not, as on IGN map, from above the next stream). A narrow firm path, easy, across scree slopes. The last part to the col looks impossible from below, but is fairly easy uphill – downhill would need considerable care with a bike and could be risky. The W side is easier; some bits are just rideable downhill. Well signposted. Good views on both sides.

A road begins just below the natural dam of the lake, which, with no apparent outlet, is worth visiting even though it is slightly longer this way. Steep narrow surfaced road from Lac d'Allos to Allos.

Allow 1½–2 hours up, 1–1½ down to Lac d'Allos.

(J. Haigh, July 1987; F. Cooke and S. Simpson, 19.6.95)

Our understanding is that bicycles are no longer permitted on this route, even when being pushed. Information found at: bit.ly/MercantourBike.

(M. Leonard and J. Olsen, correspondence, 2016)

A77 COL DE LA MOUTIÈRE   2454M

E ++

M527 or M341; IGN 1:100K map 165 & 1:25K map 3639 west sheet fold 1E; IGC 1:50K map 7 (M245 folds 10 & 23 or M81 fold 9; IGN 1:100K map 61 fold 5A)

From St-Dalmas-le-Selvage (6 km NW of St-Étienne-de-Tinée) to Bayasse (6 km N of the Col de la Cayolle) or Bonette road. A metalled road from St Dalmas to the col and just beyond, to its junction with the D9, which is a rough road from Bayasse to the Bonette road.

Since the track linking Bayasse, Moutière and the Bonette is a recognised part of the road network it is permitted for motor vehicles (in practice, 4×4s) and bicycles, and rideable with difficulty.

(M. Leonard, 10.9.17)

A85 COL DE RASPAILLON   2513M

D ++

M527 or M341; IGN 1:100K map 165 & 1:25K map 3639 west sheet fold 1D; IGC 1:50K map 7 (M245 fold 10 bottom or M81 fold 9; IGN 1:100K map 61 fold 5A)

The col is about 2½ km from the highest point of the main road over the Col de la Bonette (Jausiers to Nice), on the Nice side, and the route leads N to Jausiers. Michelin calls this the Col des Granges Communes, the 1:50K map calls it the Col de Raspaillon, with a valley to the N called the Vallon des Granges Communes, and the 1:25K map mentions two cols. See the remark at the beginning of this section. From the col a path, steep at first, descends due N, eventually becoming a rough road down the Vallon des Sagnes.

Our understanding is that bicycles are no longer permitted on this route between the Raspaillon and the Lac des Sagnes, even when being pushed. Information found at: bit. ly/MercantourBike.

A93   COL BAS   2113M
                                           M (51) +

M527 or M341; IGN 1:100K map 165 & 1:25K on two maps
(M245 folds 8 & 9 or M81 fold 7; IGN 1:100K map 61 fold 2A)

From Seyne-les-Alpes (16km SE of the dam at the Lac de Serre-Ponçon) to Le Lauzet-Ubaye, near where the Ubaye runs into the lake. There is a tarmac road to the village of St-Pons. Turn L just before the village, then, after a hamlet, fork R (marked 'Maison forestière de Bellevue'). The tarmac ends about 5km before the pass, and there is a stony track which ends at the top (a grassy, almost level, saddle, about 1km long). The path is indistinct here. At the far end of the saddle, there are two small reed-filled lakes; keep to their L, and to the L of a third small lake just below. The path is then indistinct again (bear L down the hillside). After a bit you come to a fourth small lake (keep to its R), and then you see a couple of buildings below, known locally as 'La Cabane'. Make for these. The path is then clear, through a wood; it is easy at first, later steep, zigzagging and stony. About 1½ km from La Cabane you reach a rough forest road. Go L here, and follow the road for about 5 km. Towards the end ignore a road leading L, downhill, marked 'Route forestière– Le Muretier'. Tarmac recommences just before the hamlet of Le Seuil.

Allow 5 hours for the stretch between tarmac.

(F. Wright, 12.7.86)

B. DAUPHINÉ

B05 COL DE PARPAILLON 2643M
E +++

M523 or M334; IGN 1:100K map 158 & 1:25K map 3538 east sheet fold 2B (M245 folds 9 & 10, M81 fold 8 top; IGN 1:100K map 54 fold 8D)

From La Condamine in the Ubaye valley, just N of Jausiers, to Crévoux, 10km E of Embrun in Durance valley. A tarmac road, in poor state of repair, pretty steep, zigzags up the hillside high above the stream, to a cluster of new chalets just before the Chapelle de Sainte Anne. Here the surface deteriorates a lot, but is still just rideable. The road goes along the S side of the valley, through a forest. After the forest the track is very rough, but rideable. Height 2643m inscribed on tunnel entrance.

The tunnel is furnished at each end with a large metal door. These doors are only open during the summer season, approximately 1 July–15 October. If you find the doors shut, there is a path over the top, and even if the tunnel is open the 20-minute walk up to the top can be recommended for the fine view.

There are a few shallow puddles and large potholes in the tunnel, which is 450m long and straight. (Other reports mention longer stretches under water.) The track is rideable downhill on the N side, slowly. After 1½ hours downhill tarmac is reached.

F. Wright, 29. 7. 85, and others)

B10 COL DE VALBELLE 2381M
E ++

M523 or M334; IGN 1:100K map 158 & 1:25K map 3537 east sheet fold 2J (M245 fold 9 or M77 fold 18; IGN 1:100K map 54 fold 8C)

From Guillestre to Embrun. A road throughout, metalled below about 1800m and mostly rideable above this. Just above the resort of Risoul 1850, turn L at the first junction, and at the second, soon afterwards, R. Approaching the top of the ridge, you see a road leading off to the R to a TV mast; do not take this but keep to the L, still climbing. The Col de la Coche (1791m) is met on the way down; from this col a metalled road starts down in a NE-ly direction, and a rough road goes down to the W.

There are plentiful other gravel cols in the Risoul/Vars ski area. It is equally possible to link Risoul with Le Claux, about 2km from the top of the paved Col de Vars. Climbing this way from Risoul you pass the Col de Chérine (2270m), Col de Valbelle, Col du Vallon (2466m) and Col des Saluces (2444m). The ski-area 4×4 service tracks are easily passable, if a little muddy with snowmelt in early June.

(M. Leonard, 7.6.17)

B15 COL DE FROMAGE 2301M
N SIDE E. S SIDE M ++

M523 or M334; IGN 1:100K map 158 & 1:25K map 3537 east sheet

fold 4F; IGC 1:50K map 6 (M244 fold 43 bottom or M77 fold 19; IGN 1:100K map 54 fold 9C)

From Château-Queyras (NE of Guillestre) S to Ceillac. A rough road, not shown on the 1:100K map, leaves the road to the Sommet Bucher at the 2000m contour (hairpin), and goes due S, almost level, for 3km. Here it ends, but meets the path (GR5) climbing up from a lower zigzag on the Sommet Bucher road. GR5 continues to climb gradually to the col, but descends steeply on its S side for about 500m (vertical distance) to Le Villard, where it joins a road to Ceillac.

(A. Aubert, 6. 7. 96)

B20 COL VIEUX 2806M
S SIDE M. N SIDE S +++

M523 or M334; IGN 1:100K map 158 & 1:25K map 3637 west sheet fold 3H; IGC 1:50K map 6 (M244 fold 44 bottom, M77 fold 19; IGN 1:100K map 54 fold 10C)

From the Col Agnel (on Italian frontier) to L'Échalp in the upper Guil valley, SE of Abriès, 10km r/s. Leave the Col Agnel road (D205) nearly 2km NW of the col, by the ruins of the Refuge Napoléon. CAF Refuge Agnel nearby. A fairly easy well marked path leads across meadows to the Col Vieux. By contrast, the valley to the N is wild and severe, with two lakes, Foréant and Égorgeou, at approx. 2600 and 2400m. After the lakes there is an awkward rocky step, necessitating a carry down a narrow path. Meadows scattered with larches, then a narrow path through rather thick grass. Fine view back to Monte Viso. There follows a steep descent through the forest, by a rocky path, awkward as far as the river Guil, but rideable to L'Échalp after one reaches it. No snow encountered in mid-July.

(R. Perrodin, c. 1970)

B24 COL DE NÉAL 2509M
M ++

M523 or M334; IGN 1:100K map 158 & 1:25K map 3537 east sheet fold 2B (M244 folds 42 & 43, M77 fold 18; IGN 1:100K map 54 fold 8B)

From Brunissard (on S side of Col d'Izoard) to la Roche-de-Rame (in main Durance valley, S of l'Argentière), 8km r/s, as well as rough roads. A fairly easy and pretty pass, especially during the climb. Leave the Izoard road at Brunissard and take a small road W-wards (GR5), rideable almost to the end of the forest. After steepening somewhat and becoming rougher, it turns more SW to the Chalets de Clapeyto. Climb straight up behind the chalets, on a path marked red and blue, then yellow, but not very obvious. There is a flat grassy area higher up. Climb the upper slopes ahead, then keep L-wards (SE), past two little lakes to the col.

There is an easy descent to the Lac de Néal, then an indistinct or non-existent path, not even waymarked, down the steep slopes to the valley. Keep S of the river down the valley after crossing a side stream, past some Alpine meadows, to a very steep slope, down which the path zigzags to the bottom of the Bouchouse valley. From Le Cougnet a rideable road (unmetalled?) continues down to the main valley.

B28 COL DES AYES 2477M
M ++

M523 or M334; IGN 1:100K 158 & 1:25K map 3536 west sheet fold 7D (M244 fold 43, or M77 fold 18; IGN 1:100K map 54)

From Briançon to Brunissard, S of the Col d'Izoard. Mostly GR5, and an alternative to the Col d'Izoard. From the maps, rough roads appear to go up to about 2150m on both sides, with a fairly steep path over the col. Could be combined with the Col du Néal **B25** into a circular trip from the Durance valley.

B32 COL DE PÉAS 2629M
D? ++

M523 or M334; IGN 1:100K 158 & 1:25K map 3536 west sheet fold 10D; IGC 1:50K map 6 (M244 fold 43, or M77 folds 18 & 19; IGN 1:100K map 54 fold 9B)

From Cervières, 6km N of the Col d'Izoard, to Château-Queyras in the Guil valley. Looks quite feasible (GR58 and/or small roads).

B36 COL DE FREISSINIÈRES 2782M
D +++

M523 or M334; IGN 1:100K map 54 fold 6C & 1:25K map 3437 east sheet folds 1D, E (M244 folds 42 & 41 bottom, or M77 fold 17)

From Orcières, 25km NE of Gap, to Fressinières (sic, 1:100K map), 5km SW of L'Argentière in the Durance valley. An easy pass for its height, with fine wild scenery. There is a tarmac road up to the modern ski station of Orcières Merlette (1817m). The signposted path then goes via the Forest des Estaris, but the cart tracks a bit further to the W make the climb easier, and rejoin the path near the Grand Lac des Estaris (2568m). This is a wild and beautiful spot; camping is forbidden, but there is a bothy above the S side of the lake. A steep path up slate-like scree leads to the col, with a much steeper descent at first over similar scree. Below, in a beautiful Alpine valley, long stretches are rideable, though the going is slower as you reach the treeline. A bridge takes the path N of the stream through open pastures to Dourmillouse. Here, drop down to Les Enflous and a steep path to the roadhead at 1441m. The old route along the N side of the valley from Dourmillouse has long since been abandoned, and is overgrown in places, also damaged by avalanches. The road leads down to Fressinières and the Durance valley.

Allow about 6 hours for the r/s part.

(G. Newey, August 1989)

B40 PAS DE LA CAVALE 2735M
VS ++

M523 or M334 ; IGN 1:100K 158 & 1:25K map 3437 east sheet fold 1C (M244 folds 42 & 41, or M77 fold 17; IGN 1:100K map 54 fold 6C)

From Vallouise, NW of L'Argentière in the Durance valley, to Les Auberts, at the head of the valley of the Drac Blanc, 19km to the SW. Very hard indeed, impossible if there is snow about. Scree slopes and raging torrents to cope with. Informant (1950s) spent 2½ days on the route. (But this is now GR54 – if bridges have been built across the major torrents, the route will be easier.) An update is needed.

B44 COL DU GONDRAN 2347M
E ++

M523 or M334; IGN 1:100K 158 & 1:25K map 3536 east sheet (M77 fold l8; M244 fold 43; IGN 1:100K map 54 folds 8 and 9B)

From the Izoard road, just E of Briançon, to Montgenèvre on the col of that name. The SW side is a military road, which is still in use to give access to the forts on the hills E of Briançon. The road starts about 2km E of the Briançon town sign on the main road; there is a sign '*Route militaire, très dangereuse, circulation strictement interdite …*' (this is meant for cars, and can be ignored). This side of the pass is old and worn tarmac, with very little traffic, climbing through pine woods; there is not much water to be found. On approaching the ridge at the top, go straight ahead at the crossroads. At the top, where the road is almost level for perhaps a kilometre, there are several deserted buildings, suitable for a bivouac. There are also good views of the Dauphiné mountains and the Clarée valley. The N side, which leads down to the village/resort of Montgenèvre, is unsurfaced, but has been found mostly rideable, or rideable in parts.

If approaching from Montgenèvre, turn R at a blue notice '*Zone de loisirs du bois*' at one of the first buildings on the R as you come into Montgenèvre from Briançon, about ½km before the top of the climb. Alternatively, turn off the road at a bend about ¾ of the way up from Briançon, on a track marked 'Pierres Vertes'.

(F. Cooke, 4.7.97; see also CC 80 1998, p12)

B48 COL DE L'EYCHAUDA 2425M
N SIDE M. S SIDE E ++

M523 or M333; IGN 1:100K map 151 & 1:25K map 3536 west sheet fold 2B (M244 fold 42 middle, or M77 fold 17 top; IGN 1:100K map 54 fold 7B)

From Le Monêtier-les-Bains, NW of Briançon, to L'Argentière-la-Bessée, S of Briançon, 10km r/s. The easiest start to this crossing is to take the service road for the ski lifts, which leaves Le Monêtier to the SW and climbs steadily to an old village of Peyra Juana (now only one farm and ruins). (The next two sentences, which have been written after an examination of recent maps, replace part of the original 1975 report.) This road is shown as climbing to near the top of ski lift no. 5, from where a waymarked path (GR54) goes

S by E (i. e. slightly E of S) to the col. The path swings L after the col and becomes rideable for a long way. The valley of the Torrent de l'Eychauda appears on your R, and the track descends into it by a series of long zigzags, some of which are rideable. A rough road is joined at the bottom, and this soon becomes a good tarmac surface, which gives a delightful freewheel down to Le Sarret, where turn L for Vallouise (interesting back streets) and L'Argentière-la-Bessée.

According to the map there is an alternative descent from the pass, which gets you back to the Briançon–Lautaret road. About 1km down the S side, before the zigzags, a way-marked path forks L off GR54 and contours around to the Col de la Pisse (2501m), then goes on to Serre Chevalier (2383m) and the Col de la Ricelle (2371m). From the latter path goes NW to the Serre Chevalier hilltop (2491m), then mostly N to a rough road which leads past Fréjus and down to Le Bez.

If going S→N, then just beyond Vallouise take the D4211, a lovely climb up a side valley. The road becomes a rideable track and then divides, the main track going on up the valley to a high lake and pass. Here take the R branch steeply up the hillside, with many zigzags; it is possible to push the bike almost all the way. There are good views. Once the ridge is reached, a nice rideable path leads to the col. On the Monêtier side you can ride the whole way down on a rather steep track.

Allow about 8 hours (5 or 6 if going S→N).

(A. Matthews, 1975; E. & S. Wagstaff, 10.9.97)

B52 COL D'ARSINE   2348M
M +++

M523 or M333; IGN 1:100K map 151 & 1:25K map 3436 east sheet (M244 folds 30, 41 & 42, or M77 fold 7 bottom; IGN 1:100K map 54 folds 6A, B)

From Villar d'Arène, just W of the Col du Lautaret, to Le Casset just W of Le Monêtier-les-Bains, 14km r/s; GR54. An easy crossing even with camping kit. Tarmac road from Villar d'Arène (signposted 'Refuge de l'Alpe'). From end of tarmac, a path contours the valley on R (NE) side of river, or there is an alternative rough road up the bed of the river. At the end of this rough road, the path starts climbing, crosses a stream coming in from the L, and winds steadily up alongside the river gorge. Then a slight drop to Refuge de l'Alpe—a good view here of glaciers and the source of the Romanche. From the refuge a grassy path leads up a little gully, then a long level stretch up a grassy valley, with numerous streams flowing among boulders—very pleasant. A short steep pull up to the col, views not very good, but an impressive ridge of glacial debris. Gradual drop along glacial river, numerous pools and waterfalls. (Water not drinkable on this side of the pass.)

Difficult field of boulders for about 50m (along the slope), then gradient increases on approaching the Lac de la Douche; steep zigzags (33% in places) on rather loose scree slope (care is required). Curious crossing of river where water runs under boulders, second crossing of river wet, after rain.

After the Lac de la Douche, a long descent through trees, rideable in places. Lower down in the forest are many (free) camp sites, provided with tables and seats. A forestry road down to Le Casset, a picturesque village (spoiled, unfortunately, like most other villages in this area, by corrugated iron roofs).

Allow about 6 hours.

(A. Matthews, 1975)

B56 COL DE GRANON   2413M
E +

M523 or M333; IGN 1:100K map 151 & 1:25K map 3536 west sheet fold 5A (M244 fold 42 middle, or M77 fold 8 bottom; IGN 1:100K map 54 fold 8B)

From Chantemerle, just NW of Briançon, to Granon and the Clarée valley. Metalled road from Chantemerle to top; rough road (top part officially barred to traffic, 1985) down E side, unsurfaced almost all the way.

B60 COL DE CRISTOL   2483M
S SIDE E, N SIDE M OR D? ++

M523 or M333; IGN 1:100K map 151 & 1:25K map 3536 west sheet fold 4A (M244 fold 42 middle, or M77 fold 8 bottom; IGN 1:100K map 54 folds 8A, B)

From Col de Granon B56 to Névache in the Clarée valley. Rough road to top from Col de Granon; no details of path down the N side. Both may be little used, although they are no longer in the firing range (*champ de tir*).

B64 COL DE LA VALLÉE ÉTROITE   2434M
N SIDE M, S SIDE D +++

M523 or M333; IGN 1:100K map 151 & 1:25K map 3535 west sheet fold 7B; IGC 1:50K map 1 (M 244 folds 31 and 42 or M77 fold 8; IGN 1:100K map 54 fold 8A)

From Modane to Bardonecchia, or (over the Col de l'Échelle) to Briançon, 11km r/s. Metalled road to Le Charmaix, then rough, through trees, to Le Lavoir. Bear R here (SW-wards) to avoid taking the road to the Col du Fréjus D69. The road soon degenerates into a zigzagging goat track climbing steeply to an upper dam; avoid a path across the river and continue up the R (E) side of the valley. Fine view of Mont Thabor from the col. The first 300m of the descent is very steep and rough, loose and rocky, but thereafter it moderates, and at Pont de la Fonderie a rideable road commences. This is a beautiful valley, wooded, and with imposing cliff scenery lower down; there is a CAF chalet-hotel at Les Granges de la Vallée Étroite. Metalled road starts a bit lower down the valley.

Times: Modane to summit 5 hours; down to Briançon 4 hours or less.

(W. H. Spoor, 1958, with later amendments)

Can be extended to the Colle della Rho D69 and further, as detailed in section D.

B68 COL DES ROCHILLES   2496M
W SIDE E. E SIDE M (62) ++

M523 or M333; IGN 1:100K map 151 & 1:25K map 3535 west sheet fold 3C (M77 fold 7; M244 fold 42 top; IGN 1:100K map 54 fold 7A)

From Névache in the Clarée valley to Plan Lachat, at 1962m on the N side of the Col du Galibier, 6km. r/s, as well as rough roads. A good alternative to the Lautaret and Galibier roads. From Névache, a metalled road (D301) leads past a large camping site at 1860m, and 3km later comes to the Chalets de Laval; then there is a good track along the river Clarée to the Refuge des Drayères; meteorological station (?) here. The path (GR57A) continues to the N of the river for nearly 2km, then bears L (SW) up some rocky ground (rather tough going here) to the first of the two cols (the Col des Rochilles), passing the Lac de la Clarée; then it goes along an embankment paved with stones alongside the Lac Rond. This lake, and the next, the Lac du Grand Ban, lie in a curious small basin, marshy in places, which has no visible outlet. The main col is reached just after the third lake. The path leading N from the col to Valloire crosses the Col de la Plagnette, about 2530m, and would not be too difficult with a loaded bike.

On the W side, below the col, there is a military camp, from where a stony road, probably not rideable, leads down to Plan Lachat. Some buildings on the way down provided a good bivouac in 1997.

Times: 2–2½ hours from Chalets de Laval to col, ½–¾ hour down.

(R. Perrodin c. 1970, J. Gilchrist 1997 and others)

B69 COL DU GALIBIER OLD ROAD   2642M
E? ++

M523 or M333; IGN 1:100K map 151 & 1:25K map 3535

From around 2km below the Col du Lauteret on its eastern side, rejoining the Col du Galibier road around 2km from the top. Turn R before a lay-by and the road bridge over the Torrent du Galiber. This is the old main road up the S side of the Galibier, the one the Tour de France raced until the 1930s. Seems now to be a wide track with no obvious difficulties on the map, except that it climbs in 6.5km what the new road does in 8km.

B70 COL DU JANDRI   3158M
E +++

M523 or M333; IGN 1:100K map 151 & 1:25K map 3536

From the ski station of Les 2 Alpes to the foot of the Mont de Lans glacier, about 14km r/s rising 1500m. Start at the Col de l'Alpe, by the Tourist Office, and the tarmac on the switchbacks behind the resort soon ends. Busy in the summer with downhill mountain bikers, this is apparently the highest trafficable road in the Alps (though N06 claims higher, with snow chains). The surface is sometimes loose but it is a decent 4×4 track the whole way up and though steep it is all rideable. Fine views all around even if the track is sometimes barren. This is an out-and-back route, but it

takes you above 3000m and there is a *télécabine* station and a restaurant at the top.

(W. Davies, August 2015)

B72 COL DU SOUCHET   2365M
W SIDE E. E SIDE M ++++

M523 or M333; IGN 1:100K map 151 & 1:25K on two maps (M244 fold 41 top, or M77 folds 6 & 7; IGN 1:100K map 54 fold 5A)

From Besse, 18km W of the Col du Lautaret, to La Grave just W of the same col. Rough road almost to the top of the W side. Just past the top, a path (GR54) turns off SSW to a lake perched on the edge of the Romanche gorge, with a marvellous view of La Meije, etc. From the col, an easy path goes down to La Grave.

B74 COL D'ALBANNE   1652M
E ++

M523 or M333; IGN 1:100K map 151 & 1:25K map 3435

From Albanne above the Maurienne valley to Valloire – a r/s route alternative to the Col du Télégraphe. Pass over the col and through the village and there is a road that heads into the woods and hairpins down the gorge. Just before Albanette is a hiking trailhead to Valloire. Soon the path becomes a vertiginous, rocky cliff road. At one time, brave locals may have taken a vehicle here but they are forbidden now and the avalanche warning signs seem believable. The unsurfaced stretch is not much more than 2km and it finishes on a road just below Valloire.

(W. Davies, May 2015)

B76 COL DE L'INFERNET   2656M
VS +++

M523 or M333; IGN 1:100K map 151 & 1:25K map 3435 east sheet (M244 folds 30 and 41, or M77 fold 7; IGN 1:100K map 54 fold 5A)

From Entraigues, 8km ESE of the Col de la Croix de Fer, to La Grave, just W of the Col du Lautaret. Like the Col du Souchet, not named on Michelin. Very hard indeed, with scree, landslides, etc. No path shown on recent large-scale maps, probably because of the *champ de tir* – military firing range – created since details of the pass were received. Fine views. An update is needed: our report is from the 1950s or earlier.

B80 COL DES PRÉS NOUVEAUX   2292M
M ++++

M523 or M333; IGN 1:100K map 151 & 1:25K map 3335 east sheet fold 4F (M77 fold 6; M244 folds 30 and 41; IGN 1:100K map 54 fold 5A)

From Besse, 18km W of the Col du Lautaret, to St-Sorlin-d'Arves, just E of the Col de la Croix de Fer, 16km r/s, as well as rough roads. A long route, but easy, beautiful and very rewarding. From Besse, a rideable road (unmetalled?) goes up to Bonnefin and the Chalets de la Boire. Then an indistinct path through the grass follows the E bank of the Valette torrent, which one descends to and crosses further up. Continue up the W side of the river, and cross to the E side just before its confluence with the Tirequeue torrent coming down from the E. Cross the latter and immediately turn E-wards above its N bank (faint path); in ½km cross another ravine coming from the N, and climb by many zigzags up the ridge between this last and the next ravine. This leads to wide Alpine pastures, easy going, with a faint path going up by long zigzags towards the NE, then E and almost level to the col. Exceptional panoramic view from the top.

Descend easily by Alpine pastures on the E side of the stream, past the Chalet des Prés Nouveaux, then a gradual descent for 1km before plunging by many short zigzags to the bottom of the valley. There are two small climbs out of side ravines at the Chalets de Borsa and Pravel. Still keeping E of the main river, after nearly 2km, sometimes a bit overgrown, one picks up a good track descending to the confluence of the Rieu Froid (coming down from the SW) and the main river (Arvan or Arvette, depending on which map one is using). From here a rough road goes down the W side of the valley to Pré Plan and St-Sorlin-d'Arves.

Allow 3½ hours from Chalets de la Boire to col, 3½ from col to St-Sorlin-d'Arves.

(R. Perrodin, c. 1970, with later amendments; J. Vaughan in RSJ vol. 18, no. 1, Jan. 1973, p. 16)

B84 COL DE LA CROIX DE SAVOIE 2529M
S ++

M523 or M333; IGN 1:100K map 151 & 1:25K map 3335 east sheet folds 3A, B (M244 folds 29 & 30, or M77 fold 6; IGN 1:100K map 53 fold 4D)

From the Col du Glandon to Le Fond-de-France, S of Allevard (which is 35km NE of Grenoble). Very rough and difficult; the path is often non-existent, needing much carrying over boulder fields. Not advised unless travelling light. An update is needed; our report is from the 1950s or earlier.

B88 COL DES SEPT LAUX 2184M
D ++

M523 or M333; IGN 1:100K map 151 & 1:25K map 3335 east sheet fold 2C (M77 fold 6; M244 fold 29; IGN 1:100K map 53 fold 4D)

From Allevard, 35km NE of Grenoble, to Allemond in the Romanche valley, just N of Bourg d'Oisans, 12km r/s. A hard pass, but fairly often crossed with a bicycle. At Le Fond-de-France, the end of the metalled road (16km S of Allevard), try diplomacy with the hydro-electric engineer, who may be persuaded to hoist bike and luggage to the first lake on the *téléphérique*. If not, take the stony path behind the chalet hotel, climbing slowly to Pont de la Sagne. Beyond the bridge, turn L (fingerpost), and the steep climb begins in earnest through the forest. Well-marked path; the gradient eases and steepens three times before Glézin, an open hut with bunks, but no one resident. Fine situation. There are two *téléphériques*; the one on the L follows a power line and gives the direction. From Glézin, the path is grass-grown,

following the W side of the valley in steep zigzags to the Lac Noir (tricky if under snow). From near the upper station of the *téléphérique* the plateau and lakes can be seen, together with a lot of debris from the dam-building operations. The path passes between the Lac de la Mothe and the Lac Carré, then L of the Lac Cottepens (the largest), i.e. by its E side. Cross the dam at the end of the Lac du Cos, then keep W of the lake, to the col itself. Mostly wheeling by the lakes. Fine view from the col – better still from the S side of the last of the three lakes on the S side of the col (the Lac de la Sagne). Pass E, W, E, in that order, of these three lakes, the path being almost non-existent now. The path begins to the L of the overflow from the Lac de la Sagne, and is exceedingly steep (marked as dangerous or hazardous on D&R), with about 100 zigzags down to the road. Some carrying necessary. Up-to-date information required, please!

(R. Sauvaget, pre-1958)

B92 PAS DE LA COCHE 1989M
M ++

M523 or M333; IGN 1:100K map 151 & 1:25K map 3335 east sheet fold 2C (M77 fold 6; M244 fold 29; IGN 1:100K map 53 fold 3D)

From Le Rivier-d'Allemond, on the road to the Col du Glandon from the S, to Prabert, 8km to the NW, 6km r/s. A useful and fairly easy little crossing of the Chaîne de Belledonne. An easy, well waymarked path heads N-wards from the upper (N) end of Le Rivier. This path becomes very steep through the forest; after some 2km and several sharp bends one leaves the forest to arrive at a rocky ravine. Leave this, and climb in zigzags towards the SW (pretty views to S and E), turning W-wards after a few hundred metres (bear R at a fork of paths) in the direction of a rocky gap through which runs an electric power line. This gap is the Pas de la Coche; there is an easy, but narrow and winding, path (GR549) through the rocks. There is a small lake just below the col, and a refuge on the R, at the bottom of the slope.

Either:

(i) descend from the col down the bottom of a rather uninteresting combe, then take a poor track down a boulder-strewn slope, and later descend gradually through meadows dotted with pine trees, to meet the forest road (D528) from Pré de l'Arc, which is metalled down to Prabert and the Isère valley; or

(ii) (according to the map) keep R on GR549 for about 1km past the col, and contour the hillside to Le Pré de l'Arc, whence a rough road leads S down to the car park at the end of the D528

Times: 2½ hours from Le Rivier to the col, 1½ down to D528.

(R. Perrodin c. 1970)

COL DE MERDARET   1798M

M? ++

*M523 or M333; IGN 1:100K map 151 & 1:25K map 3433 west sheet
(M244 fold 29, or M77 fold 6; IGN 1:100K map 53 fold 3D)*

From Le Fond-de-France (see B84) to Theys, 7km to
the W, or Prapoutel. From the map, the path leaves the road
above Le Fond-de-France at about 1400m, and follows the
pylon line. A rough road starts down the W side about 1km
S of the col, at 1900m approx., to Prapoutel, while the path
picks up the pylon line again on the descent to Les Ayes, on
the D280. From the col it is also, according to IGN 53, possible to take a waymarked path along the ridge to the N, over
the Grand Rocher, 1925m, to the Refuge Crêt du Poulet.

16.8.91 Cliffs above Derborence

c. SAVOY

For possible restrictions on taking bikes (especially mountain bikes) into the Parc National de la Vanoise, see Appendix II. This applies to **C16**, **C20**, **C24** and **C28**. Our correspondent Gregory C. May reports there may also be restrictions on taking bicycles on some trails in the Chamonix valley in peak season, which may affect **C73**, **C74**, **C76** and **C77**. Please follow all signs and up-to-date regulations.

C04 COL DU PETIT MONT CENIS   2183M
E SIDE E. W SIDE M? +++

M523 & M333; IGN 1:100K map 151 & 1:25K map 3634 west sheet fold 3B; IGC 1:50K map 2 (M244 fold 32, or M77 fold 9; IGN 1:100K map 53 fold 9D)

From the Col du Mont Cenis to Bramans in the Arc valley, 8km E of Modane. A rough road, with one or two short steep sections, goes up to the col from the main road col. No details of the SW side, which starts with a signed mule track going S, then SE, from the col. About 700m from the col a steep zigzag descent begins, turning R at a path junction, to the W. The path winds through cliffs to Le Planey (Le Planay, Michelin), and goes on as a metalled road to Bramans.

C06 COL DE SOLLIÈRES   2639M
AND MONT FROID   2822M
E ++

M523 & M333; IGN 1:100K map 151; IGC 1:50K map 2

From Termignon in the Haute Maurienne, the route, probably ex-military, is gravel almost from the start, full of hairpins and of decent quality. Forest until 2000 metres, but even here (and always above) views of the glacier across the valley. At roughly 2500 metres the route enters a sort of cirque and continues around it high along one side. It becomes a trail, but always wide and rideable. The Col de l'Arella (2685m) is just above, and many military buildings, including a fort on Mont Froid, which is worth the hike. This route can easily be joined to the Col du Petit Mont Cenis **C04** or to the Col du Clapier on the Italian border.

(W. Davies, August 2017)

C08 MONT MALAMOT   2917M
M (50) ++++

M523 & M333; IGN 1:100K map 151 & 1;25K map 3634 west sheet fold 4C (M244 fold 32, or M77 fold 9; IGN 1:100K map 53 fold 10D)

The approach, from W or E, is by a rough road which skirts the S side of the Lac du Mont Cenis (part of France since World War II). Coming from the E (from Susa), leave the main road after a zigzagging climb which follows a level straight stretch and brings you to within sight of the dam; turn L past a hotel and some ruined buildings, and after 2½km of rough road arrive at the large fort (Fort de Variselle) on a hill at the edge of the lake. After another ½km, or less, at the top of an uphill stretch, turn L at the white signstone 'Strada al Malamot'. From here to the top is a little over 8km, for which at least 3 hours should be allowed, and almost as much for coming down. The road, an old Italian military one, is carefully built and substantially intact, but the surface is so rough that riding up or down is possibly out of the question. After about 1¾ hours, just before passing under some electricity cables hung on pylons, fork R towards some derelict buildings, possibly barracks, one of which has the date 1899 over the entrance. Higher up there may be some snow slopes to cross. Fine views from the summit. On the summit stands a fort, over whose entrance are inscribed the words 'Caserma Malamot'.

(F. Wright, 20.7.85)

C10 COL DE LA MADELEINE ALTERNATIVE   1993M
E +++

M523 & M333; IGN 1:100K map 151 & 1:25K 3433

From Bonvillard, 13km N of Montvernier in the Maurienne, an alternative 4×4 track for some kilometres up the south side of this famous tarmac climb. Start from the valley bottom perhaps at Pontamafrey and climb the famous Lacets de Montvernier, then over the Col du Chaussy (1533m) via a rewarding balcony road. Then in Bonvillard take R turn that starts paved and becomes a track. This eventually emerges into open pastures and winds easily through scattered farmsteads and chalets before crossing a ridge and rejoining the paved Madeleine road about a kilometre from the summit.

(L. Eldret, 2014; L. Brunagel, 20.8.14; M. Leonard, 24.6.2015, etc.)

C12 COL DES ENCOMBRES   2340M
M ++

M523 & M333; IGN 1:100K map 151 & 1:25K map 3433 east sheet (M244 fold 31, or M77 fold 7; IGN 1:100K map 53 fold 6D)

From St Martin-de-Belleville, in the Belleville valley 12km S of Moûtiers (in the Isère valley), to St-Michel-de-Maurienne in the Arc valley. The 1:50K map shows a cart track over the pass, between the older paths shown on Michelin. The D&R map shows the cart track crossing the ridge at about 2365m, between two cols at 2325m and 2342m. Easy gradients, but long.

C14 COL DE ROSAËL AND   3000M
COL DE LA MONTÉE DU FOND   2977M
S SIDE M. N SIDE E ++

M523 & M333; IGN 1:100K map 151 & 1:25K 3534

From Orelle, in the Maurienne, not far from the start of the Cols du Télégraphe and Galibier, but climbing northeast, starting from the *télécabine* station, for 21km, and over to Val Thorens. The first 3km are paved; once the gravel road starts the hairpins are signed and numbered – or at least the first 19 are. After the Crêt d'Arcelin at roughly 2000 metres the track steepens to Plan du Bouchet (2344m). After this it degenerates into a rocky path up a ski slope, some pushing may be required. The sign at the ski lift at the col says 3000m, though may be a little less. Follow the ridge round towards the Col du Montée du Fond and at the *télé-cabine* station you will definitely touch higher than 3000m. From the Montée du Fond a spectacular descent on gravel ski-lift service roads to Val Thorens, the highest ski resort in Europe.

(W. Davies, August 2012 & September 2015)

C16   COL DE CHAVIÈRE   2796M

                                                      S (53) +++

M523 & M333; IGN 1:100K map 151 & 1:25K map 3534 west sheet fold 3H (M244 folds 31 & 32, or M77 fold 8; IGN 1:100K map 53 fold 8D)

From Pralognan, 18km SE of Moûtiers in the Isère valley, to Modane, 16km r/s, following GR55 all the way. See the remark at the beginning of this section. A hard pass, easiest after a dry spring and hot summer, and not advised before August because of large snowdrifts near the top. It is easier to find the way going N→S. Road from Pralognan (last eating place) to Les Prioux, then a good path continues up the L (W) side of the stream to the Refuge Péclet-Polset (food and beds if required). Easy enough thus far, but the 400m climb from the refuge to the top is very hard going, mainly boulders, landslides and snowdrifts, with a scree slope near the top. Much carrying necessary; usually the path, which is retrodden each summer, curves E-wards near the top from the direct line to the col. There are a few cairns near the top.

The southern slopes are also very steep and rough at first, but the snowdrifts are smaller. Lower down, make for the R-hand (western) torrent; the path keeps some way above it, on its E side, and takes one down to the Polset chalets. Thence a road down to the valley.

Times: from Les Prioux to top, 5 hours; from top to roadhead, 2 hours.

(R. Sauvaget, 1950s, and others)

C20   COL DE LA VANOISE   2522M

                                          W SIDE E. E SIDE M ++++

M523 & M333; IGN 1:100K map 151 & 1:25K map 3633 east sheet fold 1B, and 3534 west sheet (M77 fold 18 bottom; M244 fold 32 middle; IGN 1:100K map 53 fold 9C)

From Pralognan, 18km SE of Moûtiers in the Isère valley, to Termignon, just W of Lanslebourg in the Arc valley, 13km r/s, and GR55 all the way to Pont de Croé-Vie. See the remark at the beginning of this section. A much easier crossing than it used to be in the 1960s. Pralognan shops are closed afternoons. A rough narrow jeep track has been made all the way to the Refuge Félix Faure on the summit. The refuge has been much extended, open to all, with a warden in summer, and meals available.

Before the jeep track, a metalled road goes from Pralognan to Les Fontanettes. Above there a *téléski* chairlift leads to the Chalets de la Glière. The route follows below now, very steep in places, but eases off just before the path crosses the river into the Parc National de la Vanoise. Good campsite just outside park boundary (camping forbidden in it). The next stretch past Chalets de la Glière is unspoilt, but becomes steeper again to the Lac des Vaches, which is crossed on a causeway before the path zigzags up a scree slope to reach the grassy meadows which lead to the refuge.

Parts of the next 3km are rideable before reaching the steep rocky drop down to Pont de Croé-Vie, then there is an easier path to Entre-deux-Eaux, and about 2km SE of here a metalled road starts, which leads to Termignon.

Allow 4 hours from Pralognan to the col, 2 from the col to Termignon.

(G. Newey, 1982, amended from maps)

C24   COL DE LA LEISSE   2758M

                                                          D ++

M523 & M333; IGN 1:100K map 151 & 1:25K 3633 east sheet fold 4B (M74 fold 19; M244 fold 32; IGN 1:100K map 53 folds 9 and 10C)

From Termignon, just W of Lanslebourg in the Arc valley, to Tignes, just NW of Val d'Isère, 16km r/s; GR55. See the remark at the beginning of this section. A long hard pass. Metalled road from Termignon to Entre-deux-Eaux. From there, a narrow, gradually rising path keeps SE of the river, crossing it just before the Refuge de la Leisse, and becoming poor after passing a dam and going round the NW side of the reservoir. After the Lac des Nettes, the path ceases to exist (1958); however, as it is GR55, there is probably a well-marked path now. There were occasional paint marks and cairns as the way crossed some boulder fields, needing a lot of carrying. The pass consists of two tops nearly 1km apart, and the path is somewhat better hereabouts. There is a fine view of La Grande Motte while descending from the col, otherwise the scenery is rather second-rate. The path becomes rather rough again, with snow patches and stony areas (this part may be difficult to follow if ascending), but improves about 1km before the path to the Col de Fresse (2574m) turns off to the R. The path is rideable downhill hereabouts for some distance, then steepens down a shallow gully, afterwards contouring the hillside above the Chalet [*now Refuge?*] de Prariond, before descending to the Lac de Tignes.

(R. Sauvaget and E. D. Clements, 1958 – without bikes – and later amendments)

C28   COL DU PALET   2652M

                                                         M +++

M523 & M333; IGN 1:100K map 151 & 1:25K map 3633 east sheet fold 3A (M74 folds 18, 19; M244 fold 32; IGN 1:100K map 53 fold 9C)

From Tignes, just NW of Val d'Isère, to Champagny, 16km to the W (and 6km N of Pralognan), 14km r/s. See the remark at the beginning of this section. This is a very fine route, more rewarding even than the alternative descent of this col to Nancroix. There is a metalled road to the Lac de Tignes (lake, not town), and around its NW side. Just beyond the lake, a rather faint and narrow path (GR5) strikes up the steep hillside to the SW in a long sweep. An occasional carry may be necessary; and snowdrifts may be encountered high up, even in August. At the top, the path forks, L for Champagny. This L fork contours the slope for ½km to the Col de la Croix des Frêtes (2647m), then descends to the SW, past a small lake, the Lac du Grand Plan, to the Chalet du Grand Plan (the dot just below the 2400m contour on IGN 53). A jeep track starts here; turn L after about 1km (the track going on W is a dead end) and descend to the valley near the Refuge de la Glière. This slope is often steep. (If ascending, at the Refuge de la Glière take the path to the L, towards a wayside cross higher up – to the L of which the path goes – and about 1km after the cross turn R and keep on to the end of the jeep track; the path to the Col de la Grassaz leaves the track before the Chalet du Grand Plan). The descent from the Refuge de la Glière is now a rideable jeep road with 10 hairpins before Laisonnay. Thence, a metalled road continues down the valley to Champagny.

Times: 5 or 6 hours from Tignes to Laisonnay, an hour longer in reverse. Wheeling nearly all the way.

(E. D. Clements and R. Sauvaget, 1958, later amended from IGN 53. Crossed by tandems, 1961, R. Harrison and G. Swift, with camping gear, which necessitated a double carry from the Lac de Tignes to the top.)

C32   PAS DES BREBIS   2439M
M ++

M523 & M333; IGN 1:100K map 151 & 1:25K map 3532 west sheet fold 3J (M244 fold 31, or M74 fold 18; IGN 1:100k map 53 fold 8C)

From La Plagne, 14km SW of Bourg-St-Maurice, to Bozel, 7km to the S. The map shows a cart track (single full line) to about the 2300m contour, and about 1½km of path over the top.

C34   COL DE LA CHAL   2460M
E ++

M523 & M333; IGN 1:100K map 151 & 1:25K map 3532

From Nancroix, south of Bellentre and Landry in the Tarentaise, to Les Arcs. Cross a stream on the road just above Nancroix and then turn left on a farm track for about 8km of r/s up to the col. An always rideable ski area service road with great switchbacks above the treeline. Can be extended to the Col du Grand Renard (2455m) and the Col des Frettes (2384m). Prolonging the climb up to 2900m and the Glacier du Varet is worth the effort. Otherwise, an easy run down to Les Arcs.

(W. Davies, September 2012)

C36   COL DE LA BÂTHIE   1889M
E ++

M523 & M333; IGN 1:100K map 151 & 1:25K map 3532 west sheet fold

2D (M77 fold 17; M244 fold 20; IGN 1:100K map 53 fold 7B)

From Arèches, 4km S of Beaufort, to La Bâthie, 7km SE of Albertville, 6km r/s and rough road. Easy and fairly rewarding; the Bubbs considered the Arèches side to be rather stiff for ascent with camping gear. Metalled road (D65) from Arèches to Le Planay (Le Planey, Michelin), where take a steeply climbing path on the L, 100m before bridge over torrent. This path follows the line of a chair lift; one hour to the Chalets de Plapolets, where there is a wayside cross, and the top of the chair lift. From here, one should not take the path which seems to lead straight to the col, but a large track through woods, going S at first.

From the col, a good track goes down to the Chalet du Soufflet. Two ways lead down from here to the Chalets de la Ravoire, from where rough roads lead to Le Daru and a metalled road to the valley.

Allow 3 hours to La Ravoire.

(R. Sauvaget, updated)

C40   COL DE LA LOUZE   2119M
M? ++

M523 & M333; IGN 1:100K map 151 & 1:25K map 3532 west sheet fold 2E (M244 fold 20 bottom, or M74 fold 17; IGN 1:100K map 53 fold 7B)

From Arèches, 4km S of Beaufort, to Villoudry in the Isère valley, 6km NW of Moûtiers. No obvious difficulties from the map; start across the dam and go along the W side of the Lac de St Guérin; this is a variant of the Tour du Beaufortain.

C44   CORMET D'ARÈCHES   2109M
E ++

M523 & M333; IGN 1:100K map 151 & 1:25K map 3532 west sheet fold 3E (M244 fold 20 bottom, or M74 fold 18; IGN 1:100K map 53 fold 7B)

From Arèches, 4km S of Beaufort, to Aime in the Isère valley. A rough road above about 1700m; part of the Tour du Beaufortain.

Actually prettier than Fred says. The descent towards Aime in particular. About 5km of dirt road, driveable with care in a normal car. Passable in early June; the Refuge de la Coire has a spring and is a good place to stop for the night (unmanned until late June/July).

(M. Leonard, 2.6.17)

C48   COL DU COIN   2398M
D +

M523 & M333; IGN 1:100K map 151 & 1:25K map 3532 west sheet fold 3E (M244 fold 20 bottom, or M74 fold 18; IGN 1:100K map 53 folds 7 and 8B)

From the Lac de Roselend, on the W side of the Cormet de Roselend, to Aime in the Isère valley. The final part of the N side is very steep indeed, with practically non-existent path. (But this is now part of the Tour du Beaufortain, so there may be a path now.)

C52 COL DE BRESSON
2469M
D ++

M523 & M333; IGN 1:100K map 151 & 1:25K map 3532 west sheet fold 3D (M244 fold 20 bottom, or M74 fold 18; IGN 1:100K map 53 fold 8B)

From the Lac de Roselend to Aime, as for **C48**. The N side is a very steep boulder-strewn grass slope; the S side is easier, and views are better than from the Col du Coin. You can either take the GR5 from the Cormet de Roselend road, or follow a rough road to Treicol via the W side of the lake.

C56 COL DU PETIT ST BERNARD, ROMAN ROAD
2188M
E ++

M523 & M333; IGN 1:100K map 144 & 1:25K on two maps (M244 fold 21, or M74 folds 18 & 19; IGN 1:100K map 53 fold 9B)

From Séez, at the foot of the W side of the pass, to the pass. Road to St Germain, then a rough track, improving higher up, where it is less steep. This was perhaps the road (built by C. Gracchus in 123–122 B.C.) that Julius Caesar used to return to Rome from Gaul in 49 BC (another, short, stretch of the *Via Galliarum* can be seen at Donnaz, at the bottom end of the Val d'Aosta).

C60 COL DES FOURS
2665M
D +++

M523 & M333; IGN 1:100K map 144 & 1:25K map 3531 east sheet fold 1 (M244 folds 20 and 21, or M74 fold 18; IGN 1:100K map 53 folds 8A, B)

From the Croix du Bonhomme **C64** to La Ville des Glaciers, at the end of the road leading NE from Les Chapieux, which is 9km NW of Bourg-St-Maurice. Part of the Tour du Mont Blanc, with fine views of the SW end of the range. Very steep descent for 450m (vertically – two sections of the descent are marked as a difficult path on the 1:25K map), then much easier. There is a chalet refuge at Les Mottets (good in 1958). If you are going the other way, there is a rideable track to Le Bouillon des Tufs, then a rough traverse across the head of the Ruisseau des Tufs [*stream*] to the Tour du Mont Blanc path, which climbs to the col.

C64 COL DE LA CROIX DU BONHOMME
2443M
D (56) ++

M523 & M333; IGN 1:100K map 144 & 1:25K map 3531 east sheet fold 1J (M74 fold 18; M244 folds 20 & 21; IGN 1:100K map 53 fold 8B)

From Notre-Dame de la Gorge, 18km SW of Chamonix, to Les Chapieux, 9km NW of Bourg-St-Maurice, 14km r/s. A fine crossing, part of the Tour du Mont Blanc. Leave the D902 at Notre-Dame de la Gorge, by a wide but very rocky track (Les Rochassets) up a gradient of 17% to Nant Borrant. Much easier and sometimes rideable to Chalets de la Balme (hotel/restaurant here in 1991). Then a jeep road up the first steep slope to a hydroelectric scheme, then a very steep and rough path, with easier sections in between. A short 50m carry near the top, with possibly snowdrifts and a stream to cross. From the Col du Bonhomme **C68** here, the way divides, either S-wards down to Beaufort, with a fine

gorge between La Sausse and La Gittaz (difficulties have been experienced sometimes with landslides on this path), or SE-wards up to the Croix du Bonhomme. The latter path is often rough and difficult (note to take the uppermost path of three). This upper path continues fairly level and slightly uphill across boulder-strewn slopes and snowdrifts (early August) for 1km to the top, reaching a high point of 2479m just before the col. The refuge on the top was reopened in 1969, and was being rebuilt and refurbished in 1991.

From the refuge a fairly easy, but steep, wheelable path descends to the Chalets de la Raja, from where there is a jeep road down to Les Chapieux (or, more conveniently, in 1991, an almost level unsurfaced road, for ½km, to the Cormet de Roselend road).

Times: Notre-Dame de la Gorge to top, 4–5 hours; down to Les Chapieux, 2 hours.

(E. D. Clements, 1957, with later amendments)

C68 COL DU BONHOMME
2329M
M OR D? +

M523 & M333; IGN 1:100K map 144 & 1:25K map 3531 west sheet fold 12D (M244 fold 20, or M74 fold 18; IGN 1:100K map 53 fold 8A)

From Notre Dame de la Gorge to Beaufort. The climb from Notre Dame de la Gorge is described under **C64**. The path from the col down to Beaufort was reported to be cut by avalanches in 1961; the 1:25K map shows it as 'of uncertain continuity' and also shows a landslide or a steep-sided gorge low down on the W side, with no path here or to the W across what are presumably meadows. It might be worth trying the parallel route along the ridge from the Croix du Bonhomme refuge.

C72 COL DU JOLY
1989M
NE SIDE E (S SIDE TARMAC) +++

M523 & M333; IGN 1:100K map 144 & 1:25K map 3531 west sheet fold 11C (M74 fold 18 top; M244 fold 20; IGN 1:100K map 53 fold 8A)

From Hauteluce, just N of Beaufort, to Les Contamines, 15km SW of Chamonix. A very easy route, with fine views of the Mont Blanc range during the descent. There is now a metalled road (poor surface in parts, 1996) from Hauteluce to the summit (restaurant). A rough road (found unrideable, 1996) heads E-wards from the col to the upper end of a *télécabine* from Le Baptieu. A good path follows this down, switching to the E of it at about 1700m, to pick up another rough road from near the interchange station (restaurant) down to Le Baptieu, for Les Contamines.

There is an alternative path, striking N-wards from the col, which is not recommended: this rough track has been much cut up by rain and melting snow, and is unrideable down to 1500m, whence rough road to Le Baptieu.

(E. D. Clements, 1958; F. Cooke, 1996, reported in CC 77, 1997, p. 20)

Our correspondent W. Davies reports that in October 2017 he climbed to the Aiguille Croche, by the aforementioned télécabine *station, on a mountain bike.*

C73 COL DE TRICOT

2120M
D ++

The best map for the pass and the whole route is the IGN 1:25K sheet 3531 ET (St Gervais/Mont Blanc), fold 1D/E. Also available: M523 & M328 (Otherwise, M74 fold 8 bottom, or M244 fold 21; the LK 1:100K sheet 45 E edge – Haute Savoie – is not recommended.)

Les Contamines-Montjoie (8km S of St Gervais) to Les Houches, 6 km SW of Chamonix: 9 km r/s, 4 km track. This is part of the Tour du Mont Blanc, an alternative to the Col de Voza **C74**. The following description is from someone who combined this route with the E side of the Col de Voza. He later found there was an easier route to the Chalets de Miage [*now a refuge*], a jeep track which starts at La Gruvaz, N of and on the road below, Les Contamines. If you try this, ignore the next paragraph. From Les Contamines, take a tarmac road signposted 'Les Eccles' (also known as the Route de la Frasse). This climbs for about 100m (vertical distance) and then gives way to a steep dirt track. This climbs through trees nearly all the way to the Chalets du True at about 1700m, which is just above the trees. Accommodation, and probably a meal, is available here. You then have to descend about 170m, on a steep path to the Chalets de Miage, 1550m (more accommodation, probably meals, available here).

From here it is a steep climb on a mostly stony footpath to the Col de Tricot. If you do it early in the day you avoid the sun. The descent starts off easier, but becomes more difficult. The worst bit is just before and just after a *passerelle* (a Himalayan-style footbridge suspended on cables over a stream). Double carrying may well be found necessary at a few points here.

After the difficult stretch you go left along a path which is broadly level and often easy, though it does go up and down at times and is not always smooth. This brings you to a ridge, which you climb on a quite good track a short way to the abandoned Bellevue Hotel. The track runs roughly beside the Tramway du Mont Blanc, which climbs from the Col de Voza (and ultimately from St Gervais). It brings you down to the Col de Voza (hotel, restaurant, tramway station), from where another good track, after a brief climb, leads down, mostly steeply, to a group of houses (Les Vieilles Luges, probably about 1300m). From here a tarmac road leads down to Les Houches.

Times: Les Contamines to Chalets du Truc, 2½ hours; to Chalets de Miage, ¾ hour; to Col de Tricot, 2 hours; to Col de Voza, 3½ hours; to start of tarmac, 1 hour.

(F. Wright 15-16.7.04)

C74 COL DE VOZA

1653M
E ++

M523 & M328; IGN 1:100K map 144 & 1:25K map 3531 east sheet fold 1C (M244 fold 21 top, or M74 fold 8; IGN 1:100K map 53 fold 8A)

From Les Houches, 6km SW of Chamonix, to Bionnassay, 4km further SW. Only faint grass paths on N side in 1957, but presumably well defined now, as both GR5 and the Tour du Mont Blanc go this way.

C76 COL DES POSETTES

1997M
M ++++

M523 & M328; IGN 1:100K map 144 & 1:25K map 3630 west sheet (M74 fold 9; M219 fold 1; IGN 1:100K map 45 folds 10 and 11C)

From Vallorcine, almost on the Franco-Swiss frontier just N of the Col des Montets, to Argentière, 10km NE of Chamonix. There is a steep climb through the woods from the S end of Vallorcine, easing off as you leave the tree line. At the col you cross a variant of the Tour du Mont Blanc, which goes over the Aiguille des Posettes to the Col de Balme **F12**; the latter lies 1½km to the ENE of this col. The path meets the main Col de Balme track at about 1900m. There are excellent views of the Mont Blanc range.

(D. High, 25 and 27. 7.97)

C77 **PLANPRAZ** TO **COL DES MONTETS**

D ++++

M523 & M328; IGN 1:100K map 144 & 1:25K map 3630; LK 1:50K map 5003 or 1:100K map 105, SW corner (M74 folds 8, 9, or M244 fold 21 top, or M219 fold 1)

Planpraz (grid ref 554087 on the LK 5003) is at the top of a *télépherique* which climbs from Chamonix towards the Col du Brévent **C78**, then turns off to climb to Le Brévent (a peak). 12 km r/s. This route (part of the Tour du Mont Blanc) is reminiscent of the Faulhom traverse **G60**. Just as **G60** can be done as a day trip from Interlaken, this can be done as a day trip from Chamonix (the *télépherique*, which cost 8.50 euros in 2004, allows you to avoid the 1000m climb on a track from Chamonix). As **G60** ends with a long ride downhill from Grosse Scheidegg, this ends with a long ride downhill from the Col des Montets. The place of the Jungfrau, Mönch and Eiger is taken by Mont Blanc. Facing you, as you go along, there is a succession of glaciers (Taconnaz, Les Bossons, Mer de Glace, Argentière) and jagged peaks (Aiguille du Midi and other aiguilles, Grandes Jorasses, Les Drus).

The path does not descend, as you might hope, gradually from 2000m to 1461m. There is quite a lot of climbing and the ending is a steep descent to the Col des Montets. While the path is smooth and fairly level in parts, there are difficulties (rocks, steps, an awkward staircase), and a lot of carrying or lifting is needed. The route is well waymarked. There is no water between Planpraz and La Flegère (grid ref. 557090), and the restaurant at La Flegère has no drinkable water, but after La Flegère there are one or two small streams and one big one.

From Planpraz the path starts off fairly easy. Sometimes you have to take care to keep to the left to avoid the sheer fall on the right. Just before La Flegère there is a steep staircase, where double carrying will probably be needed.

After the Chalet des Chéserys (grid ref. 558092) there is a climb, awkward in parts, to reach the highest point on the route, just over 2100m. Ibex have been seen here. From near here a path branches off which leads down to Argentière; this is said to involve a 40m ladder. After some fairly gentle descending the path descends steeply to the Col des Montets (grid ref. 560094); a lot of carrying is needed here.

Times: Planpraz to La Flegere, 2 hours; La Flegère to Col des Montets, 5 hours.

(F. Wright 21.7.04)

C78   COL DU BRÉVENT   2368M
D (56) ++++

M523 & M328; IGN 1:100K map 144 & 1:25K map 3530 east sheet fold 4J (M244 fold 21, or M74 fold 8; IGN 1:100K map 45 fold 10D)

From the Col d'Anterne **C81** S to Chamonix. From the Chalets de Moëde [*now the Refuge de Moëde Anterne*], below the Col d'Anterne, take a good unsurfaced road towards the Col du Brévent, which can easily be seen. After about 1km turn off to the R (signpost) along a narrow, stony and often boggy or rutted path which leads down to the bottom of the valley (a pathless gorge) of the Diosaz, at about 1600m. Cross the river by a bridge and at once start climbing by a quite good path, not too steep. Near the top the path becomes stonier and steeper; some carrying, and some care, is necessary. From the top there should, in fair weather, be a good view of Mont Blanc. A steep and rather stony path leads down to Planpraz (2000m, a popular jumping point for hang-gliders), where there is an expensive restaurant and from where a steep road, with a surface of loose stones, leads down to Chamonix.

We have no details of an alternative descent to the Chamonix valley, via Planpraz and La Flégère. The path to La Flégère is very popular and should be fairly easy; it becomes rougher and boulder-strewn during the descent to Trélechamp.

Times: Chalets de Moëde to bridge across Diosaz, 1½ hours; bridge to pass, 3½ hours; pass to Planpraz, 1 hour.

(F. Wright, 4.8.91)

C80   LA ROUTE DE LA SOIF   E ++++

M523 & M328; IGN 1:100K map 144 & 1:25K map 3431

The 'Road of Thirst', referring to the exceptionally sunny nature – there are water sources available – of this 14.5km r/s between the Col de l'Arpettaz (1581m) and the Col des Aravis (1498m) and probably best done in that direction. From the Refuge de l'Arpettaz at the col take the path up past the parking; after that, it's a winding farm track that rises and falls between pastures along the edge of the Aravis massif, with views of Mont Blanc all the way.

(C. White, 2008, 2013; W. Davies, July 2010)

C81   COL D'ANTERNE   2264M
N SIDE S. S SIDE D ++++

M523 & M328; IGN 1:100K map 144 & 1:25K map 3530 east sheet fold 3H (M74 fold 8; M244 fold 21, NW corner; IGN 1:100K map 45 fold 9D)

From Sixt-Fer-à-Cheval, 15km SSE of Morzine, to Le Fayet, on the main road 12km W of Chamonix, 21km r/s.

There are at least two ways of starting the climb:

(i) (1991) Take the road from Sixt to the Cascade du Rouget. The road finishes at 1180m at the Chalet du Lignon, and there is then a steep stony track (GR5 from here to, and just over, the top), as far as a waterfall. Just above this, turn sharp L at a sign and continue along a rough path. Crossing a ridge at about 1750m, go down a short distance before climbing gently up a valley to a flat marshy area where stands the Chalets d'Anterne at 1807m [*also now the Refuge Alfred Wills*]. There is then another steep climb and another short descent to the Lac d'Anterne (2060m), before the final climb to the pass. To the R there is a good view of the rock wall of the Chaîne des Fis (or Fiz).

(ii) Take the road from Sixt to Salvagny, and on up to Chalets des Fonds (avoid posh hotel) and a small inn with accommodation on hay (deserted 1968). A well-marked path, but a long steep grind, 3km of 20%, through the pine woods, leads to the Bas du Col d'Anterne, on the edge of a sort of plateau. Here, take the path to the SE, continuing uphill; from here it is possible to see the top of the col with its cross. Later, take path down to the Lac d'Anterne (not the faint track on the L), where camping is possible (cold at night).

On the final slope to the pass there may be snowdrifts even in August, and carrying is often necessary. From the top there are fine views of Mont Blanc. There is a chalet hotel (the Chalets de Moëde) about ½ hour down the S side by a steep, rough path; from here onwards the path improves, and there are soon several ways of reaching the Arve valley—to the Lac Vert, Plaine-Joux or Servoz; all these are easy and are either good tracks or roads below 1600m.

Times: Chalets du Lignon to pass, 6 hours; Salvagny to Chalets des Fonds, 1–1½ hours; Chalets des Fonds to pass, 4 hours; pass down to Arve valley, 4 hours.

(R. Sauvaget pre-1958; J. Vaughan, 1968; F. Wright, 3.8.91)

C84   COL PELOUSE   C. 2270M
M ++

M523 & M328; IGN 1:100K map 144 & 1:25K map 3530 east sheet fold 2G (M244 folds 9 and 20, or M74 fold 8; IGN 1:100K map 45 fold 9C)

From Flaine, at the top end of an 1100m climb from the Arve valley, just SE of Cluses, to Vercland, 7km to the N, near Samoëns, or to Sixt Fer-à-Cheval (GR96). Shown as a cart track (single line) throughout on the 1:50K map, as a path on Michelin, and as a cart track (red dashed line) on the 1:100K map (1998). The col is at a T junction of tracks. The higher parts of the Mont Blanc range should be visible from the nearby Tête de Pelouse.

C88   COL DES GLIÈRES   1440M
E ++

M523 & M328; IGN 1:100K map 144 & 1:25K map 3430 east sheet (M244 fold 19, or M74 folds 6 & 7; IGN 1:100K map 45 fold 6D)

From Thorens-Glières, 12km NE of Annecy, to Le Petit-Bornand-les-Glières, 11km to the E. According to the maps,

3km of almost level path (GR96) at the top of the E side connects metalled roads.

C90 COL DE CENISE 1724M

E +++

M523 & M328; IGN 1:100K map 144 & 1:25K map 3430

From Mont Saxonnex, south-east of Bonneville, to Le Petit-Bornand-les-Glières. A steep tarmac road up through a pretty gorge that turns to a farm track for a couple of hundred metres of elevation over the col. Even steeper on the road down. Recommended.

(W. Davies, October 2009, September 2014; C. White, October 2017)

C92 COL DE LA GOLÈSE 1659M

E +

M523 & M328; IGN 1:100K map 144 & 1:25K map 3530 east sheet fold 3B (M244 folds 9 and 10, or M74 fold 8; IGN 1:100K map 45 fold 9C)

From the Col de Coux F09, 7km ESE of Morzine, to Samoëns, 11km S of Morzine. Having descended to about 1400m from the Col de Coux, leave the main path at a signpost 'Chalet de Chardonnière'. Pass through narrow openings in two fences, and in the middle of a field ignore a second sign to the chalet and take a path to the L, which climbs gently across a hillside and then enters a wood (mud here). After a short stretch of track you come onto the main unsurfaced road across the Col de la Golèse, which is steep in parts but can be ridden, apparently, with a mountain bike. Presumably it is possible to start this route from Morzine, but we have no details.

Times: Col de Coux to col, 3½ hours; col to tarmac, 1 hour.

(F. Wright, 2.8.91)

C96 COL DE BASSACHAUX 1783M

E? +

M523 & M328; IGN 1:100K map 144 & 1:25K map 3528 east sheet (M244 folds 9 & 10 middle, or M70 fold 18 bottom; IGN 1:100K map 45 fold 9B)

From Châtel, 14km NE of Morzine, to Montriond, just NW of Morzine. Road to top on NE side. The rough SW side has been described as 'very steep and awkward near the summit' and also as 'easy'; take your pick. The D&R map shows two cart tracks leaving the road end at the col; one, going downhill S by E (i.e. slightly E of S), ends in the forest after one hairpin, and the other, going level and SE for 2km, comes to a hairpin at 1800m and then descends, to meet the path coming down from the Col de Chésery F05; this presumably avoids the awkward path.

13.8.90 The road above the Stelvio; the nearer of the two
buildings is the Rifugio Pirovano, the further is the
Rifugio Livrio
13.8.90 The Rifugio Livrio from the glacier

13.8.90 The Ortler, from near the Rifugio Livrio
13.8.90 The Rifugio Pirovano, from the Rifugio Livrio; part
of the E side of the Stelvio road visible in background

6.8.95 The Drei Zinnen, from the Forcola di Lavaredo

6.8.95 The Drei Zinnen, from below the Forcola di Lavaredo

6.8.95 At the Forcola di Lavaredo, looking towards the
Rifugio di Lavaredo
16.8.90 The Ortler group from the Cima Bianca

28.7.97 On the S side of the Col du Gondran, about a mile
from the bottom
9.8.90 Eisjöchl, W side, the old military road

6.8.93 Looking S into the Valle Locana from the Colle del
Nivolet

10.8.95 At the Kreuzkofeljoch

13.8.90 Sleeping arrangements; the yellow Karrimat goes on
top of the pine twigs and grass; the white plastic bag, full
of hay, is the pillow; sleeping bag in green bag at left

15.7.94 Greina pass, at the top

28.7.97 Looking across the valley from La Grave

31.7.96 On the climb to the Tarscher pass, the wooden cross
at 2425m, looking across the Vinschgau

23.8.90 Pitztaler Jöchl, W side, probably about 2200m –
a glacier stream

The road up Mont Chaberton from the Col de Chaberton

D. PIEDMONT

This area contains many high and interesting routes, often old military roads.

D06 COL DE POURIAC   2506M

W SIDE M. E SIDE E? +++

M527 or M341; IGN 1:100K map 165 & 1:25K map 3639; IGC 1:50K map 7 (M245 fold 10 bottom, or M81 fold 9; IGN 1:100K map 61 folds 5 and 6A)

From the Col des Fourches, about 5km E of the highest point on the road over the Col de la Bonette, to Bersezio in Italy, 7km SE of the Col de Larche. The French side lies inside the Parc du Mercantour, where bikes are forbidden (see Appendix II). The ruined houses of the Camp des Fourches, on the Bonette road, provide a possible bivouac. The path in France (GR5 bis, or GR5/56 on the 1:25K map) descends sharply from the Col des Fourches, awkward in places, before climbing again at a mostly gentle slope (a herd of chamois was seen here by a correspondent). Pass two small buildings (one possibly a climbers' hut), then, ignoring paths to L and R (shown on 1:25K map), go up a small grassy valley which leads you to a flat-bottomed basin in the hills. Skirt this by the path and follow the path, which zigzags up the hillside (look out for cairns here). Just after the pass the path forks; go R here, on a narrow path across a steep slope, to the Basso di Colombart, 2461m. There is then a short descent to the river, and then a fairly good track as far as a tarmac road about 1km below Ferrere, 1869m. The tarmac road goes down to Bersezio.

(F. Wright, 13.7.86; P. Hinton, 1989, in CC 52 (1990), p. 5)

Further to Fred's description: cyclists should take the Col de la Bonette road (M2205) from St-Étienne-de-Tinée rather than the GR5. And bivouacking wild is now not permitted in this zone, the 'coeur' – heart – of the Parc, unless you are more than an hour from a road. But there is a walkers' Gîte d'Étape in Bousiéyas that has a dormitory and will allow camping or bivvying on its land. As for riding, our understanding is that bicycles are not permitted on the Col des Fourches path in the Parc, even when being pushed. Information found at: bit.ly/MercantourBike.

(M. Leonard, 2018)

D12 PASSO DELLA GARDETTA   2437M

E SIDE E. W SIDE M ++

IGC 1:50K map 7 (M245 fold 11, or M81 folds 9 & 10, top; IGN 1:100K map 61 fold 6A)

From the Colle di Valcavera (18km WNW of Demonte, or 36km W of Cuneo) to Pratorotondo in a side valley of the Valle Maira, 5km r/s as well as rough roads. At the Colle di Valcavera, leave the tarmac road which goes R over the Colle di Fauniera (or dei Morti), and descend briefly before continuing on a level or gently sloping unsurfaced road (originally military) which leads WNW. In 1988 this area was used as a source of wild herbs by collectors from the plain; certainly there is edelweiss hereabouts. After climbing a short way you come to a road junction where you can go R and after a short distance come to the Colle del Mulo, 2527m; on the other side of this pass the road, which leads down to the road over the Colle d'Esischie and to Ponte Marmora, has been overrun by one or more landslides but may well be possible r/s.

The road runs mostly above the treeline, and the grassy slopes rise to screes and rocky ridges. There is not much water, and several water bottles are recommended. The Stura–Maira watershed is soon crossed at the Colle Margherina, 2429m, and shortly afterwards at the Colle Cologna, 2394m, and from time to time there are views to the valleys on both sides. The footpath from the Passo della Gardetta has some steep and stony stretches, but is not too difficult.

Times: from the Colle di Valcavera to the pass, 3 hours (plus ¾ hour if you go to the Colle del Mulo); down to tarmac road, 1½ hours.

(F. Wright, 21.7.88)

D18 VARAITA–MAIRA RIDGE   E ++++

W end of ridge: IGC 1:50K map 6 (M245 fold 11, or M77 fold 20, bottom)

From Busca, 16km N of Cuneo, to the Colle Bicocca, 34km to the W. This is an old military road along the ridge between the valleys of the Varaita and the Maira. It crosses the road over the Colle di Sampeyre and continues for another 6km to end at the Colle Bicocca (2285m). On the way it takes in six passes: Colle di Valmala (1541m), Colle di Ciabra (1723m), Colle Birrone (1700m), unnamed (about 2050m), Colle Rastcias (2176m) and Colle Sampeyre 2284m.

There are three ways of starting the route: from the Valle Varaita through Valmala, from Rossana through Lemma and from the Rossana–Busca Road. All three meet before the Colle di Valmala. The last of the three involves the greatest length of unsurfaced road, and is the one described here.

On the road leading S from Rossana, turn R after about 2½km, just before the top of a hill (signpost Ristorante Baita di Cros). The tarmac road lasts, climbing, for about 4km; then an unsurfaced road continues uphill for 5–6km before joining the other two roads mentioned above. The one through Valmala is tarmac and is joined at a bend; turn L and follow it uphill for about 1½km to the Colle di Valmala, where the tarmac ends. There is no more tarmac on the route.

From the Rossana–Busca road to the Colle di Sampeyre is about 40km, of which 5½ are tarmac and perhaps 10–12, including the last stretch to the Colle di Bicocca, rideable (this word, of course, has no generally agreed meaning – with a mountain bike, probably the whole route could be ridden).

As on other ridge roads, care must be taken to have

enough water. There is no water between the Colle Birrone and 3km W of the Colle di Sampeyre.

There are extensive views, now on one side of the ridge, now on the other. From between the Colle di Valmala and the Colle di Ciabra the Matterhorn and Monte Rosa can be seen; the latter is 175km away.

At the Colle Bicocca is a memorial erected by the Alpini who built the road; the 'A. XVIII' on it means the 18th year of the Mussolini era, i.e. 1940.

Since 1988 the Colle di Sampeyre has been fully surfaced on both sides, and provides two easy alternative ways of ending the ride.

Times: from the Rossana–Busca road to the Colle di Sampeyre, 9 hours; from there to the Colle Bicocca, ¾ hour.

(F. Wright 18.7.88)

Also known as the **STRADA DEI CANNONI**.

D24 COL DE MARY   2637M
                                                            D +++

IGN 1:25K map 3538 east sheet fold 9A; IGC 1:50K map 6 (M245 folds 11 & 10, or M77 fold 19 bottom; IGN 1:100K map 54 fold 10D)

From the head of the Valle Maira, WNW of Cuneo, to Maljasset in France, at the end of the road in the upper Ubaye valley, 11km r/s, as well as rough road. (This has been shown on some maps as a road under construction, at least on the Italian side.) From Acceglio the tarmac road continues, steeply at times, up through Villaro, Saretto (clear green lake) and Chiappera, to about 1¼km above Chiappera. A steep unsurfaced road continues up for another 4km, to a steel chain across the road, the present limit for cars. About 300m beyond the chain turn L off the road along a sort of stone-paved causeway. This disappears at times to become merely a steep path (very steep in places). According to one report, the highest letterbox in Europe is to be found at the pass. The way down is rocky in places, necessitating short carries. There may be a little snow at the top, easy to negotiate.

Allow 2 hours from start of causeway to top, 2¼ hours down to Maljasset.

(F. Wright, 25.7.85)

D28 COL DU LONGET   2646M
                                        W SIDE D. E SIDE S +++

IGN 1:25K map 3637 west sheet fold 2J; IGC 1:50K map 6 (M77 fold 19; M245 fold 10; IGN 1:100K map 54 fold 10C)

From Maljasset, in the upper Ubaye valley, to Chianale in Italy, just SE of the road pass over the Col Agnel (Colle d'Agnello). The tarmac road ends at La Barge, but riding is mostly possible as far as Le Gâ. After this there is a narrow, steep, treacherous path along the side of a V-shaped gorge for about 1km, where double carrying (first luggage, then bike) may be necessary. The rest of the climb is not difficult. The descent is very difficult, over loose rocks, which may be slippery if wet. There is a wild camping area above Chianale.

(P. Hinton, 1989, reported in CC 52, 1990, pp. 5–6)

D33 COL DE VALANTE   2870M
                                                          S? ++++

IGN 1:25K map 3637 west sheet fold 4H; IGC 1:50K map 6 (M77 folds 19 and 20; M245 fold 11 top; IGN 1:100K map 54 fold 11C)

From Castello, below Pontechianale on the SE side of the Colle dell'Agnello, to Abriès in the upper valley of the Guil; part of the Tour du Mont Viso. Probably difficult; on the N side there is a scree slope above about 2510m, and the S side doesn't look much easier.

D37 COL DE LA TRAVERSETTE   2947M
                                                        S (51) ++++

IGN 1:25K map 3637 west sheet fold 4G; IGC 1:50K map 6 (M77 folds 19 & 20; M244 fold 44 bottom, or M245 fold 11 top; IGN 1:100K map 54 fold 11C)

From the head of the Po valley, W of Saluzzo, to the upper Guil valley, 5km r/s, as well as rough roads. A tunnel was bored through the hill below the pass in 1478–80; according to Louis Vaccarone, Le Pertuis du Viso (Turin, 1881), it was 75m long, 2m high and 2.47m wide, it sloped gently towards the Italian side, and it was built by Louis II Marquis de Saluces; according to W. A. B. Coolidge, The Alps in Nature and History (London, 1908), it was reopened in 1907. We have no reports of it, but it is shown on the 1:25K map, with a 'red' path going into it at both ends, as well as over the top; it is shown as about 50m long, and about 110m N of the col.

A very beautiful pass in a fine setting, rather hard near the top of the Italian side, where a lot of snow has been reported in early July. Shops in the upper Po valley do not open in the afternoon till 4 PM. A tarmac road goes up from Crissolo to the Albergo Pian del Re, at 2020m, and a rough road (reported to be unrideable even in descent) continues up for another 3km, to a point beyond the path to the Colle Armoine **D42**, passing close to the source of the Po. Then a path continues, contouring a spur of Monte Meidassa, and climbing a sort of corridor on the R, to a flat grassy area. Bear L, towards the back of a combe, descending a bit, then climb in zigzags up the stony or snowy slope to a ruined barracks. Behind this, climb to the L, an 'airy' path with sensational views and a short, steep and slippery climb. Bear R from the col, a rough descent across gullies (yellow way-marks). This side is easier, and in 1½ hours from the top you reach the easy Alpine meadows and the beginning of the metalled road down the Guil valley.

Half way down to the road on the W side, you cross GR58C, which goes over the Col Sellière (2834m); this lies 1½km WNW of the Traversette, and looks a lot easier on the map.

Allow at least 6 hours (from Crissolo to Abriès).

(A. J. Howarth, 1954; R. Perrodin; and others)

In 2016 a Canadian research team reported finding large amounts of animal dung carbon-dated to 200 BC, providing physical proof, they say, that this was in fact the pass used by Hannibal as he crossed the Alps for Rome.

D42 COLLE ARMOINE 2692M

N SIDE D. S SIDE E +++

IGN 1:25K map 3637 west sheet fold 4G; IGC 1:50K map 6 (M244 fold 44, or M77 folds 19 & 20; IGN 1:100K map 54 fold 11C)

A beautiful pass which connects the Val Pellice, SW of Pinerolo, with the upper Po valley: 6km r/s and rough road. The N side is not without difficulty; the S side is easy, and you soon come down to the track which leads from Pian del Re to the Col de la Traversette D37.

The starting point is the Rifugio Barbara Lowrie, 1753m, which is reached by a steep tarmac road from Bobbio Pellice in the Val Pellice. From here the path strikes steeply up the L (W) side of the valley for perhaps 200m vertically; depending on your load, double carrying may be necessary here. Then the slope eases. After about 1km you come to a gully. The way down into this is clear, the way out is not; aim to come out a bit higher than where you went in, and ignore a yellow arrow higher up, which points in the wrong direction. Higher up, at the top of another gully, a path (signposted) goes off to the R to the Colle Manzol, and soon after this you come to a small lake. Do not take the path which leads uphill from this to the R, but keep close to the lake, go downhill a bit and you will see the right path. Keep to the L (E) of the Lago Piena Sia, not far below the top.

Bear R (SW) from the top, for an easy descent over grass, with fine views of Monte Viso.

Times: Rifugio Barbara to top, 4–4½ hours; down to rough road, ½ hour.

(R. Perrodin, c. 1970; F. Wright, 16.7.88)

D48 COLLE BARACUN 2373M

E +

IGC 1:50K map 6 (M245 fold 44, or M77 folds 19 & 20; IGN 1:100K map 54 folds 11 B, C)

This is a rough road in the upper Val Pellice, which connects the Rifugio Willy Jervis at the foot of the Italian side of the Col de la Croix D54 with the Rifugio Barbara Lowrie at the foot of the N side of the Colle Armoine D42. Having crossed from France by the Col de la Croix, you can use this road to go on to the Colle Armoine, or you can go down to Villanova in the Val Pellice, following the river, by a path which is steep but occasionally rideable.

Because of the gorge above Villanova, this rough jeep track is the only road link between the upper Pellice valley (the Conca del Pra) and the outside world. The Italian plain, which is not far away at this point, can be seen from the top. On the S side tarmac is reached just before the Rifugio Barbara.

Allow 2½ hours from the Rifugio Jervis to the top, 1¼ down to the Rifugio Barbara.

(F. Wright, 16.7.88)

D54 COL DE LA CROIX (COLLE DELLA CROCE) 2299M

M ++

IGN 1:25K map 3637 west sheet fold 3E; IGC 1:50K map 6 (M245 fold 44, or M77 folds 19 & 20; IGN 1:100K map 54 fold 11C)

Like the Col de la Traversette D37 just to the S, this connects the upper Guil valley in France with Italy, but this leads to the Val Pellice. There is 8km r/s. The Italian side is a constructed mule track, difficult in places; the French side is mostly just a path, which lower down is steep and difficult at times, but higher up easier.

From the chapel at La Monta, 5km SE of Abriès in the upper Guil valley, follow the road (D947) up-valley for 250m, then turn L up a track (signpost Col La Croix, Refuge Jervis). After ½km the track peters out near a pile of stones. Take a path (no signpost) to the R, crossing a stream. The path now climbs steeply up an open hillside before entering woods and becoming less steep. (Wild boars were seen here in 1988.)

From the Italian side you have beautiful views of the Conca del Pra, a deep bowl in the hills around the headwaters of the Torrente Pellice. The encircling hills are dominated by Monte Granero. The road to the Colle Baracun D48 can be seen climbing up the S side of the valley.

On the flat ground at the bottom of the Conca del Pra stands the Rifugio Jervis (1732m) (own room and hot shower for 7000 lire in 1988).

From here you can either go over the Colle Baracun or take a path (steep but occasionally rideable), following the river, down to Villanova in the Val Pellice.

Times: La Monta to col, 3 hours; to Rifugio Jervis, 1½ hours; on down to Villanova, another 2–2½ hours.

(F. Cowsill, 1966; F. Wright, 15.7.88)

NB: In some French sources Col de la Croix is written as Col Lacroix.

D59 SESTRIERE RIDGE ROAD E ++++

IGC 1:50K map 1 (M244 folds 43 and 44, or M77 fold 9; IGN 1:100K map 54 fold 10A)

From Sestriere (the world's first purpose-built ski resort, built in 1932), at the head of the Valle del Chisone, about 60km W of Turin, an unsurfaced road (originally military) runs NE along the ridge, passing through several passes on its way. The road used to be largely rideable, but it was reported in 2001 to have got a lot worse. Just E of Sestriere a dirt road leaves the main road and climbs, with a bad surface, to the top of the ridge at about 2450m. A short descent brings you to the first pass, the Colle Basset, 2429m. The descent continues, more gently, to the Colle Bourget, 2299m. From here the road is almost level for a bit, now on the N side of the ridge, with fine views of the head of the Dora Riparia valley (Mont Chaberton D64, Monte Jafferau D79, etc.). There is a short descent to the Colle di Costa Piana, 2313m, followed by a long climb on the S side of the ridge to Monte Genevris, 2536m. The road then descends to the Colle Blegier, 2381m, before a long climb on the S side of the ridge, through the Colle Lauson, 2497m, to pass near the Testa dell'Assietta, 2567m. On this summit stands a monument commemorating a battle which took place here in 1747.

(In the War of the Austrian Succession Piemonte was invaded by the French and Spanish, and defended by the King of Sardinia, who also ruled Piemonte, and his ally, Austria; the French, under their commander Louis Charles Armand Fouquet de Belle-Isle, crossed the Montgenèvre pass and on l9 July 1747 attacked the area around the Testa dell'Assietta and the fort of Gran Serin; Belle-Isle was killed and his side, though numerically superior, was defeated and driven off with the loss of 4,900 men (against 219 for the Austro-Piemontese and their Swiss mercenaries); the battle was decisive and was followed by the Peace of Aix-la-Chapelle in 1748.)

Near here the road reaches a height of about 2540m before descending first to the Colle dell'Assietta, 2472m, and then for another kilometre or more on the S side of the ridge. There is then a level stretch of about 2km before the road makes a long descent to reach a low point of about 1800m, near a farm. From here the road climbs to a point called Pian dell'Alpe, 1917m (only 17km from Sestriere as the crow flies, but 36km along the road), where the road forks. One part goes N, climbing 2½km to the Colle delle Finestre, 2176m, and then descending to Susa (tarmac recommences at 1455m, about 10km from the pass). The other part goes S down to just E of Fenestrelle, on the road leading up the Valle del Chisone (the steeper sections, including the last 7km, are surfaced (1985 report).

In 2001 motorbikes, but few cars, were found to be using the road (there were also a fair number of cyclists, nearly all lightly loaded and on mountain bikes). Water, from streams and so on, was found to be plentiful E of the Colle dell'Assietta but scarce before then. At the Colle dell'Assietta it is possible, according to the map, to fork L, climb to a fort (Gran Serin, 2589m) and then descend to the N, to Susa or Chiomonte in the Dora Riparia valley, via Alpe d'Arguel; there are other roads leading N down into the Dora Riparia valley from the Colle Blegier and two other points; but we have no reports of any of these.

(W. Scheding 1980 and others)

This route, AKA the **STRADA DELL'ASSIETTA**, *has since become a popular bikepacking route, used in the Transcontinental Race 2015 and the Torino-Nice Rally. Our correspondent W. Davies details a larger network of unsurfaced tracks here, climbing to the ridge from several towns and some much wilder and higher than the Assietta. For more details use this web link: bit.ly/assietta.*

D64 MONT CHABERTON

3136M
E ++++

IGN 1:25K map 3536 west sheet fold 9A; IGC 1:50K map 1 (M77 fold 8 bottom; M244 fold 43; IGN 1:100K map 54 folds 9A, B)

From Fenils, a little hamlet 3km N of Cesana (the latter is at the foot of the E side of the Col de Montgenèvre, E of Briançon), an old military road climbs a vertical distance of 1800m to a fort (now ruinous) on the summit. The road used to be (just) possible for four-wheeled vehicles, and in World War II the Italians shelled Briançon from the fort, but there is now a short stretch, some way below the col (2671m), which has been overrun by a landslide. Young men on mountain bikes have been seen riding up at least some of the way, but for a touring bike the road is likely to prove, in the main, too steep and/or too rough. There are extensive views from the top, both into France (the mountains of Dauphiné, the Rochebrune, the valley of the Clarée) and into Italy (Monte Viso, etc.).

Unless you manage to ride, allow 5 hours from Fenils to the top, 4 to come down.

(F. Wright, 25.7.88)

D67 COLLE DELLA RHO (COL DE LA ROUE)

2541M
M ++

IGN 1:25K map 3535; IGC 1:50K map 1

From Bardonecchia to the French border, passing old military barracks. Leave town on the Via Pra de la Cumbe with the Rho on your left and after 3km turn L on to the Strada per Grange della Rho and climb with the Rho stream on your left. Pass through a long tunnel and over a short bridge; our correspondent reports some collapses but that they are easily passable. At Grange della Rho the route splits, both ways reach the barracks, but the R is more rideable. Just above the barracks at perhaps 2300m is the Piano dei Morti, named apparently after an avalanche in 1655 that killed a group crossing the pass. The unsurfaced road ends at the barracks and the final two kilometres to the pass is a decent hiking trail, with the last stretch unrideable: very steep, and a slippery mess. The French side is a hiking path, initially steep then quite rideable. Via the Col de la Replanette (2338m) this then links with the Col de la Vallée Étroite **B64** on the border again.

(W. Davies, September 2017)

D69 COL DU FRÉJUS

2540M
N SIDE E, S SIDE D +++

IGN 1:25K map 3535 west sheet fold 9B; IGC 1:50K map 1 (M244 folds 31, 32, 42, 43, or M77 fold 8; IGN 1:100K map 54 fold 8A)

From Modane to Bardonecchia, 4km r/s, plus 14km rough roads. The N (French) side is very easy, consisting of a good jeep track right to the top. The S side is a narrow, stony and often steep and zigzagging footpath. There are magnificent views from the higher reaches.

Just above Le Charmaix, turn R off the tarmac road along a good unsurfaced road (signposted Col de Fréjus, Col de la Vallée Étroite) through woods. At Le Lavoir (dam, small electricity plant) continue along road; the Vallée Étroite path **B64** goes R here. Road goes L up hillside, which is now steeper and mostly above trees. Carry on for several km to the top. At a small basin in the hills (good site for a tent), just after a stream, bear L, and higher up, just before a concrete avalanche barrier on the R, branch R (unsignposted) for the final, almost level, bit to the col.

The top is a small smooth saddle. Go to its R-hand end and you will find a steep path which bypasses a large snow-drift on the L (mid-July). An hour from the top you come to a large abandoned barracks with a concrete cross in front of it, and ½km below that a smaller two-storey building. Just after this you pass through a gap in a rusty barbed-wire fence and turn L (ignore a grassy track leading to the R). Less steep for a while, but the last stretch down to the road is steep and has some awkward passages.

Times: from Le Charmaix to top, 4 hours; down to road, 2 hours.

(J. & B. Vaughan, Sept. 1965; F. Wright, 13.7.88)

D74 COLLE SOMMEILLER　　　　　2993M
E　+++

IGC 1:50K map 1 (M244 fold 32 bottom, or M77 folds 8 & 9; IGN 1:100K map 54 fold 9A)

The col is named after the French engineer Germain Sommeiller who built the nearby railway tunnel in the years 1857–70, developing a compressed-air drill which greatly speeded the work. The starting point is Bardonecchia. A road, mostly metalled, goes up to Rochemolles, very steep in places. From there a rough road, just rideable where not too steep, goes to the col. Cars get to the top, and create clouds of dust as they go along (the attraction seems to be the skiing on the slopes above the col).

Allow 6 hours for the climb, 3 for the descent.

Almost certainly there is no r/s continuation from the top; no path is shown on the 1:50K map down 600m of very steep hillside (covered with snow, 1985) until the valley is reached.

(F. Wright, 21.7.85)

D79 MONTE JAFFERAU　　　　　2801M
W SIDE M. E SIDE　++++

IGC 1:50K map 1 (M244 fold 43 top, or M77 fold 8; IGN 1:100K map 54 fold 9A)

From Bardonecchia to Salbertrand. One of the best of the many fine routes in this area. It is advisable to do this route lightly loaded, because the climb from Bardonecchia is steep; to leave Bardonecchia early in the day, thus doing much of the climb in the shade; and to carry a front lamp for the tunnel on the descent. With a mountain bike the descent will be much quicker, but with a touring bike it is still possible.

Leave Bardonecchia by a steep tarmac road which climbs through Millaures to Gleise. There may be an alternative route which starts somewhere near Gleise, or La Fregiusa, and takes you to Point A in the description below, but, though less steep, it will involve covering several km in each direction. The route described here involves no backtracking.

At Gleise the tarmac ends, and is succeeded by a wide and rideable dirt road which goes past the settlements of Grand Rochas and Grande Broue. At 1922m there is a group of quite large buildings, probably connected with the ski trade; this is La Fregiusa. Shortly after this, at about 1950m, is the Hotel Belvedere. Here the road becomes a steep and stony jeep track, almost certainly impossible to ride even with a mountain bike. Just above the treeline, at about 2200m, is the bottom of a ski lift. The track follows the ski lift, climbing steeply, to its top, a short distance below the summit. The last stretch, from the top of the ski lift, is at an easier slope.

At the top there are the remains of a fort. There are also fine views of the Dauphiné mountains, the Rochebrune, Mont Chaberton, etc.

After a short steep section the way down levels out and follows the N side of a ridge, almost level and not far below the top of the ridge, for about 2½km. This part is fairly smooth. Then the track goes through a dip in the ridge and zigzags down the S side of the mountain. Here the track is steeper and rougher, mostly loose stones, and it continues like this all the way till tarmac recommences. About 2km, or less, from the dip in the ridge, a track goes off L down to Salbertrand, while if you go straight on you can, according to report, get to Bardonecchia. (This is the Point A mentioned above.)

Having gone L at Point A, you soon come to the entrance to a curved tunnel, 900m long, cut in the hillside to avoid a cliff. The tunnel is unlit and has water on the floor and dripping from the ceiling. It would be difficult to get through without a light.

The rest of the descent is long but not particularly noteworthy. It is used by motorbikes and jeeps, also some mountain bikes. Tarmac is reached at Moncellier, a hamlet at about 1250m, from where it is a quick descent to the Strada Statale 24 at about 2km E of Salbertrand (the sign has several names on it, including Frenee and Pramand).

Times: 4 hours up, 4 down (less than 4 down if you have a mountain bike).

(F. Wright, 30.7.97)

D84 COLLE DEL COLOMBARDO　　　　1898M
E　++

IGC 1:50K map 2

This pass, about 30km NW of Turin, leads from Forno in the Val di Viu in the N to Condove in the Valle di Susa. The road is an unsurfaced alternative to the Colle di Lis, a few km to the E. It starts ½km W of Forno, and after 200m of tarmac it becomes a gravel road and remains so till not far above Condove. On the N side the road is steep and the surface is loose stones. There is very little traffic. There are two small hamlets, close to one another, at 1100–1200m. Above these, two streams are crossed (there is no more water on the climb).

The slope eases before a gentle saddle which looks like the pass (this may well be the point whose height is 1898m). Here there is a large church, that of the Madonna degli Angeli (built, according to one report, in the 18th century in fulfilment of a vow). In fine weather there should be a good view from here. The church can be reached from both sides by car.

The road surface improves after the church, and the road itself turns R and follows the ridge, mostly climbing, sometimes on the S, sometimes on the N, side of the ridge. The highest point reached, probably at a little over 2000m, is 1–1¼ hours from the church and lies between kilometre posts 13 and 14.

After the highest point the road goes down the S side of the ridge, which is open and grassy, with no trees, for quite a long way. The road loses height only gradually at first, and even lower down it is less steep than on the other side. Between kilometre posts 5 and 6 some stretches of tarmac appear, but only at the steeper points. Continuous tarmac recommences between kilometre posts 2 and 3. Kilometre post 0 is at the junction with the good tarmac road from Maffiotto to Condove.

Times: from Forno to church, 4½ hours; from church to tarmac is about 16km, which might be ridden, slowly.

(F. Wright, 30.7.98)

D89 PASSO DELLA LOSA (COL DE LA LOSE) 2970M
W SIDE M, E SIDE S? (56) +++

IGN 1:25K map 3633 east sheet fold 10A; IGC 1:50K map 3 (M74 fold 19; M244 fold 33; IGN 1:100K map 53 fold 11C)

From Pont St Charles (2050m), E of Val d'Isère, on the N side of the road over the Col de l'Iseran, to a point on the road up the S side of the Colle del Nivolet **E09**, at the head of the Valle di Locana in Italy. (Warning: the French side is part of the Parc National de la Vanoise; mountain bikes are not allowed, and an attempt may be made to refuse entry to touring bikes; see Appendix II.) Many maps fail to show this pass, and instead show the Col de la Galise, which is some 600m to the N. Despite the height of the pass, the French side is not particularly difficult. From the road at Pont St Charles, an easy path leads up the valley to the Refuge du Prariond (65 francs for a night in 1991). There is then a steeper, but still mostly quite easy, climb to the pass. A herd of about 30 ibex, and four chamois, were seen here in 1991. We have no details of the Italian side; the first part of the descent, which is thought to start some 200m S along the ridge from the top of the climb, may be difficult, and the D&R 1:50K map marks the path (to the Col de la Galise) with blue crosses, i.e. a *passage dangereux*.

(F. Wright, 9.8.91)

3.8.91 Les Fiz from the Col d'Anterne

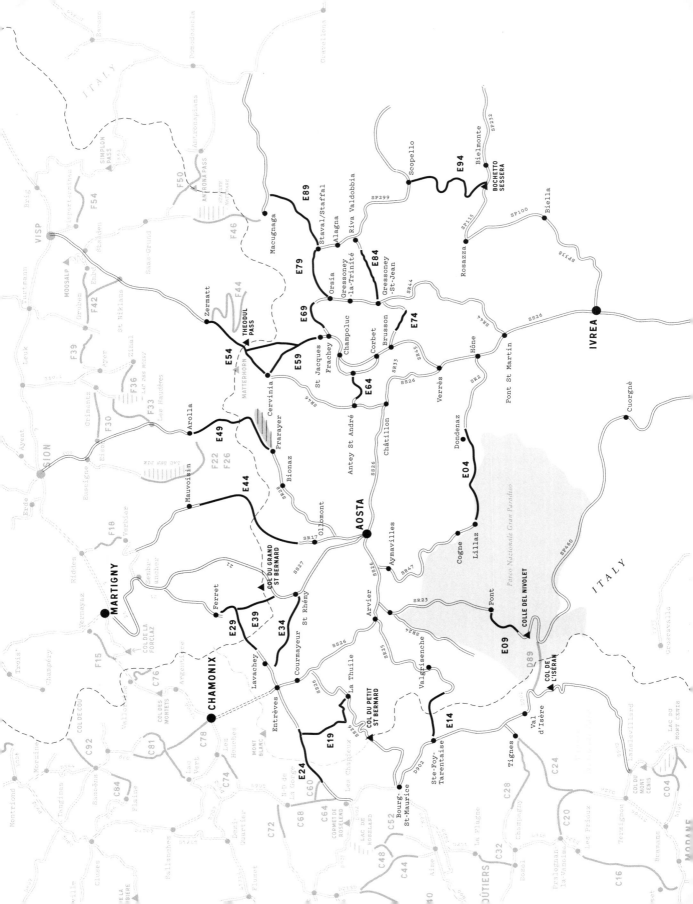

The Val d'Aosta and the region to the N (Section F, Canton Wallis) contain some of the highest and most challenging routes in the guide. For an explanation of the Landeskarten (LK) map references, see Appendix III.

E04 FENÊTRE DE CHAMPORCHER
2826M
M +++

IGC 1:50K map 3

From the head of the narrow, wooded Cogne valley, S of Aosta, to the head of the Champorcher valley, which leads into the bottom end of the Val d'Aosta. A pleasant and not very difficult route. The start is at Lillaz (1617m), some 3km above Cogne. A steep, narrow, tarmac road zigzags up an apparently nearly impossible hillside, through trees, to bring you to the quiet and unspoilt valley at whose head lies the pass. The road is barred to all but authorised motor traffic, and only the steeper bits are tarmac; higher up there is no tarmac at all.

About 5km from Lillaz, go L at an unsigned fork. 1km further on, at 2020m, there is a small chapel, rebuilt in 1982 by the ANA (Associazione Nazionale Alpini). At about 2300m, after a steep stretch, ignore a turning to the L, and shortly afterwards, at a bridge over the river, also ignore a yellow arrow saying Fenêtre de Champorcher (the arrow is for walkers). Passing a farm on your R, you come to another turning to the L and another yellow arrow for the Fenêtre de Champorcher. This time obey the sign and descend a short way towards the river. Do not turn L over the river but continue on a level and then climbing road to where the road ends, at an electricity pylon, at about 2500m. This spot, Peradza, is about 13km from Lillaz. The pass is now visible ahead as a notch in the skyline, with an electricity line on pylons running across it.

There is now a good footpath, smooth and distinct though steep in places, to the pass. At the pass itself there are two buildings (possible bivouac) and a good view in both directions; to the WSW you see the Gran Paradiso.

On the other side the path is no steeper but stonier and rougher, and some carrying is needed, but eventually the path becomes a grassy track, which joins a jeep track. After some 3km on the latter, at about 2150m, you reach the first settlement, Dondena or Dondenaz. The buildings here include a rifugio.

Below Dondena the road widens; there are short stretches of old and worn tarmac, but mostly it is a gravel road of uneven quality. Continuous tarmac, in good condition, is reached 5.2km below Dondena; from here the road descends a steep slope into the valley of Champorcher.

Times: from Peradza to pass, 1 hour; from pass to jeep track, 1¼ hours.

(F. Wright, 28.7.98; W. Davies, E side, September 2016)

E09 COLLE DEL NIVOLET
2612M
N SIDE M. S SIDE TARMAC (58) ++++

IGC 1:50K map 3 (M74 fold 20; M244 fold 33; IGN 1:100K map 53 fold 11C)

From Pont at the head of the Val Savarenche (1960m, 25km SSW of Aosta), S to the head of the Valle di Locana, 8km r/s. A road link was proposed over this pass, but the northern section, from Pont to the top, has never been completed, and as far as is known the plan has been shelved in order to preserve the character of the Gran Paradiso National Park. At Pont, cross the torrent coming down from the R (W), and then climb by a well-marked path in the direction of the rocky escarpments. The path is easy at first, then steep and zigzagging as far as Croce della Roley (a cross at the top of the steep bit). Turn SW-wards here, without crossing the river (an alternative path, not recommended, does cross the river and takes you up a steep slope onto the stretch of the road which has been completed), past some rocky knolls and up a wide flat valley. Here the path is almost level and mostly over grass. Pass a group of chalets on the L, cross the main river soon afterwards, and continue past the Chalets de Nivolet, below the stretch of completed road, which you reach either by following the track or by striking off to the R and climbing up the slope. From here the road is rideable, and soon becomes metalled to and over the col. There are fine views of the hills around the Gran Paradiso on the way up; from the top the view is mostly to the S, into the Valle di Locana.

Allow 3 hours for the climb.

(F. Wright, 6.7.86 and 6.8.93)

E14 COL DU MONT
2639M
W SIDE D. E SIDE M ++++

IGN 1:25K map 3532 east sheet fold 10B; IGC 1:50K map 3 (M74 fold 19; M219 fold 11, or M244 folds 21 & 22 bottom; IGN 1:100K map 53 fold 10B)

From Ste-Foy-Tarentaise, 10km E of Bourg-St-Maurice, over the frontier into the Italian Val Grisenche, 11km r/s. From Ste-Foy take the tarmac road through Les Masures to Le Crôt (no need to go via Le Miroir, though this is a fascinating village). Leave the road here and climb up to the R by a good track (rideable in descent) along the N bank of the stream. After the steep climb, it is possible to ride a short way across pastures, past some chalets, to La Motte (1¾ hours from Le Crôt). Here there is a refuge, offering food and accommodation. Climb up behind the chalets, on grass, straight ahead at first, then with many zigzags to the col. The path is little used and not waymarked, but easy enough to follow, a pleasant steady plod to the col, where one is suddenly confronted with one of those classic Alpine panoramas. Even the Matterhorn is visible. No carrying is necessary. The path on the Italian side is (1991) easier and better than on the French. At a farm you reach a jeep track, and then it is easy going. Michelin shows a road along the SE side of the Lago di Beauregard; this was used in 1982, but in 1991 it was found to be quite easy to go along the NW side of the lake; there was an unsurfaced, almost level, road which became surfaced about half way along the lake.

Times: 1¾ hours from Le Crôt to La Motte, 2 more from there to pass; 1¼ hours down to start of jeep track.

(G. Newey, 1982; F. Wright, 10.8.91)

E19 COLLE DI CHAVANNES 2603M
N SIDE D, S SIDE E (63) ++++

IGN 1:25K map 3531 east sheet fold 2I; IGC 1:50K map 4; LK 1:50K map 292, grid ref. 553066 (M74 fold 18 top; M244 fold 2I; IGN 1:100K map 53 fold 9A)

From La Thuile, 8km S of Courmayeur, to the path over the Col de la Seigne, at the SW end of the Mont Blanc massif, 6km r/s, as well as rough road. From La Thuile take the road towards the Petit St Bernard pass. After 3km you come to a bridge over the river; this is Pont Serrand. Here turn R off the road, and follow a jeep road, probably originally military, which goes up first in steep zigzags, then contours the NE side of the valley. (If approaching from the Petit St Bernard, you can leave the road near one of the zigzags before Pont Serrand, and take a small path which winds round a grassy hillock before descending to a bridge over the river; then you have a steep pull up the grass slope opposite to the jeep road.) The road, or track, remains fairly easy (rideable with a mountain bike) as far as the col, where there is an old fort, a possible bivouac.

There are two paths from the col. One strikes L down the scree slope, soon to pass by a steep hidden névé (inadvisable with bike). The other strikes down to the R, a distinct path across the scree slope, but requiring care. It is quite steep, and for the first 200m or so (vertically) it may be found necessary, or advisable, to double-carry (first luggage, then bike). The path then bears L along a grassy ridge, descending slightly, towards the Col de la Seigne **E24**, before going R and zigzagging down a second steep slope, grassy this time, and much easier than the scree. The river from the Col de la Seigne is easily forded in good weather at about 2200m, and from there you can join the track to that pass on the N bank. (Or, if heading to Courmayeur, you can stay on the R bank of the river and after ½km cross to the L bank by a footbridge.)

If approaching from Courmayeur, you can turn L off the track just after the Rifugio Elisabetta and the old barracks, cross the river by a footbridge and take a faint path for ½km up the R bank; or stay on the track almost to the end of the level expanse, then ford the river.

There are magnificent views of the Gran Paradiso during the climb, and of the Mont Blanc range during the descent. Altogether a very rewarding crossing.

Times: La Thuile to top, 4½–5 hours; descent to Col de la Seigne path, 1½–2 hours.

(E. D. Clements & R. Sauvaget, 1958; F. Wright, 25.7.98)

E24 COL DE LA SEIGNE 2516M
M ++++

IGN 1:25K map 3531 east sheet fold 2I; IGC 1:50K map 4; LK 1:50K map 292, grid ref. 550066 (M74 fold 18 top; M244 fold 2I; IGN 1:100K map 53 fold 9A)

From Les Chapieux, 9km NNW of Bourg St Maurice, to Courmayeur, 10km r/s. There is a good tarmac road from Les Chapieux to the Refuge de Seloge (4km up), where bunk beds are available; then a rough track for 1km to Ville des Glaciers. Here you can carry on up the track to Les Mottets, or stay on a path on the L (SE) side of the stream; the latter saves a bit of up and down, but is rather rough. The zigzags up the hillside above Les Mottets are the hardest part of this easy climb; this section is rutted and rocky. Easier higher up, with fine views of the Mont Blanc range as you approach the col, which is marked by a large cairn.

The descent on the E side is easier, with a tricky stretch above and below a derelict building. At about 2200m there is a level plain nearly 1km long. This is the Alpe Inférieure de la Lex Blanche. At its far end, on the L, is an abandoned barracks (the Casermetta Seigne) [*now restored*] and above this a refuge (the Rifugio Elisabetta). From here the road (loose stones) descends in zigzags to another level area (marshy) about 1km long and a bit less across. This is at about 1950m. The road crosses this area by a low causeway and comes to a small lake on the L, the Lac de Combal. This lake was deliberately dammed in the late 17th century as a defensive measure in the war between the kingdom of Savoy and Louis XIV of France, the Sun King. After the lake the road crosses by a bridge to the L bank of the river. There is now intermittent tarmac, which becomes continuous at about 1900m. At about 1750m there is a barrier to stop cars going any further; at 1700m a restaurant, the Chalet du Miage; after a descent, two pleasant-looking camping sites, Aiguille Noire and Cuignon; and finally a steep descent to Courmayeur.

Allow 6½ hours altogether.

(E. D. Clements, 1958; F. Wright, 2.8.85)

E29 GRAND COL FERRET 2537M
M ++++

IGC 1:50K map 4; LK 1:100K map 46 (tourist 105); 1:50K map 292 (tourist 5003), grid ref. 572082 (M74 fold 9; M219 folds 1 & 2, or M244 fold 22; IGN 1:100K map 45 fold 11D)

From Ferret, at the head of the Swiss Val Ferret, 22km S of Martigny, to the head of the Italian Val Ferret, 10km r/s. In 1884 a certain de Vautheleret wrote a proposal to build a railway tunnel under this pass, but nothing came of it (information kindly supplied by Swiss Federal Railways).

This very fine route is part of the Tour du Mont Blanc, and a justly popular r/s route. The metalled road (mostly steep, with views of the towering E side of the Mont Blanc range on the R) up the Swiss Val Ferret ends 1km beyond Ferret. Two tracks continue: the one ahead leads to the Fenêtre de Ferret **E39**; the one to the R crosses the La Drance stream by a bridge and zigzags up to La Peula, a summer steading for cattle, which used to be the Swiss customs post.

This is the way to the Col Ferret. Above La Peula the hillside has been worn by the cattle into many parallel ruts contouring the grassy hillside. This hard going lasts for perhaps 1km, and becomes easier as the gradient eases and the ruts lessen. The grassy hillside continues all the way to the top, with occasional red, white and black waymarks. A magnificent view of the Mont Blanc range has opened up, and the 1km extra walk to the Tête de Ferret, 2713m, improves it still further. 3km away to the NNW is Mont Dolent, where France, Italy and Switzerland all meet, while to the W the many great peaks line up, culminating in Mont Blanc itself.

The descent from the col is rather steeper, about 30%, but should not present any difficulty. After dropping about 500m, you come to another summer steading, Pré de Bar, which used to be the Italian customs post. From here a rough jeep road, partly rideable, descends steeply to the floor of the Italian Val Ferret, down which runs a metalled road to Entrèves and then Courmayeur.

Snow should not present much of a problem on this route; the steep descent to Pré de Bar faces SW, and snow does not linger here.

Allow about 5 hours for the crossing: 3 up, 2 down, either way. No carrying necessary.

(E. D. Clements, 1955; F. Wright, 24.8.85; and others)

E34   COLLE DI MALATRA   2928M
                                                    S ++++

IGC 1:50K map 4; LK 1:100K map 46 (tourist 105); 1:50K map 292 (tourist 5003), grid ref. 572076 (M74 fold 9; M244 fold 22; IGN 1:100K map 45 fold 11D)

From St Rhémy, on the road over the Great St Bernard and 4km S of the pass, to Lavachey-Praz-Sec in the Italian Val Ferret, 5km NE of Entrèves (at the entrance of the Mont Blanc tunnel). The climb is over spurs along a steep ravine, across hundreds of metres of snow. The summit itself is an arête, capped with ice and girded with about 50m of sludgy scree; it is so sheer and footloose that double carrying is necessary at the end. From the summit there is a view of the Grand Combin, Monte Rosa and the Matterhorn far to the E, and in the W, much closer, Mont Blanc and the threatening black pinnacle of the Grandes Jorasses.

(C. Ingram 20–21.7.86 or 87, in CC 42 (1987), p. 13)

E39   FENÊTRE DE FERRET   2697M
                                                    M +++

LK 1:100K map 46 (tourist 105); 1:50K map 292 (tourist 5003), grid ref. 577080 (M74 fold 9; M219 fold 2, or M244 fold 22)

From Ferret at the head of the Swiss Val Ferret, 22km S of Martigny, to the road over the Great St Bernard, about 2km W of the pass, 10km r/s. The metalled road ends a little beyond Ferret; keep straight on up the main valley for nearly 2km. At the second steading on the L, Plan de la Chaux, the path zigzags steeply up the hillside in an ESE direction, across innumerable contouring cowpaths, which make for hard going, especially at first. This rather rough and stony 500m climb brings you to the first of the three Lacs de Fenêtre. Pass the W edge of this; the going is easier now. (If going the other way, do not go down the L bank of the stream but cross the rough-and-ready dam and go ahead.) Then go between the other two lakes and up the final pull to the col. It is still fairly easy going down to the Great St Bernard road.

If going the other way, look for red marks and arrows on rocks on the L, near a farmhouse by the main road. As you come up the road, a conspicuous overhanging rock tower (Tour des Fous) comes into view; the path goes just to the R of a smaller rock tower just beyond this, not up the scree slope between them. About 400m beyond the farmhouse the path turns L across a stream, then climbs and passes over a stretch of sloping rocks. Just after this it forks; take the R fork, ford a stream and keep going for the col.

Despite the altitude, snow should not present too much of a problem from July onwards. If coming from Italy, quite a lot of carrying is necessary on the climb, but only for short stretches. There are very fine views of the Mont Blanc range during the climb from the Val Ferret.

Allow about 5 hours from Ferret to the Great St Bernard road, or 4 if going the other way.

(E. D. Clements ,1969; F. Wright, 9.8.93)

E44   FENÊTRE DE DURAND.   2797M
                                                    S(51) ++++

LK 1:100K map 46 (tourist 105); 1:50K map 293 (part of route) (tourist 5003), grid ref. 593084 (M74 fold 10; M219 fold 2)

From the Barrage de Mauvoisin, at the head of the Val de Bagnes (the next valley to the E of the Great St Bernard), to Ollomont, N of Aosta in Italy. A long hard pass, with very fine scenery, a good alternative to the Great St Bernard road. There is a tarmac road to the Mauvoisin dam (hotel), then a good track along the W side of the lake. At 2041m, the track crosses the stream and zigzags up the hillside (unrideable), then descends to the stream again. At the lowest point turn R off the main track (signpost to 'Tour des Combins') to cross the stream by a smaller track over a bridge, then climb the hillside to two stone buildings (one ruinous, one new), where the track ends. From here on it is only a path, uphill, but one that is easy to follow. In early July there was found to be much snow on the higher parts, and small instep crampons were found useful; it may be advisable to do this pass in August. At the top there is a plaque in memory of Italy's first post-war president, Luigi Einaudi, who fled over this pass in September 1943 from Mussolini's troops; the reformer Calvin also fled over it in 1536 to avoid persecution in Aosta.

Just below the top on the S side there was (in early July) a steep and rather difficult snow slope, and lower down you come onto an unsurfaced road, which it may be best to follow (from the map, it goes through Doues and joins the road down from Ollomont), because the direct descent to the roadhead of the Val d'Ollomont is steep and pathless, through trees and shrubs, unless you happen to strike a track.

Allow 6–7 hours from the dam to the top, 2–2½ from there to the unsurfaced road.

(F. Wright, 4.7.86)

E49 COL COLLON

3114M

VS (52) +++++

LK 1:100K map 46 (tourist 105); 1:50K map 283 (part of route) (tourist 5006), grid ref. 605090 (M219 fold 3)

From Arolla, at the head of the Val d'Hérens (SE of Sion), to Prarayer or Praraye at the head of the Valpelline in Italy. A very hard pass, on which, if you take the wrong way at a certain point, you have to cross a glacier which has hidden crevasses in it. The scenery of glaciers, icefalls and high mountains is remarkable. There is a short ladder at one point, so straps are needed in order to carry the bike on your back. Short crampons may also be found useful. It is said that cattle used to be driven across the pass; records show it as having been in use in 1544.

From Arolla take the tarmac road, almost level, which leads up the valley, past an electricity works, for about 2km before petering out into a jeep track. This ends at a car park just after crossing the stream by a good bridge. Two paths start from here: we have no report on the one to the R, but it may well be easier than the one to the L, which starts with a climb over rocks up the hillside and on which much carrying, and some double carrying, is needed. About 2½ hours from the car park you come to a kind of terrace in the hillside, where the rock overhang is supported on concrete buttresses – it would be possible to bivouac here. Just before the terrace, turn R down a path signposted 'Les Bouquetins'. This is easy and almost level, and soon brings you onto a miniature glacier closely hemmed in by the valley walls. The surface is firm, and the glacier only lasts for 200–300m. There follows a short stony zigzagging climb ending in a metal ladder of 13 rungs, spaced 30 cm. apart (you need straps – see Appendix II).

Just after the ladder is the point where you must turn R in order to go up the L (W) side of the main glacier (L here means left looking downstream, as usual). (The path most used by walkers, straight ahead, leads to the Cabane des Bouquetins, on the R (E) side of the glacier.) We have no report of this part of the route, because our description is from someone who followed the obvious path up the R side of the glacier, and then had to cross the glacier (where he fell into several crevasses).

Probably about an hour, or a bit more, after the ladder, with the main glacier on your L, you come to a tributary glacier coming down from the R at a fairly steep slope. The surface on this glacier is firm, but because of the slope progress is not fast, and double carrying may be needed. Provided you have crampons, the ice gives a better grip than the soft snow.

From the top, the descent is difficult. The only path found by our correspondent was a line of tracks in a steep snow slope. Although he was double carrying, with crampons, he lost his footing and slid with his bike into a stream.

After that there are scree slopes, and after a bit you come onto a path, which leads to the Rifugio Collon, 2818m, run by the Club Alpino Italiano, run by a friendly custodian (6000 lire for the night, plus 4000 for breakfast, 1987).

Below the hut the path, though now mostly distinct and marked with yellow paint, is still steep, narrow and difficult, calling for careful footwork and much double carrying. About 3 hours from the hut you reach the floor of the Combe d'Oren, a large steep-sided corrie. An easy stretch follows, but then you ford the stream and there are more difficult bits, with double carrying. The stream is crossed by at least one snow bridge. About 5 hours from the hut you come to a *malga* (summer steading) and soon another one. By now the path is much easier. Still marked in places with yellow paint, it leaves the valley bottom near the second *malga* and contours the hillside high above the blue waters of the Lago di Place Moulin. About 3km from the malga it joins a level tarmac road, which lasts for about 2km before passing through a tunnel and becoming a dirt road descending steeply to the dam at the end of the lake. Then a good tarmac road takes you to Bionaz and the lower Valpelline.

Times: allow a day from Arolla to the Rifugio Collon, and most of another from there down to Bionaz.

(F. Wright, 12–13.8.87)

E54 THEODUL PASS

3317M

S (51) +++++

LK 1:100K maps 46 and 47 (tourist 105); 1:50K (tourist) map 5006, grid ref. 621088 (M219 fold 4)

From Zermatt to Cervinia, 19km r/s. The name ('God's slave') is that of a late-4th-century bishop of Octodurum (Martigny) who, according to legend, descended from heaven to go to Rome and receive the confession of the Pope. The Pope in gratitude gave him a bell, and he entered into a contract with the Devil that he (the Devil) would carry the bell back to Sion, and if he got there first, then the saint would give the Devil his soul. The story involves two cocks on the church of Valère at Sion, one white (the saint's) and the other black (the Devil's). The white one crowed first, meaning that the saint (presumably crossing the pass later named after him) had won. The saint is now the patron saint of vineyards and (in South Germany) of Alpine pastures.

According to W. W. Hyde, writing in *Scientific Monthly* (1937), in 1895 54 coins, dating from the reign of Nerva (A.D. 96–98) to that of Theodosius the Great (379–95), were found in the ice at the top of the pass.

Raphael Reinhard, in his book *Pässe und Straßen in de Schweizer Alpen* (Lucerne, 1903), says the first crossing with a bike was by an American on 6 September 1899; so this pass may be to r/s Alpine cycling what the Rocciamelone (climbed in 1358) is to Alpine mountaineering. Unlike the Rocciamelone, it is high by our standards, in fact the highest route in this edition of the guide.

It is advisable not to try the route before late July or August. It is a long slog rather than technically difficult, though the stretch on the glacier may prove slow going in soft snow (here short crampons may be found useful). There are magnificent views on a good day. On the descent to Cervinia (formerly known as Breuil) you pass a mere 3km from the summit of the Matterhorn.

To start, go up the main street of Zermatt and keep straight on, up then down to a bridge. Do not cross it; continue past another bridge. About 1½km from the centre of Zermatt, fork L, following the sign to the Gandegg hut; you go over a third bridge and then uphill to Zum See. Just above Zum See you come to a road. You can cross this and continue on the path, or turn R along the road to Stafel, then take a path which leads to Schwarzsee; here shelter is possible in or near the small church. It is a long climb (about 1300m) from Zum See to the hut; the path is rough in places, but always easy to follow. Soon after the Gandegg hut, you come to the top of a ridge of boulders, the moraine of the glacier. The glacier itself is wide and smooth, and its surface nowadays is likely to have been fashioned into ski pistes by machines on caterpillar tracks. This, and the gentle slope, makes it easy to push the bike up, though you may sink in a bit. At the top there is a rifugio run by the Club Alpino Italiano. There is no glacier on the Italian side, just snow down to about 3000m, which may be easier going than the boulders nearby. Lower down there is a bulldozed track, steepening as you get nearer to Cervinia. At the start of the track, at about 3000m, there are some buildings, one on stilts, where you could bivouac, and lower down, at Plan Maison, there is a place which looks like a hotel.

In 1997 A. Aubert found that it was possible to combine this route with the next one in this guide, the Colle Superiore delle Cime Bianche **E59**, bypassing Cervinia, as follows: at the Capanna Bontadini, 3025m, turn L along a jeep track which leads first to a lake at 2808m, then to the refuge at 2800m (see **E59**).

Allow 7 hours from Zermatt to the Gandegg hut, 3 more from there to the top, and a further 4 down to Cervinia.

(A. J. Howarth, 1956; F. Wright, 31.7.86; A. Aubert, 6.8.97)

E59 COLLE SUPERIORE DELLE CIME BIANCHE   2982M

N SIDE E. S SIDE D +++

LK 1:100K maps 46 and 47 (tourist 105); 1:50K maps 293 and 294, grid ref. 619085 (M219 fold 4)

From Cervinia, at the head of the Valtournenche, to St Jacques at the head of the Val d'Ayas. The N side is a good jeep track, the S side is a footpath. There are good views of the Matterhorn and nearby hills as you go up, and of the hills to the S from the top. The route would be much harder if taken from S to N.

Start at Cervinia from near the *funivia* terminus (where the cable car goes up to Plan Maison and beyond); there are signposts for Routes 22 and 23 Lago Goillet and Colle delle Cime Bianche. There is a refuge at 2800m (food available). At the top the track turns L to follow the line of a ski lift. Leave the track here and follow yellow arrows across a low ridge of scree, till you see the path, which from then on is easy to follow.

There are two stages in the descent. The first, which lasts till about 2300m, consists of easy level stretches interrupted by steep hard ones. On the steep stretches some carrying is necessary. A stone building, probably good for a bivouac, is passed at just over 2400m. At 2300m you get your first proper sight of the Val d'Ayas, and the second stage begins. This is almost uniformly stony and awkward, mostly quite steep and often inundated by streams. Much carrying is necessary. The Alpe Ventina at 2179m was a good bivouac in 1988.

The difficulties are over at Fiery (hotel, small chapel). Here it is probably best to turn L, go past the Casa Alpina, cross the river and take the unsurfaced road, which gives an easy descent to St Jacques.

Times: Cervinia to pass, 3½ hours; pass to Fiery, 4½ hours; on to St Jacques, ½ hour.

(F. Wright, 31.7.88)

E64 COLLE PORTOLA   2410M

D +

LK 1:100K map 46; 1:50K map 293, grid ref. 617072 (M219 folds 3 & 4)

From Antagnod, near Champoluc in the upper Val d'Ayas, to Antey St André in the Valtournenche. The E side is very steep and boulder-strewn near the top; the W side is grassy.

E69 COLLE DI BETTAFORCA   2672M

M +++

LK 1:100K map 47 (tourist 105); 1:50K map 294, grid ref. 626079 (M219 fold 4)

From Champoluc, in the upper Val d'Ayas, to the head of the Val di Gressoney, 10km r/s. An easy route, with a jeep track all the way; no carrying is necessary. From Frachey, 2½km up the main valley from Champoluc, a tarmac road leads uphill, but soon gives way to a jeep track. After about ½ hour turn R at an unmarked fork, pass under the wires of a ski lift and cross some open land on which there are ski-lift buildings (marked Sciovie Mandria 1 & 2) and an old farm building (good bivouac). Soon after, at another unmarked fork, go L, uphill, to a farm, Alpe Taconet; higher up there is another cowshed (another possible bivouac?). Pass under the ski lift again, and later go straight on at another fork (the R-hand fork leads to the Lago Ciarciero). After a short descent past a small lake, follow the jeep track to and over the top. The track is probably rideable in places down to Staval, which is 3km up-valley from Gressoney-la-Trinité.

Allow 4½ hours up, 1½ down.

(F. Wright, 18.8.87)

E74 COLLE DI RANZOLA   2170M

W SIDE E. E SIDE D ++

LK 1:100K map 47; 1:50K map 294, grid ref. 628067 (M219 fold 4)

From Brusson, half way up the Val d'Ayas, to Valdobbia in the Val di Gressoney. There is a wide, well-surfaced road from Brusson up to about 1700m (a small hamlet, perhaps the one shown on the map as La Croix). Then the tarmac is often worn and potholed, and at about 1850m it stops altogether, giving way to an unsurfaced road which lasts for 2½km, is at first rideable and ends at a farm (2080m). From there a stony footpath (or a grassy alternative) leads after a short climb to the pass. Attached to a stone wall just above the pass is a metal plaque commemorating the crossing of the pass by 'Il grande poeta' Tolstoy in June 1857.

From the pass there is a choice of ways down. One (shown as a mule track on the 1:50K map) goes off at a gentle slope to the R; it may well be better than the one described here, and may lead to the top of the road from the Val di Gressoney. The other, more directly ahead, is generally steep and difficult. There are many rocky places and many stone step-like obstructions, probably designed to prevent erosion but making the path difficult to negotiate with a bike. However, the path is through woods and is shaded. Near the valley bottom you come to a poor jeep track, which soon leads to a road; this brings you to Gressoney in 5 minutes (according to a map it climbs to about 1750m in the other direction but does not go very near the pass).

Times: last farm to pass, ½ hour; from pass to beginning of jeep track, 1½ hours.

(F. Wright, 12.8.91)

E79   COLLE D'OLEN
2881M
D ++++

LK 1:100K map 47 (tourist 105); 1:50K map 294, grid ref. 633080 (M219 fold 4)

From Gressoney-la-Trinité, at the head of the Val di Gressoney, to Alagna Val Sesia, at the head of the Val Sesia, 16km r/s. From Orsia, about 1km up the valley road from Gressoney-la-Trinité, follow the yellow sign and take a narrow mule track which goes round a small chapel. This track is partly paved, and has a good surface. It is marked with a red '6' on a white background. After a while it turns into a grassy path across open pastures, and leads you to a station on the cable-car (ovovia) line called Bedemie. Here you can either take the steep jeep track or keep on the mule track; the latter becomes rather rough (carrying needed) and joins the jeep track again anyway. About 2½ hours up from Orsia you reach Alpe Gabiet, the terminus of the cable-car line; there are two rifugi (small hotels) here, several other buildings and possibilities for bivouacking.

Above the Albergo del Ponte (one of the hotels), follow a steep jeep track for ½km; here the mule track, marked with red '6's, forks R, but it is stony, hard going and not always easy to find. It is much better to keep to the jeep track, running up close to the chair lift. The two ways link up again before the chair-lift terminus, 1½ hours from Alpe Gabiet. Above the terminus there is no jeep track, just the path, an easy 40 minutes to the top. From the top four ibex were seen, high up, in 1987. No snow was reported, on either side. There is a choice of ways of starting the descent, but it may be best to take the level path to the L, to the two rifugi

(one closed, the other with a good view of Monte Rosa, etc., to the N and E). The path goes on down from them, marked red and yellow, with sometimes a black 5. The descent is long and tiring, often requiring carrying (but not double carrying). You come to a *malga*, then a *rifugio*, then a cable-car station at Alpe Oltu. Here the worst is over. There is a grassy track for about 1km, then a reasonable dirt road, which becomes a steep tarmac road not far above Alagna.

Allow 5–5½ hours for the climb from Orsia, 4–4½ for the descent.

(F. Wright, 19.8.87)

E84   COLLE VALDOBBIA
2480M
D ++

LK 1:100K map 47; 1:50K map 294, grid ref. 633070 (M219 fold 4)

From Riva Valdobbia, just S of Alagna, in the upper Val Sesia, to Gressoney-St-Jean, in the upper Val di Gressoney. The E side is fairly easy except for a steep rough section about midway; the W side is steep and rough for almost the whole way. There is a poor reward scenically compared with the Colle d'Olen.

E89   COLLE DEL TURLO
2738M
S SIDE M, N SIDE S +++

LK 1:100K map 47 (tourist 105); 1:50K maps 284 and 294 (tourist 5006), grid ref. 640083 (M 219 folds 4 & 5)

From Alagna Val Sesia, at the head of the Val Sesia, to Macugnaga, at the head of the Valle Anzasca, 19km r/s. A long and tiring route, lacking the really spectacular views from the Colle d'Olen. The S side is very much easier than the N side.

From Alagna a tarmac road goes on up the valley to a car park at 1500m. Continue on a wide track for about 200m, and turn R up a narrow path marked with red and yellow paint marks and the figure 7A. The path leaves the valley track about 20m before a wooden bridge; it is easy to miss the sign. The rather rough and rocky stretch through the woods soon improves to become a long but surprisingly easy ascent, mostly of good surface, past Alpe Faller and Alpe Grafenboden (these names reflect the fact that German-speaking people (the Walser) from Canton Wallis came over the Monte Moro pass, F46, in the 13th century and settled in the Valle Anzasca and neighbouring parts). Higher up the slope is steeper, but the surface is still mostly good, requiring only an occasional short carry. This old road was built about 1930 (there are inscriptions at the top and on the N side referring to the 6th and 8th years of the Mussolini era, i.e. 1928 and 1930); it is in many places a stone causeway, perhaps a metre high, winding over the hillside and reminiscent of Hadrian's Wall; there is no fear of getting lost, at least until after Alpe Schena, well down the N side. At the top there is a rock seat and a rock table, and a plaque, in the Walser dialect, commemorating the meeting there of representatives of the Walser people, including some from Saas and Zermatt, on 30 August 1970.

There are over 50 zigzags in the first 300m of descent, perhaps 150 on the whole of the N side. It is fairly easy going as far as Alpe Schena, where the well constructed 'walled road' ends. Then a poor path continues, soon turning W-wards down to the valley. This path has many awkwardly projecting rocks, and much carrying and lifting is needed. Double carrying may be necessary at times, if you are climbing. The path descends in zigzags down a steep slope covered with bushes and trees, and reaches level ground at the valley bottom (La Piana). For a short distance the going is easier, but the path then becomes rocky, difficult and tiring all the way down to the beginning of a dirt road, at some deserted houses (at 1358m). Even this dirt road is not easily, if at all, rideable; the alternative is a stepped track to reach the main road at Borca or Isella, for Macugnaga, a short way up the valley. There is a hut (no warden) at Lanti (2140m) on the N side.

Allow 5½ hours for the ascent from the car park, 7½ for the descent to Borca.

(E. D. Clements, early September 1969; F. Wright, 1.8.87; A. Aubert, 9.8.97)

E94 BOCCHETTA BOSCAROLA   1425M
                                               E ++

LK 1:100K map 47; 1:50K map 294, grid ref. 651065 (M219 fold 15)

From the Bocchetta di Sessera, 1382m (*bocchetta* is another word for pass), 10km due N of Biella and just W of the resort of Bielmonte, to Scopello in the Val Sesia. This is an easy unsurfaced road through rolling wooded hills which lie in a publicly owned forest or reserve of some kind; no unauthorised motor vehicles are allowed, and there are very few houses along the way, no signs to indicate the way or to name individual places, and very few people of whom to ask the way if you are not sure.

From the Bocchetta di Sessera a gravel road, rideable in parts even with a laden touring bike, goes downhill to a bridge over a river at 1190m. The road then rolls along a wooded hillside, and 13km after the Bocchetta di Sessera, having crossed several streams, comes to a second river, the Torrente Dolca, which has a pronounced valley of its own. The road then starts to climb gently (many horseflies were encountered here), and 2½km after the Dolca it comes to a hairpin bend. There is a small concrete building on the L, and two small houses just off to the R. What looks like the principal road goes L at the bend. Do not follow it, but go ahead up a small road, or track, with a metal barrier and a notice '*Divieto d'Accesso*'. This road takes you, after another 2½km, to the Bocchetta Boscarola. The track continues for a third 2½km down the other side, then comes to a wider and more frequented gravel road. There are fine views of the Sesia valley and Monte Rosa. After 600m of this better road you come to a steep but wide and mostly well-surfaced tarmac road which leads down to Scopello (7km).

Times: with a mountain bike you could probably do the 21km (tarmac to tarmac) in under 2 hours; it will take longer with a touring bike.

(F. Wright, 4.8.98)

F. **CANTON VALAIS** (WALLIS)

This section includes the San Giacomo **F69**, which lies on the border of Canton Ticino (Tessin). For an explanation of the Landeskarten (LK) map references, see Appendix III.

F03 **COL DE TANAY** 1440M

E ++

LK 1:100K map 41 (tourist 105); 1:50K map 272, grid ref. 554132 (M217 fold 14; IGN 1:100K map 45 fold 10B)

From Vouvry, 10km S of Montreux, a tarmac road leads to the village of Miex at 1000m, and ends shortly afterwards at a car park at 1080m (turn L at the fork just above Miex, and again at the top end of the car park). The remaining 360m is done in 1.9km (average gradient 18.8%), on a road whose surface is not tarmac and yet is fairly smooth, so that 4-wheel-drive vehicles can get up. (According to Denzel the gradient reaches 35%.) From the pass, a short descent on the other side brings you to the small village of Tanay (hotel/restaurant, etc.), set beside a picturesque lake in a site protégé.

Allow 1 hour from the car park to the pass.

(F. Wright, 18.8.91)

F05 **COL DE CHÉSERY** 1995M

E? +

IGN 1:25K map 3528 east sheet; LK 1:100K map 41 (tourist 105); 1:50K maps 271 and 272, grid ref. 551116 (M244 fold 10, or M74 fold 8 top; IGN 1:100K map 45 folds 9 and 10B)

From Morgins, near the French frontier W of Monthey, to the Lac de Montriond, just N of Morzine, in France. No obvious difficulties, from the Swiss 1:50K map.

F07 **PORTES DU SOLEIL** AND 1950M
PORTES DE L'HIVER 2099M

E +++

LK 1:100K map 41 (tourist 105); 1:50K maps 271 and 272, grid ref. 552115.
(M217 fold 14; IGN 1:100K map 45 fold 10B; 1:25K map 3528 east sheet)

From Champéry, 10km SW of Monthey, to Morgins. Our report is short on detail. From the map it seems that the Portes du Soleil are most easily reached by a narrow road running up from Val d'Illiez (which is 3km down-valley from Champéry). From the pass (an excellent viewpoint for the Dents du Midi) a path leads SW for 1km, then goes NW over the Portes de l'Hiver to the Col de Chésery **F05**. On the N side, a mule path starts from a farmstead at 1866m and becomes a track which closely follows the L (W) side of the stream (the Vièze de Morgins) down to Morgins.

(D. High, 30.8 and 5.10.97)

F09 **COL DE COUX** 1925M

E ++

IGN 1:25K map 3530 east sheet fold 3A; LK 1:100K map 41 (part of route) (tourist 105, also part of route); 1:50K map 272 (part of route), grid ref. 550111 (M217 folds 13, 14 bottom; M244 fold 10, or M74 fold 8; IGN 1:100K map 45 fold 9C)

From Champéry, 10km SW of Monthey, to Morzine, in France. Above Champéry, the road (the map shows two alternative roads) steepens and narrows, and after about 1½km becomes unsurfaced. It becomes rougher and stonier, but is still a jeep track of sorts as far as the pass. Here there is an unattended customs post, a possible bivouac.

The other side is a footpath which may be muddy (the mud can get under your mudguards and jam your wheels). The first of the following descriptions is of the way to the neighbouring Col de la Golèse **C92**, bypassing Morzine, and the second is of the way to Morzine.

(i) After descending 500m (vertically), leave the main path at a signpost 'Chalet de Chardonnière'. Pass through narrow openings in two fences, and in the middle of a field ignore a second sign to the chalet and take a path to the L, which climbs gently across a hillside and then enters a wood (more mud here). After a short stretch of track you come onto the main unsurfaced road across the Col de la Golèse.

(ii) Continue on the path/track through the forest, down to a farm, then follow a well-marked gravel road down to the Mines d'Or, where there is a café and souvenir shop. From here it is a tarmac road, quiet and gently descending, to Morzine.

Times: Champéry to the pass, 2½ hours; pass to Col de la Golèse, 3½ hours.

(F. Wright, 1.8.91; J. Mackle, July 1996, reported in CC 76, 1996)

F12 **COL DE BALME** 2205M

M +++

LK 1:100K map 46 (tourist 105); 1:50K map 282 (tourist 5003), grid ref. 563097 (M219 fold 1; M244 fold 10, or M74 fold 9; IGN 1:100K map 45 fold 11C)

From Trient, 8km SW of Martigny, on the road to the French frontier and Chamonix, to Argentière, just NE of Chamonix. This is part of the Tour du Mont Blanc. The N side is steep, and starts as a footpath from the hamlet of Peuty (grid ref. 565099 on the LK 5003), where there is a *gîte* or refuge. The path soon enters a wood and climbs steeply, but it is surprisingly smooth and easy (there are a few steps in two places). Above the wood there is a fairly easy footpath to a small building (farm?), Les Herbagères (grid ref. 564097) at 2036m, and from here a jeep track, rough at first and better later, leads to the pass. On the other side there is a choice between: a footpath, which is sometimes difficult and steep, and a track, which is longer (it goes past the Col des Posettes **C76**) but much easier.

From the top there is a good view of the Chamonix valley and the Mont Blanc range.

There is an alternative approach from the N, which starts as an easy level path by the side of an artificial watercourse, at the top of the Col de la Forclaz, crosses the Trient stream just below its glacier, and climbs to the col from the E; but this has been found to be difficult and awkward.

F13   COL DE LA FORCLAZ TO BOVINE TO CHAMPEX
                                            S (69) ++

LK 1:100K 46 (tourist 105); 1:50K tourist 5003 (M74 fold 9, or M244 folds 10, 11 bottom (France), or M219 folds 1 and 2 top (Switzerland)

8 km r/s, 2 km track. This is part of the Tour du Mont Blanc (an alternative to the path over the Fenêtre d'Arpette).

The path from the Col de la Forclaz (grid ref. 566100 on the LK 5003) starts smooth and easy, but it soon becomes stony and difficult, with very variable gradients, on its climb to the highest point of the route, at 2049m. Difficulty is caused not only by rocks but also by tree roots. On the climb there is one stream, concealed from sight but given away by the sound, also a farm.

The highest point (grid ref. 569100) is reached just before the farm at Bovine (grid ref. 570100). From this high point an easy path soon brings you to Bovine, and continues even easier, level, for over ½km. Then the descent proper begins. This, which is mainly responsible for the S grade, is steep and difficult, and the bike must be carried nearly all the way. Lower down, you cross three streams in succession. The slope becomes easier, but the rocky path is still like an obstacle course, and it is seldom possible to put the bike down and push. Finally you come to the start of a fine, broad, smooth, rideable unsurfaced road. After 2 km, at a farm, this becomes a tarmac road, which descends a short way to the main road, joining it about 4 km below the village of Champex (grid ref. 575097), on the Martigny side of the village.

Times: 2½ hours for the climb, the same to the start of the unsurfaced road.

(F. Wright 23.7.04)

F15   MARTIGNY OR VERNAYAZ TO FINHAUT   E +

LK 1:100K map 46 (tourist 105); 1:50K map 282 (tourist 5003), grid ref. 565104 (M217 fold 14, bottom; M219 fold 1; IGN 1:100K map 45 fold 11C)

A good quiet alternative to the road over the Col de la Forclaz. There are two ways up to Salvan from the Rhône valley:

(i) A tarmac road from just N of Martigny, crossing the River Trient by a bridge (said to be the highest in Europe, at 187m above the river) over the gorge

(ii) A track/path from Vernayaz (½km N of bridge over the Trient)

A recent report on the latter would be welcome. From Salvan, climb on a tarmac road to Les Marécottes, where

there is an open-air Alpine zoo (entry fee 5 francs, 1987), and Le Trétien. From here it is an unsurfaced road to Finhaut. For the unsurfaced road between Le Trétien and Finhaut, allow 1½ hours going up, ½ hour going down.

F18   CROIX DE CŒUR   2174M
                                                         E ++

LK 1:100K map 46 (part of route) (tourist 105); 1:50K map 282 (part of route) (tourist 5003), grid ref. 584107 (M219 fold 2, top)

From Riddes, 14km NE of Martigny, to Verbier, 8km to the S. It is a good tarmac road from Riddes to Mayens-de-Riddes (1500m, resort, with hotels); then it is unsurfaced but quite rideable. The road goes through conifers at first; higher up there are good views of the hills on the N side of the Rhône valley, and, looking S from the top, of the Grand Combin and part of the Mont Blanc range. On the S side only the first 4km or so are unsurfaced; tarmac recommences above Verbier.

(F. Wright, 26.8.87)

W. Davies adds that from the Croix de Cœur you can follow a r/s ridge road that passes through a long tunnel and to the Col des Mines (2320m), so named for the lead and silver extracted here until 1861. Heading east along a picturesque cliff road you climb to the Lac and then the Col des Vaux (2705m?) and eventually to the Col de Chassoure (2739m). He also reports that C. White made it higher, to the Col des Gentianes (2894m).

F22   COL DE RIEDMATTEN   2919M
                                                         S (52) +++

LK 1:100K map 46 (tourist 105); 1:50K map 283 (tourist 5003), grid ref 599096 (M219 fold 3)

From the Lac des Dix, at the head of the Val d'Hérémence, S of Sion, to Arolla, at the head of the Val d'Arolla. The pass is named after a 16th-century bishop of Sion, who used it (cf. the story of the Theodul, **E54**). There is a tarmac road as far as the top of the dam (the Grande Dixence, at 285m one of the highest in the world) which holds in the Lac des Dix, then an unsurfaced road along the W side of the lake. There are two alternative ways up to the pass. The second is the easier. For the first (E of the glacier), cross an inlet at the top end of the lake by a metal suspension bridge and climb a steep metal staircase of 79 steps; double carrying will be necessary here. There is then a narrow, steep and little used, but discernible, path. Higher up there is a difficult gully, full of rocks, to get across, and then some expanses of boulders, probably moraine. Here the path disappears, but there are splashes of paint on the rocks. Some carrying is necessary. It is easy to miss the way to the last climb up to the ridge on your L, because there does not seem to be any signpost; but if you find it, it is short, steep and stony. For the second way up (W of the glacier), take a path which climbs up the hillside to the R before the suspension bridge; this is often steep but is well used, because it leads to the Cabane des Dix, a hut overlooking the Cheilon glacier. From the hut, or a point before it, go L across the glacier (firm surface), taking care to follow the track used by walkers. You will then have to go down-valley, over the moraine, for a short way, looking out for the way up to the gap in the ridge on your R which is the pass.

The other side of the pass is easier. There is an easy path down to about 2500m, then a jeep track down to Arolla.

Allow 5½ hours from the Grande Dixence dam to the pass, 2 hours down to Arolla.

(F. Wright, 3.8.86 and 11.8.87)

F26 PAS DE CHÈVRES 2855M
S (52) +++

LK 1:100K map 46 (tourist 105); 1:50K map 283 (tourist 5003), grid ref. 599096 (M219 fold 3)

This pass is just S of the Col de Riedmatten **F22**. It is better used than the Col de Riedmatten, because it offers a slightly more direct route from the Cabane des Dix to Arolla than the other. The approaches from both sides are as for the Col de Riedmatten. On the W side, after crossing the glacier from the Cabane des Dix, you cross a short stretch of moraine and then climb a ladder, or to be precise two ladders, one long and the other, adjacent to it, short. Their combined height is about 20m. For the ladders, you will need straps to carry the bike on your back (see Appendix II).

(F. Wright, 3.8.86 and 11.8.87)

F30 PAS DE LONA 2788M
M ++

LK 1:100K map 41 (tourist 105); 1:50K map 273 (tourist 5006), grid ref. 606111 (M217 fold 16)

From Eison or (see below) Évolène in the Val d'Hérens to Grimentz in the Val d'Anniviers; this is an alternative to the Col de Torrent **F33** just to the S. Our description is from someone who took part in the Grand Raid Cristalp, the biggest and most famous of Swiss mountain-bike races, which goes from Hérémence to Grimentz. The route he describes involves a climb from the Val d'Hérémence to Mandelon, then over and down into the Val d'Hérens at Évolène. From here he climbed to the Pas de Lona; there was some dirt track up to 2400m, and from then on he had to carry his bike to the top. On a good day, the views are said to be beautiful. The 1800m descent to Grimentz was found to be thrilling, on a steep hairpinned rocky track with large drainage gullies.

Our correspondent did the route (from Hérémence to Grimentz) in 5 hours 9 minutes, but he was in a race, on a mountain bike and presumably without luggage.

(D. High, 25.8.96, reported in CC 77, 1997, p. 8)

F33 COL DE TORRENT 2919M
M (52) +++

LK 1:100K map 46 (tourist 105); 1:50K map 283 (tourist 5006), grid ref. 607108 (M219 fold 3)

From Les Haudères in the Val d'Hérens to Grimentz in the Val d'Anniviers, 13km r/s. This is a splendid route, fairly easy despite its height, commanding fine views throughout most of its length. However, snow may limit the possibility of crossing to between mid-July and late September in an average year. There is a metalled road as far as Villa, above Les Haudères. In Villa, turn R just over the bridge (signposted 'Col de Torrent'). There are two alternatives:

(i) a mule track throughout, stony at first, and keeping L at most forks, provided the L fork goes uphill

(ii) a track to Les Lachiores, then a path heading N to pick up the mule track higher up. Follow the red and white striped markings on the rocks. The two ways join up at around 2370m, and higher up, at around 2500m, the path levels off and bends more round to the E, past a little lake; soon after this it steepens again for the final zigzag climb. The path is adequate, if narrower than before, but still all wheelable. There is a cross on top, with very wide views. An equally easy path descends the E side (snow may be late to clear here, but the odd patch should not give any trouble), and is rideable for some distance past the Lac des Autannes. There is a large cowshed at about 2400m, then a jeep track down to the Moiry dam. There is a very fine S-ward vista from this track, of the Valais peaks. In ascending, when you come to the cowshed you must leave the jeep track and strike uphill, where there seems to be a path. There is a metalled road from the Moiry dam down to Grimentz and beyond.

Allow about 7 hours from Villa to the Moiry dam, 6 if going the other way.

(E. D. Clements, 1963, M. A. Stephens, 1980, F. Wright, 10.8.87)

F36 COL DE SOREBOIS 2850M
E SIDE E. W SIDE M ++

LK 1:100K maps 41 and 46 (tourist 105); 1:50K maps 273 and 288 (tourist 5006), grid ref. 611110 (M219 fold 3)

From Zinal in the Val de Zinal (the top end of the Val d'Anniviers) to the Lac de Moiry, 8km r/s. Following the road which goes up the valley, turn R, just before Barma, up a jeep track which leads to the Sorebois Restaurant. From there continue on the jeep track, which climbs towards the pass. (You can take a cable car up to the restaurant, for 8 francs.) When you reach the ridge, do not go R but L for 200m, to reach a narrow track which leads to the Lac de Moiry.

(A. Aubert, 12.8.97)

F39 FORCLETTA PASS 2874M
E SIDE D. W SIDE M (63) +++

LK 1:100K map 41 (tourist 105); 1:50K map 273 (tourist 5006), grid ref. 616114 (M217 folds 16 & 17)

From Gruben (1829m) in the Turtmanntal, to Ayer (1465m) in the Val d'Anniviers. From the food shop in Gruben follow the tarmac road up-valley for just over 1km, then turn R, across the river, along a gravel road which climbs the W side of the valley in long traverses, through conifers. There are fine views of the Weisshorn (4506m), with its two glaciers. At 2488m you come to a farm called Alp Chalte Berg, at the end of the road. (This claims to be the highest alp, i.e. mountain cow farm, in Europe.) In the middle of the grassy slope above the farm stands a signpost indicating the direction of the pass. The path is at first easy, though narrow; later it is often steep and rocky, sometimes rutted and continually making small changes of direction. Towards the top there are some short but steep and difficult sections on loose gravel and grit.

From the top, looking W, you have a remarkable panorama of near and distant peaks. The view to the E is undistinguished. The first 300m (vertical) of descent is down a grassy slope with many rocky sections. The path, though rather tiring, is much better than on the other side. Then you come to fairly level grassy ground, over which the path leads to a farm, with cows, at the start of another gravel road. This farm is at about 2500m, like Alp Chalte Berg. The road, for about 1½km, is gently sloping and rideable, but thereafter it is steeper and rougher. At first it gives fine views of the jagged peaks at the head of the Val de Zinal, and after 11km it brings you to a tarmac road just N of Ayer.

If you are going the other way, go to Ayer, take the turning for Chandolin and St Luc, and after 1km turn R up the gravel road signposted 'Alpage de Nava 6km'.

Times: Alp Chalte Berg to pass, 2¼ hours; pass to start of gravel road, 1¼ hours.

(F. Wright, 7.8.98)

F42 AUGSTBORD PASS 2894M
E SIDE S. W SIDE D (63) +++

LK 1:100K map 42 (tourist 105); 1:50K map 274 (tourist 5006), grid ref. 624117 (M217 fold 17)

From the Mattertal (Embd, St Niklaus or perhaps Moosalp) to Gruben in the Turtmanntal. According to Reinhard (see E54), this pass used to be paved and rideable, i.e. with a horse. Wherever you start, it is a long hard climb, both because of the height to be climbed (1550m from Embd, more from St Niklaus) and because the path, higher up, is difficult. The pass would be much easier if taken in the opposite direction. The following description is of a climb from Embd by a route which, up to about 2000m, is not claimed to be the only one possible, or even the best.

From Embd (about 1350m, reached by a steep road from Stalden), where there is a food shop, a narrow but well surfaced tarmac road climbs above the village for about 1½km, before turning into a gravel road and then a footpath. At about 1600m there is a wooden cross by the side of the path, and another path goes off up to the R here. Our correspondent was advised to take this path to the R, and did so, but it is steep and tiring. It takes you past several small houses, and near the top of these you come to a second wooden cross. Here it is probably advisable to go R, climbing till you reach the right path, which is well used and not difficult. The path then goes L through a wood at a gentler slope. At about

2100m it leaves the wood and crosses to the R bank of a stream which comes down from the R (the W) over grassy slopes in a small steep valley. The path remains easy for some way. At 2150m it is joined from the L by another path coming from St Niklaus and Jungen, and at 2200m it crosses back to the L bank of the stream.

At about 2300m there are six stone houses built adjacent to one another in a row down the slope. These seem to be unoccupied and secure against entry. After these the path becomes much rougher and steeper, and remains so (with some fairly level bits) to the top. Another path from Jungen joins at about 2600m. The last bit is particularly hard. There are good views in both directions from the top.

On the other side there is a steep and rocky stretch to start with; then the path is level or gently climbing, easy going. Another steep stretch requires care, but on the whole the path on this side is better than the one on the other side. At about 2500m you come to a small farm, and shortly afterwards a gravel track, which leads down (4km) to the main road just below Gruben, where there is a food shop (opening hours 9.30–12.00 and 14.00–18.30) and a hotel.

There is no refuge or hut on the route, and our correspondent saw no good bivouac sites offering shelter from the weather.

Times: from Embd to pass, 7 hours; from pass to gravel track, 2 hours.

(F. Wright, 6.8.98)

F44 GORNERGRAT 3135M
E ++++

LK 1:100K map 47 (tourist 105); 1:50K map 284 (tourist 5006)

Starting from the heart of Zermatt, taking the signed route up to the Gornergrat ridge. Initially, it heads up a good gravel road through a light forest, getting above the tree-line as it reaches Sunnegga (2288m). The next stretch from Sunnegga is the only complicated part of the route. The higher road next to the cable car station seems possibly too steep to ride, so an option is to take a hiking trail down and past two little lakes, Leisee and then Moosjisee. From here there is a short, steep, rocky road on the left, just past Moosjisee, that soon joins a good-quality road that goes all the way to the summit (ignore the hiking sign here or you'll be hiking steep lacets). Above Grünsee is a not difficult but fabulous stretch of cliff road heading higher. Turning the corner, above Riffelalp, the route runs beside the tourist train for a long stretch. From this point on, the route is difficult – steep – but still a rideable gravel road to the top. The tourist train stops at 3089m, the Kulm Hotel and Observatory are at 3120m and the viewing platform is 3135m. Amazing views of the Monte Rosa massif and the Matterhorn. There are plenty of possible routes up and down but some of the more direct ones, e.g. towards Riffelalp, will require a lot of carrying.

(W. Davies, August 2017)

F46 MONTE MORO PASS

2868M

S (53) ++++

LK 1:100K map 47 (tourist 105); 1:50K map 284 (tourist 5006), grid ref. 642094

From Macugnaga, at the head of the Valle Anzasca in Italy, to Saas Grund in Switzerland, 10km r/s. The pass was used by the Walser (see **E89**) in the 13th century, and there was a mule track by 1440. It is a beautiful but very hard route, especially hard if taken S→N, because the S side is nearly twice as high as the N. There are good views of the E face of Monte Rosa. Unless lightly loaded, expect much double carrying higher up. (It is possible to avoid all except the top part of the climb by taking your bike up from Macugnaga in the cable car; this cost about £7 in 1997 according to A. Aubert.)

From the main square (post office, etc.) in Macugnaga, follow a street which leads up-valley past the funivia terminus. Pass between a church (the Chiesa Vecchia) on your R and a large lime tree (used as a meeting place since 1200, according to the notice) on your L. Just before a wooden bridge over a stream turn R up a metre-wide constructed mule track (signpost: Moro Pass). This peters out after just over 1km, and you follow quite good path to the first station on the *funivia* (1700m). The map shows a path heading E from here, but our correspondent was advised to take a path, marked by red and yellow paint marks, which led up the hillside, almost without zigzags; this starts rough and steep and becomes rougher. Above a certain height (2400m?) there is really no path, just paint marks on the rocks. Accommodation for the night is available just below the top on the Italian side, either at the top end of the *funivia* or at a *rifugio*. An ibex was seen near the top in 1988.

The highest part of the route is over large boulders (follow the paint marks), past a metal statue of the Madonna on the ridge itself. One quite large snowfield was met on the N side, at about 2750m, in early August. There is much rock and boulders on the N side too, but you reach continuous grassy slopes at about 2300m. There is a rough road from the S end of the Mattmarksee.

If you are going N→S, you will probably have difficulty in finding the start of the way down. There is no proper path, but you should soon see the hut and cable terminus; head to these, or to their L.

Times: from Macugnaga to refuge, 7 hours; from refuge to Mattmarksee, 5 hours.

(E. D. Clements (without bike), September 1969; F. Wright, 8-9.8.88)

F50 ANTRONA PASS

2838M

W SIDE M. E SIDE S (54) +++

LK 1:100K map 47 (tourist 105); 1:50K map 284 (tourist 5006), grid ref. 645098 (M219 fold 5)

From Saas Almagell, in the Saas valley S of Visp, to Antronapiana in Italy. The Swiss side is both shorter (900m compared with 1500m r/s climbing) and much easier than the Italian side. The pass seems not to be much used by walkers.

Until Napoleon built, or improved, the road over the Simplon, in 1801–5, this was the main way of getting from the Upper Valais into Italy, and stretches of the original mule track remain on both sides, but especially on the Swiss side.

From Saas Almagell follow the main road up the valley for 1km to an unsignposted crossroads. Here turn L up a narrow tarmac road, which lasts for about 1½km and brings you to the Restaurant Alpina and the top of the chair lift at Furggstalden (about 1900m). Pass the Restaurant Alpina on your L and go straight on, not turning R into a field. The path is not difficult, being apparently the former mule track. After a stretch of wide, almost level, track you round a corner and look into the Furggtal. There are two well-built stone buildings here, a possible bivouac.

The track continues quite easy, climbing gently on the R (NE) side of the stream. A herd of about 30 chamois was seen here in 1989. Only at the top end of the valley does the going get harder, as the path steepens to get past a mass of loose rocks, possibly old glacial moraine. There are plenty of red and white paint marks and small cairns.

At the top you look over a precipice down to the small dark blue Lago di Cingino, 600m below. The path is to be found by turning R, climbing a little along the Italian side of the ridge and then forking L from a path which follows this side of the ridge. At one point the path is only a narrow ledge, and even when it gets down to scree care is needed. There are no paint marks, only occasional cairns, and sometimes you have to make your own line across the scree. At about 2500m the mule track reappears (there are still no paint marks).

From the dam at the lake (on whose steep downward side an ibex was seen in 1989, licking salt off the stone), a path, liberally marked with yellow paint, leads down to the valley. This path is difficult – worse than the mule track above the dam, of which it may not be a continuation – and much carrying is needed. At the valley bottom, at about 1650m, there is a stone bothy, where you can bivouac. From here on the slope is a bit easier, mostly, but the path does not really become easy till just before another dark blue lake, the Bacino di Campliccioli (1350m). Near the far end of this lake is the start of a tarmac road down the valley.

Times: from Furggstalden to the pass, 5 hours; to the dam by the Lago di Cingino, 3 hours; to the valley bottom, 2½ hours; to the start of the tarmac road, 2 hours.

(F. Wright, 10.8.89)

F54 SIMPLON PASS TO
VISPERTERMINEN

2602M

2202M

M ++

LK 1:100K map 42 (tourist 105); 1:50K map 274, grid ref. 641123 (M217 folds 18 & 17)

From the Simplon Pass to Visperterminen, 4km S of Visp. Quite an easy route, much of which could probably be ridden with a mountain bike. Little or no carrying is needed. The Simplon hospice (14 francs for a bed, 1989) is a convenient starting point. Much of the route is above the treeline, and there are views of the hills to the N of the Rhône valley, later also of the Mischabel range to the S. From the road leading to the Gebidum Pass the Aletsch glacier can be seen. There are no signposts till the Gebidum Pass, but the path or track is always clear, and doubt only arises at junctions.

From the car park on the S side of the Hotel Simplonblick, take a tarmac road leading N, and almost at once fork R, downhill. The road then bears L, goes down and then up, and 1km from the hotel becomes unsurfaced. Soon afterwards it reaches Stalden, which consists of a large white building (a holiday home for nuns) and some smaller ones below it. About 100m before the large building turn L (no signpost) up a grassy track, and pass a small lake on your L. Just over 1km beyond this lake, at the top of a rise, turn R up a smaller path, which after 1km joins a track coming from below. There is a climb, then a level stretch, then a point where four paths meet. The one to the R goes down to the Rhône valley, the one to the L to the Inneri Nanzlicke (2580m) and the one ahead to the Üsseri Nanzlicke (2602m). Take the last of these, which after the pass descends easily to the Nanztal. There is a proper jeep track from about 2100m down to the valley bottom, and up the other side to the Gebidum Pass (2202m). Soon after this pass you reach Giw (1964m), the top of a chair lift and tarmac road from Visperterminen.

Times: from the Simplon Pass to the Üsseri Nanzlicke, 3 hours; to the Nanztal bottom, 2 hours; to Giw, 2 hours.

(F. Wright, 13.8.89)

F57 FURGGEN PASS   2451M
E +++

LK 1:100K map 42 (tourist 105); 1:50K on three maps, grid ref. 652133 (M217 fold 18)

From Grengiols, at the top of a side road, 10km NE of Brig, to Heiligkreuz and the Binntal just below Binn. An easy unsurfaced road with good views of the Berner Oberland. Just above Grengiols fork L towards Bächerhäusern, and about 2½km above Grengiols, where the tarmac ends, take the R-hand of two unsurfaced roads (signpost Breithorn and Säflisch). The road is dusty (probably muddy when it rains).

Allow 3 hours to the top, 2½ down to Heiligkreuz (less if you manage to ride).

(F. Wright, 11.8.88)

F60 ALBRUN PASS   2409M
D (68) +++

LK 1:100K map 42; 1:50K map 265, grid ref. 666135 (M217 fold 19)

From Binn, up a side valley 15km ENE of Brig, to Goglio, up another side valley 20km N of Domodossola. The approach roads on both sides have quite long tunnels, below Binn and below Alpe Devero; the latter (in 1993) was particularly difficult, being curving and unlit. From Binn there is a tarmac road up to Im Feld. The Binntal used to be known for its mines, and at Im Feld there is a quarry where visitors can try their hand at finding crystals, etc.

Here do not take the tarmac road on the same side of the river (this leads to the quarry) but cross the bridge and turn R up an easy jeep track (an old smugglers' road, apparently). Follow this for about 5km; then, at a signpost 'Binntalhütte, Albrunpass', turn R off it onto a footpath, where some carrying is needed. A night at the Binntalhütte cost 22 francs in 1993. From the hut it is a short climb, up a quite carefully constructed mule track, to the pass. Some carrying is needed here. The descent is rougher, for some way. At the first small lake cross by the broken dam to take an easy path down the R bank of the stream. Roughly ½km before the large lake (Lago di Devero) cross by a wooden bridge to the L bank, and skirt the lake along its SE side by an easy path, which after a short steep climb joins a wide track (perhaps rideable) leading to the end of the lake and then down to Campriolo, the first settlement. The road remains unsurfaced down to, and for ½km beyond, Alpe Devero; it is then tarmac down to Goglio.

Most of the Italian side is a national park, and from the Lago di Devero there are striking views of the mountains along the Swiss frontier. Cars are not allowed above Alpe Devero.

Allow 4 hours from Im Feld to the pass, and 4 from the pass to Campriolo.

(W. G. Stoll 1989, F. Wright 11–12.8.93)

F63 GRIES PASS   2462M
D +++

LK 1:100K map 42; 1:50K map 265, grid ref. 671145 (M217 fold 19)

From Ulrichen, where the road over the Nufenen Pass joins the road up the Rhône valley, to Riale at the head of the Val Formazza in Italy: 2.9km rough track, 5.4km r/s. This pass was probably used by German-speaking colonists from Oberwallis (the upper Rhône valley), who settled in the Val Formazza in the 13th century; to this day the villages in the Val Formazza have German and Italian names. For those who have cars, a popular outing is, having parked the car where the road to the Griessee leaves the Nufenen road, to do a circuit of the three passes Corno **F66**, San Giacomo **F69**, Gries; with a mountain bike this can be done in a day, on foot it usually takes longer.

Climbing the Nufenen road from the N, you see a dam high up on your R. About 1½km before the Nufenen Pass, where the road bends L, a road leads off to the R towards this dam. It is tarmac, and for ½km the slope is little or nothing; after that it is variable. After 1.8km the road forks; the R fork leads after a short climb to the dam, which holds in the Griessee, the L fork soon ends in a car park. Take the L fork, and leave the car park by a broad stony track, which after ½km comes to a wooden cross and a stone building. Go L, uphill, here, following what soon becomes a rough footpath. This more or less follows the contour line 50–100m above the lake. A glacier can be seen descending almost to the water's edge opposite. There are some tricky bits, which you don't see till you are on them. Almost 2km from the car park you come to a signpost where you turn L for the Corno Pass.

Going ahead here, you cross first a stream, then a snowfield about 100m wide, and after a climb descend perhaps 50m to the pass.

Here there is a small unmanned *rifugio* with a metal roof. A notice near the door says that at this spot the composer Richard Wagner, on 18 July 1852, began his spiritual pilgrimage to Italy.

The descent begins about 150m to the L of the *rifugio*. It is down a steep hillside into a flat-bottomed basin in the hills. At first the path is mostly smooth and easy, but it becomes rougher and harder lower down, and a lot of lifting and some carrying is needed. An easy path across the bottom of the basin brings you, near the far side, to a wide track which is easily rideable with a mountain bike and perhaps even, in places, with a touring bike. This descends, beyond the outlet of the basin, in several traverses to the Lago di Morasco, where people park their cars. From here the road, though not tarmac, is used by cars and leads down to Riale (tarmac recommences at the dam).

(See CC 21, 1980, and 39, 1986; also F. Wright, 28.7.02.)

F66   CORNO PASS
2540M
E ++

LK 1:100K map 42 (tourist 101); 1:50K map 265, grid ref. 672145
(M217 fold 19)

A rough alternative to the top part of the (comparatively recent) road over the Nufenen Pass, 6km r/s. It is very easy going, and more scenic and quiet than the road, much superior even to the old Nufenen footpath. Leave the new road by (or near to) the hairpin at Alp Cruina di Bedretto; there is a very good well-defined path, steep in places, to the Corno hut. Above the hut the path is still excellent (rideable in descent) as far as the beginning of the summit lake. Take the R-hand (uphill) fork here; it is very stony over the top as far as two locked huts (1956), and there may still be snowdrifts here late in the season. A fine view of the Oberland peaks opens up as you start to descend – keep these in front of you and the new reservoir on your L. Soon you meet the reservoir access road (see **F63**), which leads on to the main road.

Allow about 2 hours for the rough section.

(E. D. Clements, 1956, etc.)

F69   PASSO DI SAN GIACOMO
2313M
S SIDE E. N SIDE D   +++

LK 1:100K map 42 (tourist 101); 1:50K map 265, grid ref. 677145
(M217 fold 19)

From Riale (a small village with no shops) at the head of the Italian Val Formazza, to or near All'Acqua in the Swiss Val Bedretto, 11km WSW of Airolo; 6km r/s. Some maps have been known to show a road over this pass into the Val Bedretto; according to W. G. Stoll, Mussolini made an offer to the Swiss to build a road, at his expense, over and down to Airolo, but the Swiss did not want the Italians so close to their fortresses on the Gotthard. Everyone who has tried this pass from either direction has experienced difficulties in

finding the path on the Swiss side.

Just before Riale, as you approach from the Val Formazza, a rough and stony road, passable for 4-wheel-drive vehicles, turns R and zigzags up the hillside, giving views of the Lago di Morasco (see **F63**) and nearby mountains; Shortly before the dam which holds in the Lago di Toggia, there is a rifugio/restaurant on the L. After a short climb to the dam, the road follows the W shore of the lake, and then climbs a short way to the pass. It ends just after a dilapidated yellow-painted building on the L, perhaps suitable for a bivouac. A rutted path now climbs ahead for a short way, to the L of what looks like an outdoor lavatory, to a wooden cross. From here you can see, about 1km away and below you, a small white chapel and, close to it, a modern building. This chapel is the spot referred to on signposts as San Giacomo.

From San Giacomo three waymarked paths lead down to the valley. All three were investigated by a correspondent in July 2002, one with a bike, two without. None was found to be very easy:

(i) The easiest is probably as follows: at San Giacomo go ahead (sign All'Acqua), and after 10 minutes you come to a fork, with a signpost. Both paths are shown as leading to All'Acqua. The L one is called the *vecchia mulattiera* (old mule-track), the R one is shown as going first to Stabbiascio. Go R here. The path is in many places either rocky or else a narrow rut. In addition it hardly loses height for some way. Then it comes to the top of a cable hoist and descends for perhaps 100m before turning R and levelling off again. It comes to Stabbiascio, a large cowshed, and just beyond this there is a sign which marks the beginning of a fairly easy path descending to the valley, just down-valley from All'Acqua. If coming the other way, take a short tarmac road from All'Acqua leading down to a bridge over the stream (the Ticino), turn L along a track, after 200m pass a building on the R (a possible bivouac) and soon after that bear R climbing up the path (sign Stabbiascio).

Time: from cross to All'Acqua, 2½ hours.

(ii) Not much less suitable is the following, which has the advantage of meeting the valley road up-valley from All'Acqua and so reducing the vertical distance on r/s by about 200m. At San Giacomo turn L (sign 'Capanna Corno–Gries, Passo del Corno'). At first it is a rutted path over grassy slopes, crossing a stream at one point, undulating but not steep, and not losing height overall. After ¼ hour you come to a small building on the L. Immediately after this turn R downhill at a small red sign 'Paltano'. The path is sometimes rocky, sometimes narrow and rutted, sometimes so steep that double carrying may be needed. Lower down the slope moderates. Just before the bottom you reach a bulldozed gravel track, which takes you down to a wooden bridge over the stream, and the road. (Whatever Paltano is or was – a farm, probably – our correspondent saw no sign of it.) If coming the other way, leave the road about 2½km up-valley from All'Acqua, at a point 300m along the road above the higher of two close-set hairpin bends (look for a signpost and a bridge over the stream).

Time: from cross to main road, 2–2½ hours.

(iii) The most direct but also (as our correspondent thought) much the hardest is the *vecchia mulattiera* mentioned under (i) above. For this, take the L fork as described under (i). After about 20 minutes you come to a cowshed ('Val d'Olgia' on signposts). Below this the path is fairly easy for a bit, over a grassy slope, but then it enters a wood and is often steep, narrow and with awkwardly projecting rocks. It is, however, easy to follow, with many paint marks. If coming the other way, turn R after the bridge at All'Acqua – see (i) – along a broad grassy track, parallel to the stream, over an open hillside. The track soon enters a wood. About 10 minutes after the bridge, after crossing a stream, turn sharp L, uphill, at a sign 'Passo San Giacomo'.

Time: from cross to All'Acqua, 2½ hours.

(E. W. Stocks, 1965; F. Wright, 8.6.82 and 29–30.7.02)

F72 RIONDA AND   2156M
LA TOURCHE   2198M
                                     E +++

LK 1:100K map 41 (tourist 105); 1:50K map 272

From Morcles, 15km N of Martigny. One of the toughest road climbs in Switzerland, up 29 numbered hairpin bends to the village of Morcles. After another 4km the tarmac ends, leaving a good gravel track with some fabulous balcony stretches. Views into the Rhône Valley and towards Lac Leman. At the fork keep going for a flat traverse to Rionda; or turn left to head north to La Tourche, where there is a refuge and restaurant that's on the Via Alpina trail and therefore popular with hikers.

F75 PAS DE CHEVILLE   2038M
              E SIDE D. W SIDE E (56) ++
LK 1:100K map 41 (tourist 105); 1:50K map 272, grid ref. 581126 (M217 fold 15, or M243, SE corner)

From Erde, 5km W of Sion, to Gryon, in the hills 7½km NE of St Maurice, 10km r/s. A fine, varied pass, hard going on the E side, very easy on the W. Try to cross in dry weather, and avoid if there is snow about. The wildlife in the higher parts of the pass includes (report dated 1981) capercaillies, eagles and 700 chamois.

There is a marvellous cliffhanger of a road from Erde to Derborence, with a couple of tunnels. At Godey, 2½km before Derborence, there is a small shop; also a restaurant by the lake at Derborence, a lake created by huge rock avalanches from Les Diablerets, in September 1714 and again in 1749. Right by the restaurant, a sign points up a steep narrow path towards farm buildings. This is quite a struggle, as is also the next stretch through the woods to Les Penés. There follows 1km of much easier going along the S bank of a stream to some shepherds' huts at the foot of a cirque of steep slopes.

The way here is N across the stream and up a steep grassy slope, indicated (in 1957) by a large arrow, not W-wards up the obvious path in front. This tough slope leads to a cleft in the cliff which is a bit tricky, and a few short carries are needed; maybe it is easier in descent. Above the cleft, the going becomes easier as you approach the col, which is right underneath the huge southern cliffs of Les Diablerets.

The descent on the W side is extremely easy. A gravel track descends gradually to Anzeindaz (restaurant). From there to Solalex (restaurant) there is a steep and loose jeep road, used by a six-wheel-drive taxi, and tarmac recommences (1991) at Solalex.

Allow at least 3 hours from Derborence to the col; 2 hours down to Gryon; in reverse 3 hours up from Gryon, 2 down to Derborence.

(E. D. Clements, 1957; G. Newey, 1982; M. Haxell, 1985; F. Wright, 16.8.91)

F81 COL DU SANETSCH   2243M
           N SIDE M. S SIDE TARMAC +++
LK 1:100K map 41 (tourist 105); 1:50K maps 263 and 273 (tourist 5009), grid ref. 588131 (M217 fold 15, or M243 SE corner)

From Gsteig, 17km NNW of Sion, to Sion or Conthey. This is a very fine route, best taken from N to S. From the centre of Gsteig, a narrow metalled road leaves the main road at a signpost, and goes SE for 1½km, to become a jeepable track up through the woods. An hour's climb brings you to a sign 'Sanetschstrasse 1½ hours, Sanetschpass 3 hours' (in German). Nearby, a short path leads W to the Sanetschfall, worth the short diversion. The main path crosses the stream a second time, and the surface deteriorates a lot, with many loose stones; higher up you appear to be climbing into a ring of cliffs, from which there is no exit. (There is no difficulty here; the path is always wide.) Follow the yellow paint marks, though the track is unmistakable anyway. A stream comes down the cliffs at one point, necessitating a short carry where it crosses the path. Soon after this you meet an unsurfaced road, which leads in a few hundred metres to the dam, at 2034m.

From the other end of the dam a good tarmac road leads to the top of the pass, and, on a fine day, a magnificent panorama of the Valais peaks. All the highest peaks of Switzerland, except those of the Oberland, are visible. A little way down the S side is an extensive limestone pavement, a must for botanists, etc. If you follow the road down, there is a very dark tunnel at one point, followed by another shorter one. According to the Michelin map these can be bypassed by taking the original path past Tsanfleuron and Glarey. This was in good condition in 1963, before the construction of the road, but may now have fallen into disrepair, as it is very steep. If you are making for the Pas de Cheville F75, it should still be possible to follow the old cart road to Daillon, Erde, etc., without descending to the Pont du Diable and the Rhône valley. This would save a 300m climb.

(E. D. Clements, 1957 & 1963; F. Wright, 23.8.85, etc.)

F87 RAWIL PASS 2429M
D (51) +++

LK 1:100K map 41 (tourist 105); 1:50K map 263 (tourist 5009), grid ref. 600136 (M217 fold 16, or M243 SE edge)

From Iffigen, at the head of the Ober-Simmental (19km NNE of Sion), to Ayent, 6km NE of Sion, 13km r/s. Berchtold V of Zähringen tried to take an army over this pass in 1211, but was driven off by rockfalls. There is a narrow road up from Lenk to Iffigen, partly metalled. At Iffigen (hotel), a signpost points the way, not up the main valley, but due S up a fairly wide boulder-strewn path through the pines, up the hillside, whose general angle is hardly less steep than that of the S side of the Gemmi **F90**; but there is less bare rock, and more trees and grass.

The cliff section is about 250m high, but the path is narrower and rougher than that on the Gemmi cliff. At one point you pass close to a waterfall, then under dripping rocks. A chamois was seen near here in 1986. At the top of the cliff stands the Blatti hut (2018m), after which the gradient eases slightly, but the climb to the Rawilsee (2349m) is still rough and very steep for a considerable distance. Soon after the lake, you reach the top. Views are disappointing, as a nearby ridge cuts off any distant views of the Valais peaks.

For about 3km the path descends very gradually (over the so-called Plan des Roses), but the surface is boulder-strewn, a succession of dried up river beds. Then quite suddenly the path begins to descend in earnest, and after about 1km passes through a small steep tunnel (note, when ascending, to turn L on emerging, as the R-hand fork leads only to a farm). The descent continues down a sort of cliff, a very steep but quite good zigzag track, with a surface of loose stones; by now you get fine views of the Valais peaks across the Rhône valley. There is another farm at the bottom, where a reservoir (the Lac de Tseuzier, 1777m) has been built. A good track along the W side takes you to the Tseuzier dam, from which a metalled road with three tunnels descends to Ayent and eventually the Rhône valley.

Allow 6 or 7 hours either way between Iffigen and the Tseuzier dam.

(M. A. Stephens 1970s; F. Wright, 29.7.86.)

F90 GEMMI PASS 2316M
M ++++

LK 1:100K tourist map 105; 1:50K map 263 (tourist 5009), grid ref. 613138 (M217 folds 16, 17)

From Leukerbad, up a side valley from Leuk (which is 22km up-valley from Sion), N-wards to Kandersteg, 8km r/s. The name means 'playing field'; the pass was used for wrestling bouts between the Bernese and the Valaisans. The pass was first mentioned in 1252. The startling S side of the route is the result of improvements by Tyrolese workmen in 1736–41 (plus, no doubt, recent maintenance). Until the 19th century (information from W. G. Stoll), small two-wheeled horse-drawn carriages took people over the pass.

The Gemmi is one of the most spectacular of all Swiss passes, justly popular. At Leukerbad the road ends, and a good path heads straight for an almost vertical cliff, 600m high. The path climbs this cliff in a remarkable piece of mule-track engineering. There are numerous zigzags, and often the path is cut out of the cliff itself. It is rather like a spiral staircase; sometimes one bit of path almost overhangs the bit below. The gradient is mostly 25–33%. No carrying is needed. The path is seldom less than 2m wide, and is well used and fairly smooth. Some parts, especially higher up, have been concreted. There are, however, some troublesome steps, or beams set transversely into the path, over which you have to keep lifting your bike (these are especially frequent higher up). There are occasional bits of wooden handrail in the more dangerous spots, but it is probably safer not to try the route if there is snow about. During the climb, the marvellous panorama of the Valais peaks steadily widens. There is a large hotel at the top, and usually many tourists, because a cable car also climbs the cliff from Leukerbad.

A good wide path, nearly always rideable, and of easy gradients, leads from the top, past the shallow Daubensee (which has no visible outlet), for about 10km, till a fantastic view opens up to the E. 500m below is the Gasterntal, with a grand array of peaks at its head. Here also is the top of a cable car coming up from Eggen, above Kandersteg. Here the path begins a headlong descent with many zigzags. The surface is very good, so some of this descent can be ridden, with extreme caution. The gradient is mostly 25%.

Allow 5–6 hours for the route, either way.

(E. D. Clements, 1958; G. Newey, 1966 & 1980; F. Wright, 27.7.86, etc.)

Our correspondent W. Davies advises that the S side, from Leukerbad, is now closed to bikes. But the N, from Kandersteg, is still stunning. So it is still possible to cross this pass, if touring, using the cable car from Leukerbad.

F93 LÖTSCHENPASS 2690M
N SIDE S. S SIDE D (54) +++

LK 1:100K map 42 (tourist 105); 1:50K map 264, grid ref. 621140 (M217 fold 17)

From Kandersteg, 25km SW of Interlaken, to Ferden in the Lötschental. There are fine views of the Gasterntal and the Kanderfirn (glacier) on the N side, and of the Lötschental and the Bietschhorn on the S. In fine weather quite a lot of walkers can be expected.

The pass was already well known in 1352. It was the scene of several battles (in 1384, 1419 and 1656) between the Bernese and the Valaisans; a mule track on the N side was built in 1698. It became less popular after the improvement of the Gemmi **F90** in 1736–41.

There are two unsurfaced roads up the Gasterntal, an almost level valley between towering cliffs; the one on the R (N) side of the valley is probably the better. Fifteen minutes' walking (according to the signpost) before Selden fork R down a road which soon crosses the river and ends at a farm. A steep and often rocky and irregular path, requiring some carrying, leads to the hotel/restaurant/farm at Gfällalp. Above here the path improves a little, but then steepens again to climb past the snout of the glacier. A level and easy path, over firm snow, crosses the glacier, whose midstream section is crevassed. The crevasses are visible, run parallel to the path and can be avoided. Beyond the crevassed part the glacier's surface is covered with small rocks, where the bike can still be pushed but there are no paint marks; you head for a snowfield with a track running across it, which is visible from afar. A small bergschrund, which has to be jumped, marks the edge of the glacier. After this the rocks are bigger, and some carrying is needed, but the path is well marked by paint and often easy enough to see.

The snowfield is probably only 50m across, but it slopes steeply enough to make crampons useful, though probably not essential. After it there is a steep rock section, where double carrying will probably be necessary. The slope then eases, and the pass itself is a broad smooth rocky saddle, easy going. A hut here provides refreshments and possibly accommodation.

The descent starts at a gentle slope but then becomes steeper, calling for careful footwork and some carrying or lifting. An unsurfaced road, which starts at Kummenalp (2083m), leads down to the Lötschental. It becomes surfaced 1½km before reaching the main square (church, water trough) at Ferden.

Times: from Selden (or the fork in the road) to the pass, 5½ hours; on to Kummenalp, 1½ hours.

(F. Wright, 7.8.89)

F95   RIEDERALP AREA   E +++

LK 1:100K map 42 (tourist 105); 1:50K map 264, grid ref. 645136 (M217 fold 18)

This area is just NE of Brig, on the SE side of the ridge which borders the Aletsch glacier on the S. For most of the route there are fine views across the Rhône valley to the Pennine Alps. You can put your bike on a cableway to go from Fiesch (15km NE of Brig) to Kühboden (2226m) (note that the youth hostel which used to be here has been closed); or you can climb the 1200m by a zigzagging road, later a track, which starts at Lax, just SW of Fiesch. From Kühboden follow a path for 2km along the slope, WSW, to the Hotel Bettmerhorn (2173m), then fork R and descend to the Bettmersee (2006m). Skirt the L bank and take a good path, uphill, to the small clear Blausee. Shortly after this, reaching the crest of the ridge (the Moosfluh), you have a view of the Aletsch glacier, the longest in Europe. The path descends on the other side of the ridge, almost reaching the Aletschwald, which is claimed to be the only forest growing above a glacier. Then it reaches the crest of the ridge again, at a lower point, the Riederfurka (2064m), and becomes a mule track along the SE side of the ridge, passing through Riederalp, Greicheralp and Bettmeralp. There are several cableways going down from this stretch, which can be used to get back down to the valley; the one from Riederalp starts just before the Hotel Spycher.

(W. G. Stoll, undated, and leaflet by Swiss Youth Hostels, 1982)

F97   FURKA OLD ROAD, OR PATH   2431M
                                                          M ++

LK 1:100K maps 37 and 42 (tourist 101); 1:50K maps 255 and 265 (tourist 5001), grid ref. 674158 (M217 fold 19)

From Gletsch, on the W side of the Furka Pass, to Realp, on the E side. There is an old path over the pass, boggy soon after leaving Gletsch, and cut by several rock falls on the E side. (1963 report.)

16.8.91 Pas de Cheville, E side, top

G. **BERNER OBERLAND** ETC

Some of the later routes in this section, starting at **G72**, are in the cantons immediately to the E of Canton Bern.

G04 <u>COL DE JAMAN</u>   1512M
E +

LK 1:100K map 41 (tourist 105); 1:50K map 262, grid ref. 564144 (M217 fold 14, or M243)

From Montreux, at the E end of Lake Geneva, to Montbovon, 12km to the NE, in the Haute Gruyère. A very easy, but popular, low pass, with fine views to the Savoy Alps and across Lake Geneva. The climb up the W side from Montreux is steep (20%), but metalled right to the top. It passes a girls' finishing school on the outskirts of Montreux, after which the gradient eases for a while; however, it is not clear from the report which way this refers to – there are two roads, via Caux and via Les Avants. Either way leads to the top, from where it is worth climbing the Dent de Jaman (1875m) by a steep zigzag path up its N ridge. The descent on the E side is by a well-trodden gravel path (some mud), which joins a smooth tarmac road down the Hongrin valley about ¾km after passing the railway (assuming that the road from the Hongrin dam is metalled).

(M. Haxell, 1985)

G08 <u>MONTBOVON</u> TO <u>AIGLE</u>   E +

LK 1:100K map 41 (tourist 105); 1:50K map 262, grid ref. 570140 (M217 fold 14)

From Montbovon (see **G04**) to Aigle, in the Rhône valley about 10km above Lake Geneva. The Lac d'Hongrin reservoir has been built since this route was done. It may be possible to cross the dam (though the 1:100K map shows no short cut across it) and pick up the path shown on Michelin. The map shows about 6km of rough road around the NE side of the lake. Recent information required, please.

G12 <u>LES MOULINS</u> TO <u>LA LÉCHERETTE</u>   E +

LK 1:100K map 41 (tourist 105); 1:50K map 262, grid ref. 574143 (M217 fold 15)

Les Moulins is 2km SW of Château d'Œx, on the N side of the Col des Mosses, and La Lécherette is higher up on the same side of the pass. This route is a footpath avoiding most of the road on the N side. (1950s report.) The 1:100K map shows 2½km of single-line cart road, the rest as a rough road.

G16 <u>COL DE BRETAYE</u>   1806M
E +

LK 1:100K map 41 (tourist 105); 1:50K map 272, grid ref. 572130

(M217 folds 14 & 15)

From Villars, in the hills 7½km ESE of Aigle (see **G08**), to La Forclaz, 8km ENE of Aigle. The route has been done, but we have no report. This pass is shown on Michelin, but the Landeskarte 1:50K only shows a little railway, and a nearby track, which passes the Col de Soud (1523m) on the way to the Col de Bretaye; it also shows a pass between Villars and La Forclaz at 1806m, on an E–W ridge.

G20 <u>COL DE LA BALLISAZ</u>   1414M
E +

LK 1:100K map 36 (tourist 104); 1:50K maps 252 and 253, grid ref. 585167 (M217 fold 5, or M243)

From Schwarzsee, at the end of a small road 17km SE of Fribourg, to La Valsainte, 7½km to the WSW and at the end of another small road 10km ENE of Bulle. A short and very easy route, well marked through pretty pre-alp country, useful as a continuation after the pretty road from Riggisberg (S of Bern). From Schwarzsee, a stony road leads W-ward; bear to the L and climb through the forest on a zigzag track. Note that the correct route zigzags sharply N-wards at a path junction at one point, soon to bear round W-wards through alpine pastures to the col. There are some chalets at the end of the forest, and a direct path may cut out the final zigzag anyway. The descent is gradual and mainly rideable; before meeting the forest again, take the R-hand path to La Valsainte, where you meet the metalled road. The L-hand path also soon meets a road down the other side of the valley to Charmey, but it is mostly unsurfaced.

Allow 1½ hours up, ¾ hour down.

(Anon. 1955)

G24 <u>ZWEISIMMEN</u> TO <u>SAANENMÖSER</u>   E +

LK 1:100K map 41 (tourist 104); 1:50K map 263 (tourist 5009), grid ref. 590152 (M217 folds 16 & 15, top)

From Zweisimmen in the Simmental, 40km WSW of Interlaken, to Saanenmöser, where the railway goes over a pass before descending to Gstaad. This is a metalled road along the SE side of the river to Oeschseite, then a rather undulating cart track following the railway line.

(1982 report)

G28 <u>REULISEN PASS</u>   1715M
E +

LK 1:100K map 41 (tourist 104, where the name is Rümlisse); 1:50K map 263 (tourist 5009), grid ref. 595147 (M217 folds 15 & 16)

From Gstaad to Grodei (or Grodey), about 9km to the ENE in the Ober-Simmental. Between the same valleys as the Trüttlisberg **G32**; easier and shorter, but the path (3km connecting rough roads) is not always easy to find.

G32 TRÜTTLISBERG PASS 2038M
D ++

LK 1:100K map 41 (tourist 105); 1:50K map 263 (tourist 5009), grid ref. 595141

From Lauenen, 6 km SSE of Gstaad, to Lenk in the Ober-Simmental. The following (6.7.06) is from someone who crossed the pass without a bike. The start, from Lauenen, is up a road signed 'Altersheim Sonnibühl', about 100m N of the information office (near the church), which issues free *Wanderkarten* (path maps). This climbs up a mostly grassy hillside, with scattered chalets and a network of tarmac roads. The road provides an easy way up to a small settlement called Flue. Just before the road ends above Flue, go L up a steep gravel track which is mostly clear and easy to follow. The exception is at a point where the track goes through a wooden gate and then downhill to cross a stream. Here (so our correspondent was told) do not go through the gate but go R following a smaller track which leads to the pass. Unfortunately our correspondent went through the gate and arrived at the Türli, 1986m, from where he had to take a path to the Trüttlisberg pass.

The descent starts as a muddy but easy path which loses height gradually. There are several narrow metal gates and a barrier made of two short ladders. After rain the path can be soft and sometimes wet. Lower down, you come to one or two small farms approached by rough tracks. It may be better to keep to these and ignore the official red-and-white posts and paint marks, which are meant for walkers, not people with bikes, and which indicate a path which is often narrow, rutted and difficult even without a bike. Lower down this path comes to a good dirt road but soon abandons it to go down several flights of wooden steps and cross a stream (again, it may be best to stick to the road). After the stream the path improves, losing height gradually, comes to the route of a cable car and soon reaches tarmac and an easy descent to Lenk.

Times (allowing for a bike): W side 3 hours, E side 2½ hours.

G36 HAHNENMOOS PASS 1950M
E +

LK 1:100K map 41 (tourist 104); 1:50K map 263 (tourist 5009), grid ref. 604144

From Lenk in the Ober-Simmental to Adelboden in the Engstligental. Very easy; the E side is all tarmac, and only the top 2km on the W side is unsurfaced (mostly rideable downhill anyway).

(1986 report)

G40 BONDERCHRINDE (OR BUNDERCHRINDE) 2384M
S ++

LK 1:100K tourist map 104; 1:50K map 263 (tourist 5009), grid ref. 614148

From Kandersteg to Adelboden in the Engstligental. The following (10.7.06) is from someone who crossed the pass without a bike. On the route described here the path has in a few places been washed away. An alternative (which would take longer because there is no cable car) would be to take the road leading to the Gemmi pass F90 and turn right up a road to a road junction at 1595m (Usseri Üschene), then take a path to meet the other one near the pass.

From Kandersteg take the cable car (10 francs in 2006) to Allmenalp, 1725m (restaurant, dormitory accommodation). An easy path leads up to Obere Allme (farm, milk etc. for sale). The path climbs from here and continues up the valley to a yellow signpost which points left to Bonderchrinde. You now cross, still uphill, a wide field of scree, the path being easily visible. You might be able to push a bike over the rocks, or you might have to carry it. After the scree a path, not steep till near the end, leads to the top of the ridge (the Alpschelegrat). The path is mostly broad and easy, but in one or two places it has been carried or washed away.

From the top of the ridge (2315m, turnstile to keep cows away) you look half right and see the path leading to the Bonderchrinde, not far away. The path, easy at first, is steep towards the end. From the pass there is a fine view of Kandersteg, the Öschinensee, the Hohtürli G44, the Blümlisalp group and in the distance the summits of the Eiger, Jungfrau and Mönch. In the other direction you see Adelboden and the surrounding hills.

The descent is steep at first, over loose stones. Lower down the path crosses scree and comes to grass. It is often uneven and rocky, and carrying will probably be needed from time to time. A dirt road, which soon becomes tarmac, is reached at Bonderalp (Bunderalp), which seems to be the name of a small farm as well as a restaurant a short way down the road.

Times (allowing for a bike): E side 3 hours, W side 2 hours.

G44 HOHTÜRLI 2781M
VS ++

LK 1:100K map 42 (tourist 101); 1:50K map 264 (tourist 5004), grid ref. 625151 (M217 fold 17)

From Kandersteg to Griesalp, at the head of the Kiental. The following (11.8.58 and 9.7.06) is from two people who crossed the pass without a bike. Extremely hard. The top 300m (vertically) on the W side, and nearly 600m on the N side, are scree, though the surface of the path itself is not bad. Both sides, higher up, are very steep, and the highest part of the N side is so steep that it has been furnished with flights of wooden steps, like ladders, and ropes and chains to hold onto. It maybe possible to negotiate this stretch by holding the bike in one hand, with the front wheel secured, and the rope/chain in the other; double carrying may well be needed. On the W side it is probably advisable to take the path which goes up to Oberbärgli from the lake, rather than the other one which climbs the hillside from near the restaurant, Läger, etc. and keeps well away from the lake. On the N side, rather than the uneven and troublesome footpath that connects Griesalp with Bundalp, 1840m, you can take a good tarmac road.

Times (allowing for a bike, and starting the W side from the Oschinensee); W side 5 hours, N side 2 hours.

G48 SEFINENFURKE 2612M
S (54) +++

LK 1:100K map 42 (tourist 101); 1:50K map 264 (tourist 5004), grid ref 628153 (M217 fold 17)

From Stechelberg, at the head of the Lauterbrunnental S of Interlaken, to Griesalp, at the head of the Kiental. A popular pass with walkers. There are views of the Gspaltenhorn ridge, the Schilthorn and other more distant peaks. From the roadhead in the Kiental the Gamchi glacier can be seen at the head of the valley. There are some steep stretches on both sides.

From Stechelberg take either a path across the river (no reports) or a path to Sichellauenen, then across the river and along the hillside, through woods, to the entrance to the Sefinental. The path follows the L (N) bank of the stream for nearly 3km, as a narrow road, not tarmac but with a good surface and easily rideable where the gradient allows. At a gap in a fence, a footpath takes over, climbing, often steeply, away from the stream.

Near the tree line it is easy to miss a small path branching off to the L from the main path; the signpost 'Rotstock Hütte' is badly placed. This small path leads across a stream and then up a grassy slope to the Rotstock hut (a bed cost 12 francs in 1989). After the hut the path is steep, rutted and rocky for some way, then eases before the final slope, which is steep and consists of loose rock debris partly compacted with wet rock dust.

The W side is even steeper. For the first 50m or so (along the slope) there is a fixed rope, which you can hold in your R hand while carrying the bike in your L. The path remains steep for some way, over the same rock debris.

Times: Stechelberg to Rotstock hut, 5 hours; to pass, 2¼ hours; to beginning of road, 2 hours.

(RSJ 28, no. 6, Nov./Dec. 1983; W. Stevenson in CC 41, 1987; F. Wright, 5.8.89)

G52 GRÜNENBERG PASS 1553M
E ++

LK 1:100K map 37 (tourist 101); 1:50K map 254, grid ref. 632179 (M217 fold 7)

From Schangnau, 16km N of Interlaken, to Habkern, 5km N of Interlaken. On the descent from Schangnau, turn L at a crossroads by a cheese factory (*Käserei*); the signpost is for Gemmi-Chilbi. The road descends to the river (the Emme) and crosses it through a covered bridge, after which it climbs steeply. At Rotmoos it becomes unsurfaced, and after climbing for some way it descends to Trüschhübel. Here, at about 1100m, turn L up a track (signpost Grünenbergpass). There follows a rough track of varying quality, in parts rocky and uneven though it could be traversed by a motor-bike and, with difficulty, by a jeep.

There is no view from the top, because of the trees, but just after it there is a view of the Oberland peaks. The S side has a much better surface, of smooth gravel.

(F. Wright, 30.7.89)

G56 KLEINE SCHEIDEGG 2061M
E +++

LK 1:100K map 37 (tourist 101); 1:50K map 254 (tourist 5004), grid ref. 640159 (M217 folds 8 bottom and 18 top)

From Wengen, on the slope just E of Lauterbrunnen, and 10km SE of Interlaken, to Grindelwald. Access to Wengen from Lauterbrunnen is by a cog railway or a steep track; the latter is a good easy track and causes no problems. From Wengen it is a very good wide footpath or rough road throughout. There are fine views, but the path is very popular with tourists.

G60 FAULHORN TRAVERSE 2620M
D (54) +++++

LK 1:100K map 37 (tourist 101); 1:50K map 254 (tourist 5004), grid ref. 642169 (M217 fold 8)

From Wilderswil, just S of Interlaken, to Grosse Scheidegg, 32km r/s. This is a panoramic route of the highest class; the ever-changing views of the famous Oberland trio (Eiger, Mönch, Jungfrau) demand a fine, clear day. Almost all is wheelable, occasionally you can ride.

If coming from Interlaken, turn L just before the Wilderswil/Schynige Platte railway station; if from Bönigen, turn L at the Gasthof Hirschen. From the covered wooden bridge at Wilderswil, a stony path beside the cemetery is signposted Schynige Platte. After countless zigzags, the path emerges on an alp 900m above the valley. The main path continues up, but soon a L-hand branch leads to the Breitlauenen hotel and station on the rack railway (a modest hotel compared to the 'palace' on the Schynige Platte). This path continues round the back of the hotel to rejoin the main path higher up. After ascending another 250m, the path contours the steep slopes below the ridge (hay barn hereabouts in 1989), before making the final climb to the Schynige Platte hotel. The 1400m climb from the valley has been up a very well-made, smooth path for most of the way.

From the hotel, ride down to the station and take the path straight ahead; fairly soon it becomes very boulder-strewn for nearly 2km (in 1957), but the marvellous view is always there. Contouring the Laucherhorn, the path improves, and climbs again to a slight col, switching to the N side of the Sagisen ridge and temporarily losing the view. Rounding another corner, the path turns sharply back to the SW, climbing up a rough rocky trough to another col on the ridge (tiny café, the Weber Hütte, 1989, selling drinks). Here the path turns E-wards again up a short steep rocky 'ladder', which will probably entail a double carry. It is the only awkward bit on the whole route, but there is no danger. The rest of the way to the Faulhorn is much easier as you gain a broad grassy ridge. The summit is about 60m above the top of the path, up some wide, easy zigzags. There is a little hotel/restaurant at the top, touristy, because it is one of the finest viewpoints in the Alps.

A wide and very popular path, a bit rough and boulder-strewn at times, leads down to the Bachsee [also called Bachalpsee], from where a very good, mostly rideable path leads to First, the upper station of the cable railway from Grindelwald. Here you lose the tourists. There is a road from First to Grosse Scheidegg. It is not tarmac, but the surface is quite good and it is certainly rideable. At Grosse Scheidegg there is a hotel/restaurant, popular with climbers.

Since 1985 or before, there has been a tarmac road over the Grosse Scheidegg, except for some unsurfaced stretches on the Meiringen side. There is a fine gorge and waterfall just above Rosenlaui to the SE, and the backward views hereabouts to the Wetterhorn are very fine. If you want a direct route to Innertkirchen, there is a good track which leaves the road at one of the hairpins and goes via Geissholz to meet the main road above the hairpins just W of Innertkirchen. (These hairpins on the main road avoid the Aar gorge, which is well worth the walk, and is nice and cool on a hot day. It is not known whether bikes are allowed through the gorge.)

Times: the route can be done as a round trip from Interlaken (turn R at Grosse Scheidegg and come back through Grindelwald); for this allow 14 hours, including meal stops. Or you can turn L at Grosse Scheidegg and go down to Meiringen; this would probably take about 13 hours.

(E. D. Clements, 1957, 1960; F. Wright, 3.8.89)

G64   BRIENZERSEE   E +

LK 1:100K map 37 (tourist 101); 1:50K map 254 (tourist 5004), grid ref. 643175 (M217 fold 8)

From Kienholz, at the E end of the Brienzersee, to Iseltwald, about half way along the SE shore. There used to be a good quiet path here, then a road from Iseltwald to Interlaken. It was still pleasant in 1982, despite the motorway, a lot of which is in tunnels here.

G68   SÖRENBERG TO SCHANGNAU   1316M
                                                  E +

LK 1:100K map 37 (tourist 101); 1:50K map 244 (tourist 5023), grid ref. 642185 (M217 fold 8)

From Sörenberg, on the road over the Glaubenbüelen Pass, 7½km N of Brienz, to Schangnau (see G52), 16km N of Interlaken. Mostly a small metalled or rough road, with a 3km connecting path, sometimes rideable in this, the downhill, direction. (Our report is from the 1950s.)

G72   SEEWENEGG   1749M
                                                  E +

LK 1:100K map 37 (tourist 101); 1:50K map 244 (tourist 5023), grid ref. 649192 (M217 fold 8)

From the Glaubenberg Pass (1543m), 22km SW of

Lucerne, to Flühli, 7km to the W. Rideable to the top and down to the lake at Seewen; keep N round the lake, and go S on meeting the rough road down to Flühli. (1950s report.)

G76   TANNENALP   2010M
                                                  E ++

LK 1:100K map 37 (tourist 101); 1:50K map 255 (tourist 5023), grid ref. 668181 (M217 fold 9)

From Engstlenalp, at the head of the Gental, 12km NE of Innertkirchen, to the head of the Melchtal, 6km to the W. A very good path to Melchsee-Frutt, then a very steep road (average 11%) down to the Melchtal.

G80   JOCH PASS   2209M
                        N SIDE D. SW SIDE E ++

LK 1:100K map 37 (tourist 101); 1:50K maps 245 and 255 (tourist 5023), grid ref. 672181 (M217 fold 9)

From Engelberg, 25km SSE of Lucerne, to Engstlenalp, at the head of the Gental (see G76), 10km r/s. There is a r/s climb of about 1200m from Engelberg, but only 350m from Engstlenalp; this may influence your choice.

From Engelberg there are two ways up to the Trübsee: a well-kept path to the E of the cable railway, very steep up the final zigzags below the cables; and a jeep track leaving the road to Unter Trübsee at Unter Trübsee. The latter makes for the W shore of the lake. There are also two ways up from the Trübsee to the pass, both very steep. In 1953 the one below the ski lift was easier; the other, a little to the E, crosses an awkward scree slope low down. It may be possible to take your bike up in the ski lift.

There are good views from the top, especially of the Titlis, but any long views are restricted to the W and N. The way down to Engstlenalp is steep and rocky at times, but mostly not too difficult if you avoid the short cuts made by walkers.

Times: we only have times for a trip done the other way, viz. 1½ hours from Engstlenalp to the top, 2½ hours down to Unter Trübsee.

(E. D. Clements, 1953; F. Wright, 17.8.89, etc.)

G84   GÄTTERLI PASS   1192M
                                                  E ++

LK 1:100K map 32 (tourist 101); 1:50K map 235 (tourist 5008), grid ref. 685208 (M217 fold 10, top)

From Lauerz, on the Lauerzersee, just W of Schwyz, to Gersau, on the N shore of the Lake of Lucerne (Vierwaldstättersee). There is a forest track to the top, while the S side is tarmac. There are good views to the S. (The ferry from Beckenried to Gersau cost 5 francs in 1989, and took ¼ hour.)

G88 SEELISBERG TO BAUEN   M +

LK 1:100K map 37 (tourist 101); 1:50K map 245 (tourist 5008), grid ref. 686200 (M217 fold 10, top)

Seelisberg and Bauen are both on the W side of the Urnersee (which is the E end of the Lake of Lucerne). Michelin shows a rough road from Seelisberg to Wissig, which is 300m above Bauen. In 1956 Wissig and Bauen were connected by an interminable stepped path with many zigzags. Recent information required, please.

G92 SURENEN PASS   2291M
                                                       D +++

LK 1:100K map 37 (tourist 101); 1:50K map 245 (tourist 5008), grid ref. 684187 (M217 folds 9 & 10)

From Engelberg, 25km SSE of Lucerne, to Altdorf. A long, hard pass, not too bad on the W side, but with two or three very long, rough and steep descents on the E side. The path is easy to follow.

G96 SUSTEN PASS OLD ROAD   2259M
                                                       E ++

LK 1:100K map 37 (tourist 101); 1:50K map 255 (tourist 5001), grid ref. 677175 (M217 fold 9)

This is a quiet alternative to the modern road over the pass, from Innertkirchen to Wassen. It is still usable in a number of places, particularly a long stretch on the E side; the surface is rough, but sometimes rideable. (Our report is from the 1950s.)

H. NORTH-EASTERN SWITZERLAND

For an explanation of the Landeskarte (LK) map references, see Appendix III.

H10 HAGGENEGG
1417M
E +

LK 1:100K map 33 (tourist 110); 1:50K map 236 (tourist 5008), grid ref. 695209 (M216 fold 19)

From Einsiedeln, 14km NE of Schwyz, to Schwyz. A metalled road up the valley to a little beyond Alpthal, then a very easy track to the pass, with a narrow metalled road for the descent.

H20 HINTERHOHI PASS
1416M
E +

LK 1:100K map 33; 1:50K map 237 (tourist 5015), grid ref. 730226 (M216 fold 20)

From Nesslau to Amden (both N of the Walensee). Short and easy.

H30 WIDERSTEINER FURGGE
2013M
D? +

LK 1:100K map 33 (tourist 110); 1:50K map 237 (tourist 5015), grid ref. 730210 (M216 fold 20, and M218 fold 3)

From Murg, on the S shore of the Walensee, to Engi in the Sernftal, 14km to the S. Take a private road up the Murgtal to Merlen, at the top of sixteen zigzags, and continue up to Mornen (1335m). Then go through a sparse wood of mixed evergreens, to reach first the lower Murgsee and then the upper Murgseen, where there is a mountain hotel, the Fischerhütte. The path continues over meadows to the pass. The descent to the S is steep but on a well-marked path as far as the Übli huts, from where a rideable road leads down to Engi.

(Leaflet by Swiss Youth Hostels, 1984)

H40 SAREISERJOCH
(AND THREE MORE IN LICHTENSTEIN)
2008M
M +

LK 1:100K map 34 (tourist 109); 1:50K map 238 (tourist 5012), grid ref. 766218 (M216 fold 22)

From Malbun, 7½km SSE of Vaduz the capital of Liechtenstein, to Nenzing, just across the border in Austria. There is a good track to the Sareiser Höhe, then a narrow path to the summit, with a steeper rocky descent to Nenzinger Himmel. An equally easy pass, perhaps, on which we have no details, is the Bettljoch, 2108m, from Steg (between Vaduz and Malbun) to Nenzing; this consists of a jeep road to Alp Gritsch (1897m), a mule track thence to the summit and a path down the other side. The following two look very much harder from the map: Barthümeljoch, 2305m, from Jenins (just N of Landquart) to Nenzing; Chlei

Furgga, 2243m, from Seewis (6km ENE of Landquart) to Nenzing. These can be found on M216 fold 22, bottom; the last two also on M218 folds 4 & 5, top.

H50 RUOSALPER CHULM
2178M
M ++

LK 1:100K map 38 (tourist 110); 1:50K map 246, grid ref. 705193 (M218 fold 2)

From Muotathal, 10km ESE of Schwyz, to the road over the Klausen Pass. A tarmac road goes up the Bisistal through Dürrenboden, followed by an unsurfaced road, then a path over the pass, which later goes SW to the Klausen road. There are no difficulties in good conditions.

H60 RICHETLI PASS
2261M
D +

LK 1:100K map 38 (tourist 110); 1:50K maps 246 and 247, grid ref. 724195 (M218 folds 2 & 3)

From Linthal, 14km SSW of Glarus, to Elm in the Sernftal, 14km to the E. The W side is a long, steep and rough ascent; the E side is somewhat easier.

H70 RISETEN PASS
2189M
S ++

LK 1:100K map 38 (tourist 110); 1:50K map 247 (tourist 5012), grid ref. 737204 (M218 fold 3)

From Weisstannen, 8km SW of Mels or Sargans, to Matt in the Sernftal, 13km to the WSW. The route starts as a tiny tarmac road from Weisstannen, with some gravel. At a junction at 1175m, 4km from Weisstannen, keep N of the main river (the jeep road crosses to the S here). From a farm at 1661m a rough footpath begins, heading SSW, not well trodden, marked with occasional painted stones. It took three hours pushing a fully laden bike to get to the top (including crossing electrified cattle wires). The descending path is very steep and narrow, with turns too tight to think about riding down. Double carrying was necessary for the first hour.

Once on gravel again, it is a fine descent into Matt; the descent took two hours.

(S. Fishpool, 22.8.92, supplemented from the LK)

H80 PANIXER PASS
2404M
S ++

LK 1:100K map 38 (tourist 110); 1:50K map 247, grid ref. 727190 (M218 fold 3)

From Panix (Pigniu), 7½km WNW of Ilanz in the Vorderrheintal, to Elm in the Sernftal. Very long and very hard going, but rewarding. There are some very rocky sections, especially on the N side, requiring carrying.

This pass was the scene of a celebrated crossing (from N to S) by the Russian general Suvorov, with 15,000 troops and 1,400 French prisoners, over snow and ice, in October 1799. *(See Cycloclimbing 87, p. 15.)*

H90 CHRÜZLI PASS   2347M

S +

LK 1:100K map 38 (tourist 110); 1:50K map 256 (tourist 5001), grid ref. 700175 (M218 fold 1)

From Amsteg, 13km S of Altdorf, to Sedrun in the Vorderrheintal, 6km WSW of Disentis. Before the opening of the route through the Schöllenenschlucht (below Andermatt), this was the preferred mule track for trade and travel from the N to the Ticino over the Lukmanier Pass. From Amsteg (519m) take the road to, and through, Bristen (770m), and 2km after Bristen take a cart road which doubles back up into the side valley to a flat space, the Etzliboden (1330m). From here a footpath climbs steeply to cross two steps in the valley floor, Rossboden and Gulmen. Where the main valley and path turn 90° L, at Müllersmat (just below 2000m), there is a sign pointing to the nearby Etzlihütte. From Müllersmat the path climbs up the Chrüzlital and over scree to the pass. The descent into the Val Strem is on a broad mule track, which remains on the R bank of the stream until almost at the bottom of the valley.

(Leaflet by Swiss Youth Hostels, slightly amended from the map for the benefit of cyclists)

9.8.91 At the Col de la Galise, me

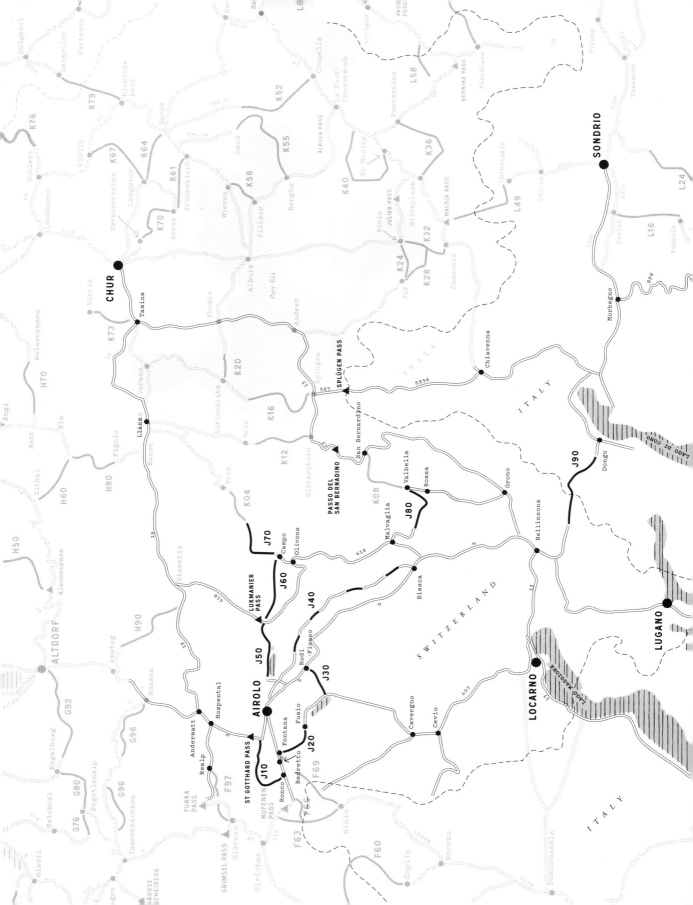

J. CANTON TICINO (TESSIN)

J10   ST GOTTHARD PASS TO RONCO   M +

LK 1:100K map 42; 1:50K map 265 (tourist 5001), grid ref. 685154 (M217 fold 20, top)

An old military road contouring high above the Val Bedretto, with a steep path down to Ronco. There are good views of the Valle Leventina and the Val Bedretto. This route is easier if started at the Gotthard end; otherwise you start with a climb up one of several hard paths. It can be started, at the Gotthard end, at two different points. Point A is where, as you come down the new road from the pass, the gallery open to the L ends and the tunnel proper begins. Point B is reached by a tarmac road which leaves the main road at the bottom end of the tunnel (signpost Sentiero Alto Val Bedretto, Villa, etc.). The route can also be finished at several different points on the Nufenen road: Villa, 1354m; Bedretto, 1402m; and Ronco, 1482m. The following description is of the route from Point A to Ronco.

From Point A a steep and stony path climbs for about 100m (along the slope), then becomes level, wider and easy. In a few places landslides make carrying necessary. After about 1km there is a restaurant, and after this for about another 1km, as far as Point B, there is an unsurfaced road (giving access to the restaurant), easily rideable with a touring bike.

After Point B the route is a stony jeep track for some way. It climbs to reach its highest point at a farmhouse (Alpe Fieud, 2116m) and then descends gently but not losing much height. At one point a bridge has been washed away, making the road impassable for cars and motorbikes. Near, but above, here is another farmhouse, Alpe Cavanna (2015m), and it is apparently soon after this that the path to Villa leaves the track.

From here on, the track is at times merely a narrow but easy footpath. Our correspondent met a 30m stretch of snow. Eventually the track ends abruptly, and you have to take a footpath down to Ronco. This path, through fly-infested woods, is the most difficult part of the route. It takes the best part of an hour. Generally steep and narrow, often difficult and rutted, it requires a lot of carrying. It is, however, mostly easy to see, and, where not, well waymarked.

Time: from Point A to Ronco, 4 hours (less if you manage to ride any part of the route).

(F. Wright, 10.7.94)

J20   PASSO DEL NARÈT   2437M
                                            M +++

LK 1:100K map 42; 1:50K map 265 (tourist 5001), grid ref. 686148 (M217 fold 20; M218 fold 11)

From Fusio, 32km NNW of Locarno, in the Valle Lavizzara, to Fontana in the Val Bedretto just W of Airolo. The tarmac road from Fusio goes up past the Lago Sambuco to the Lago di Narèt, to the N end of one of the two dams which hold in the lake. From here go L along the dams, and

follow the road around the lake as far as you can (this looks easier than going R around the lake on a footpath, which is hard at times). Then take a level path, still skirting the lake, to join the path which climbs to the L, away from the lake, up to the pass (a short climb, 130m vertically).

Just over the pass is a refuge, apparently deserted but in good condition. The path bears L here, is easy for 200m and then crosses a patch of scree. Some 400m after the scree turn R down a distinct and quite easy path, which leads past a cowshed to the path that comes up from the Val Bedretto to the Capanna Cristallina. (The nearby Passo di Cristallina has been crossed by W. G. Stoll, but found to be hard and unrewarding.) Turn R down this path, which is not difficult and brings you to the top of an unsurfaced road about 400m above the Alpe Cristallina (farm buildings). At this Alpe turn R down the unsurfaced road; at the next signpost, ¼ hour on, keep to the road (signpost Ossasco) rather than the path (signpost Airolo); and at a road junction (Bosco di Ossasco, 1536m) turn R (signpost Fontana).

Times: Lago di Narèt (end of first dam) to pass, 1¼ hours; pass to Alpe Cristallina, 2 hours; Alpe Cristallina to Nufenen road, 1¼ hours (less if you ride it).

(F. Wright 5.8.88)

J30   PASSO DI CAMPOLUNGO   2318M
                                                S? ++

LK 1:100K map 43 (tourist 110); 1:50K map 266 (tourist 5001), grid ref. 697146 (M217 fold 20, or M218 fold 11)

From Rodi-Fiesso or Prato, 10–12km ESE of Airolo, in the Valle Leventina, to Fusio (see J20). Apparently this is a well-used path, but there is a long steep climb through woods from the Valle Leventina, and several other steep sections.

J40   STRADA ALTA VALLE LEVENTINA   M +++

LK 1:100K map 43 (tourist 110); 1:50K map 266 (tourist 5001), grid ref. 705150 (M218 folds 11 & 12)

From Airolo, at the head of the Valle Leventina, to Biasca, at its foot. This route has been highly recommended for its fine views. It is largely tarmac roads, with some intervals of r/s. Our correspondent strongly recommends cyclists to ask the tourist office at Airolo for a booklet with a plan of the route; he also says the route is popular with walkers, so that the accommodation (see below) tends to be booked up, but you can descend to the valley to find other accommodation. The route is marked from time to time with yellow signs.

The first place to head for from Airolo is Madrano. The road starts either from Valle, a kind of eastern suburb of Airolo, or from a point on the main road below Airolo, just above where it crosses the River Canaria, which comes down from the NE. From Madrano the road goes through Brugnasco and Altanca (1390m), reaching a high point at Cresta (1421m); then through Ronco (1368m) and Deggio (1208m) to Catto (1241m). From Catto, there is a track for 1km, later a footpath, over very steep ground, through the Bosco d'Öss, to Freggio (1037m—just before here there is a stream, good to bathe in), then a road, climbing steeply, to Osco (1157m). Here there are two alternatives:

(i) Take the road which climbs to Tarnolgio (1595m), just below Predelp, and contours the hillside to Croce (1622m) and Molare (1488m). Then descend, still on the road, to Calpiogna (1143m)

(ii) Take the road downhill, and at the first hairpin take a path (which looks fairly level on the map) through the woods to Calpiogna (1143m)

Here again there seem to be two alternatives:

(i) Descend by road through Primadengo, and soon after this village take the road which climbs to Rossura and Tengia

(ii) Take a fairly level path through the woods to Figgione and then Rossura

From Tengia, either:

(i) Take a path along the hillside to Paschirolo (1208m), then a track to Calonico, then a road to Anzonico (984m), or

(ii) Take a path uphill to Sorsello (where there is a hut), continue uphill to the Monti di Cò (1362m), and then descend, mostly on a track, to Anzonico

There is then a road through Cavagnago (1020m) to Sobrio (1091m). Just beyond Sobrio there is a car park and a children's playground, from where you see, ½ R and below, a meadow. The descent to the meadow is the steepest and most dangerous part of the route ("Absolutely not for people who get dizzy," says our correspondent). The path crosses a stream and comes to Bifre (a few houses), from where there is a rideable unsurfaced road to Bitanengo (909m), and finally an extremely steep but well surfaced zigzag road down to Bodio, just W of Biasca. (It is possible, from Bitanengo, to continue on paths and tracks, through Diganengo and Conzanengo, down to Pollegio, but our correspondent does not recommend this.)

To sum up, there are five r/s stretches on the route: Catto–Freggio, Osco–Calpiogna (with a long alternative by road through Tarnolgio), Calpiogna–Rossura (with an alternative by road through Primadengo), Tengia–Calonico or Tengia–Anzonico, Sobrio–Bitanengo.

The above route can be very hot in summer (our correspondent did it in January), and so in summer you may prefer to take another high route, along the SW side of the valley. This starts at Fiesso. According to the map it is tarmac, through Prato, as far as Dalpe, then unsurfaced to Chironico, where you have to descend to the valley again.

Accommodation is (in 1999) available at Airolo, Altanca, Catto, Osco, Calpiogna, Predelp, Calonico, Anzonico, Cavagnago, Sobrio and Biasca; in the case of Airolo, Catto, Osco, Calpiogna, Predelp and Calonico, the accommodation includes dormitories.

(W. G. Stoll, undated, and a leaflet from the tourist office at Airolo)

J50   PASSO DELL'UOMO   2218M
M ++

LK 1:100K maps 38 and 43 (tourist 110); 1:50K map 266 (tourist 5001), grid ref. 701156 (M218 fold 11)

From Airolo, just S of the St Gotthard Pass (or Piotta, 5km down-valley from Airolo), to the Lukmanier Pass, 15km to the E. From Airolo, take the road to Altanca, and on up to Piora, at the W end of the Lago di Ritom, a long steep climb. (On the way, you pass what is supposed to be the steepest railway in the world – it is funicular – with a maximum gradient of 87.8%.) From a tunnel near here there is a breathtaking view of the Valle Leventina. A gravel road runs along the N shore of the lake, climbs from the E end of the lake, passes another lake (the Lago Cadagno), then a large farmhouse and then a mountain hut (the Capanna Cadagno, 1987m), and continues towards the Passo del Sole (found to be unrewarding by W. G. Stoll). Just after the Capanna turn L up a path across the grassland, keeping always to the N of the main streams. The path is sometimes rocky and rutted, and quite a lot of carrying is needed. On the other side, the descent of the Val Termine is easier. There is a wide jeep track all the way, though in its middle section this is very rocky and it is hard to imagine even a jeep getting up or down. Just before the Lukmanier Pass, the track goes along the S end of a reservoir; here it is rideable and ordinary cars can get along it.

Times: from Capanna Cadagno to top, 1¾ hours; from top to Lukmanier Pass, 1¼ hours.

(E. D. Clements, 1955; F. Wright 13.7.94)

J60   PASSO DI GANA NEGRA   2430M
M +

LK 1:100K maps 38 and 43 (tourist 110); 1:50K map 266 (tourist 5001), grid ref. 707156 (M218 fold 12, top)

From the Lukmanier Pass to Campo (also known as Campo Blenio), just N of Olivone. There is a steep climb from the Lukmanier summit, needing care higher up, where the path goes close to the edge of a cliff; it is easy and often rideable thereafter.

J70   PASSO DELLA GREINA   2378M
D (59) ++

LK 1:100K map 38 (tourist 110); 1:50K map 256, grid ref. 716163 (M218 folds 12 & 2)

From Olivone, 19km N of Biasca, NE via the Diesrut Pass K04 to the Valle Lumnezia and Ilanz in the Vorderrheintal. At Campo Blenio do not turn L up into the village but go straight on (signpost Ghirone, Luzzone). Just before a church, where there is a sign 'Luzzone' pointing to the R, go straight on; ignore two turnings to the R; cross the river by a bridge; and continue on the tarmac road till just after the last settlement (Daigra, 1419m – about ten houses). There is then a good jeep track (easily rideable with a mountain bike), past a farmhouse (bivouac possible in cowshed, at about 1900m), to a kind of basin in the hills (an old mine here?). The track ends here, and our correspondent had about 400m of level going across a sloping snowfield. After this the path zigzags steeply up a grassy slope, runs level for 200m, zigzags upwards again and climbs for about 400m to the top. Our correspondent met snow for this last 400m, and also for about 1km of level going at the top. The path then descends gently, giving easy going, to the main river, which here follows a flat-bottomed and almost level valley, too high for trees.

Do not cross the river to the L bank, but stay on the R bank, following a level and mostly easy path. To reach the Diesrut Pass, it is probably best, if you can spot it, to take a path which climbs gently up the hillside to the R, towards the gap in the hills. The alternative is to follow the river to a bridge just before the Terri hut, then turn R up a very steep path which also leads to the pass.

Times: from Daigra to pass, 4 hours; from pass to bridge before Terri hut, 2½ hours.

(F. Wright, 15.7.94)

J80 **PASS GIÜMELA**   2117M
N SIDE VS. S SIDE S (67) ++

LK 1:100K map 43 (tourist 110); 1:50K map 267, grid ref. 727137
(M218 folds 12 & 13)

From Malvaglia, 6km N of Biasca, to Valbella, at the head of the Val Calanca. A very difficult pass, owing to the steepness and awkwardness of the path; also on the S side it is often hard to find the path.

From Malvaglia, take the road up the Val Pontirone, which goes through Pontirone and Fontana and ends, ¾km after Fontana, at Biborgh (1313m). This valley is lonely and lacks accommodation. From Biborgh the path starts as a series of rock steps, climbing steeply through a wood. There is then an easier, almost level, stretch past the hamlet of Prato Dentro, and then a path into a wood. Soon the path becomes more steep, difficult and awkward. Emerging from the wood you come to a small farm with pigs and goats, the Alpe di Lesgiüna (1472m, 2km beyond Fontana). There is then a descent to the partly dry course of a stream, on the far side of which the path climbs what is nearly a cliff in a series of steep zigzags, largely through trees. To your R there is a large waterfall. At the top you come to a grassy open hillside with a stone building (possible bivouac?), and climbing across this you reach another small farm, the Alpe di Giümela. Turn L here (path not easy to find) and continue climbing, partly through trees and on an awkward path, to the pass. Double carrying may be needed just before and just after the pass.

On the other side, after a steep bit, there is an area where paint marks on rocks indicate the direction (there is, as often on this side, no visible path). Another steep short descent brings you to an open grassy slope with no visible path and few if any paint marks. At the bottom of this is a path at right angles to your descent. Go L here (going R will take you to the Alpe di Naucal, and eventually to Santa Domenica, S of Rossa) and soon bear R, downhill, over an open grassy space (with a bathtub in the middle, serving as a trough) into a wood. Here the path is often indistinct, nor are there enough paint marks to guide you, but eventually, at about 1550m, you arrive at a wide gravel road, apparently still being built at some expense. This goes downhill to the R, becomes tarmac after about 1½km and brings you to the hamlet of Valbella, 1334m.

(Leaflet by Swiss Youth Hostels; F. Wright, 31.7.02)

J90 **PASSO DI SAN JORIO** (SANT'IORIO)   2014M
S +

LK 1:100K map 43 (tourist 110); 1:50K map 277, grid ref. 733114
(M219 fold 9, top)

From Bellinzona to Dongo, on Lake Como near its N end. Long and hard, also difficult to find the path on the Swiss side.

K04 PASS DIESRUT

2428M

D (59) ++

LK 1:100K map 38 (tourist 110); 1:50K map 256, grid ref. 721166
(M218 fold 2)

From the Passo della Greina **J70**, with which it can conveniently be combined, to Vrin in the Valle Lumnezia. For the approach from the Passo della Greina, and the W side of the pass, see **J70**. The descent on the E side follows the R bank of the stream down to about 2100m, then crosses to the L bank. It is moderately difficult, not all that steep. A farmhouse provides a possible bivouac in a cowshed (Alp Diesrut) at about 1900m. The path continues, still moderately difficult but rideable for short stretches, till it joins an unsurfaced road 1km before, and a little below, the first village, Puzzatsch.

Times: from bridge near Terri hut to pass, 1 hour; from pass to Puzzatsch, 2¼ hours.

K08 PASSO PASSETTI

2081M

S OR VS? +

LK 1:100K map 43 (tourist 110); 1:50K map 267, grid ref. 732144
(M218 fold 13)

From Valbella, at the head of the Val Calanca, 24km NNE of Bellinzona, to San Bernardino, just S of the pass of that name. The Val Calanca, seldom visited by cyclists, is quiet and pretty, with a clear trout river. There is a tarmac road as far as Valbella, then an unsurfaced but level and rideable road for just under 2km to a spot called Pian d'Asc, 1341m, where the path begins. The route is thought to be steep and awkward, and it would probably be easier if started at San Bernardino (there would be less to climb). It could be combined with the Pass Giümela **J80**, which leads to Valbella from the W.

K12 VALSERBERG

2503M

D (59) +++

LK 1:100K maps 38 and 43 (tourist 110); 1:50K maps 257 and 267, grid ref. 735157 (M218 fold 13)

From Vals, near the head of the Valsertal, 17km S of Ilanz in the Vorderrheintal, to Hinterrhein, just N of the San Bernardino Pass. Vals Platz and Valé (or Vallée) seem to have merged into one built-up area. Near the middle of Vals, having passed the Information Office on your R, turn L over a bridge onto the R bank of the river, then go R and leave the town by a road signposted Zerfreila. Follow this, climbing among conifers, for about 1km, and where it makes a hairpin bend to the R go straight on (signpost Kiosk Peil, 4km) along an unsurfaced road, still among tall conifers. To reach Wallatschalp (which is how it is written locally) there are two alternatives, neither without difficulty:

(i) About 500m before the little settlement of Peil a sign 'Valserberg' points to the grassy hillside on the L, where there is little indication of a path.

(ii) Just before you cross the river to Peil, there is a sign 'Valserberg' directing you past a farmhouse (where fresh milk may be available) to a path up the hillside, which is quite well marked and easy to see but extremely steep. From the Wallatschalp farmhouse, which can just be seen from the bottom of the second (steep) path, the path climbs much more gently over a grassy open hillside. There is a section where it goes along the top of a steep drop to the R, then it goes over grassy slopes again. At about 2200m there is a little wooden hut, just below a signpost saying (among other things) 'Zum Hirt 2221m'.

Rounding a corner, you see the final climb to the pass. Our correspondent reports about ½km of fairly steep snow, for which short crampons were useful. At the pass there is a substantial stone building (a mountain hut, perhaps, which opens in August), where a bivouac may be possible (part of the building was open). From the top there is a beautiful view of the mountains around the upper valley of the Hinter Rhein, and the San Bernardino road pass can be seen.

The S side was found to be snow-free. The path starts broad and easy, but then an arrow points to the R over irregular ground, and just below two poles in the form of a St Andrew's cross there is a steep, zigzagging, rutted section which requires a lot of carrying. Then you cross a small stream, and the going becomes easier. Finally you come to a jeep track, at about 2100m, with much loose gravel on it; turn R down this to reach Hinterrhein.

Times: from Peil to pass, 4 hours; from pass to jeep track, 1¼ hours; down track to Hinterrhein post office, 1¼ hours.

(F. Wright, 17.7.94)

K16 SAFIENBERGPASS (SAFIERBERG, SOME SOURCES)

2490M

D +

LK 1:100K map 38 (part of route) (tourist 110); 1:50K maps 257 and 267, grid ref. 740160 (M218 folds 13 & 3)

From Splügen, in the upper valley of the Hinterrhein, to Safienplatz in the Safiental, 14km to the N; 12km r/s. For its height, the scenery is rather poor; the S aspect is rather walled in. Views are best during the initial very steep ascent out of Splügen; also the view of the head of the Safiental from Thalkirch is impressive. A sign in the village square (not noticed in 2002) says 'Safienplatz 23km'. The start is by a narrow and steep tarmac road leaving the main road about 1km WSW of Splügen village square; this leads to Gadenstadt (Gadenstatt), about 350m above Splügen. The tarmac road continues, even more steeply, to about 1850m. From here a path leads to the Stutz Alp, 2019m, where you can spend the night in simple accommodation in a hut next to the cowherd's small house (the price seemed not to be fixed in 2002, but 15 francs was accepted). The cowherd was willing to show how he made cheese, how he milked the cows, etc. After Stutz Alp the path is better still, and even rideable for a short while. There is a short descent to the stream, but the path, as shown by paint marks, stays on the same side for several hundred metres until it crosses by a bridge of wooden planks. After crossing, the path, well supplied with paint marks and usually clear to see, goes uphill on grassy, slightly boulder-strewn slopes. Higher up the going is easier. The top is WNW from the point where the stream is left. Just over the pass there is a stone-built hut; this belongs to the military (who in 2002 were trying to sell it) and is unlikely to be open to the public. Descend at first by a short scree slope; then a very good rideable path descends a grassy spur till it steepens. Suddenly it turns R to cross a subsidiary stream, and at once the going becomes very bad indeed, stony where the path does exist, but quite a lot of it has been obliterated by avalanches. These require carrying; one in particular contains huge boulders. At Bodenalpli a rideable cart track descends to the Turrahus (1694m), where there is a hotel. From there to Versam, a distance of 24km, the road, though mostly not tarmac, is smooth and easily rideable. Shortly before Versam there is a 3km stretch of tarmac, which includes the well lit Aclatobel tunnel, 1.7km long.

In 2002 four black salamanders, in four different places, were seen on the path between the Stutz Alp and the pass. These creatures, which have been seen on other routes in this guide, are about 12 cm long, slow-moving and like shiny black plastic toy lizards in appearance. About 10 chamois were also seen near the top on the other side of the pass.

Time: about 7 hours.

(E. D. Clements, 1956, amended from the LK; F. Wright, 2–3.8.02)

K20 GLAS PASS 1846M
E +

LK 1:100K map 38 (tourist 110); 1:50K map 257 (tourist 5002, part of route), grid ref. 746171 (M218 folds 3 & 4, bottom)

From Safienplatz, 9km WSW of Thusis, to Thusis on the Hinterrhein, 18km SSW of Chur. Very easy, with a road down the E side. The scenery is second-rate.

K24 STALLERBERG 2579M
D +

LK 1:100K map 44 (tourist 109); 1:50K map 268 (tourist 5013), grid ref. 766146 (M218 fold 14)

From Juf, near the head of the valley of the Averserrhein (23km SE of Splügen, or 20km WSW of St Moritz), to Bivio, 6km W of the Julier Pass. This is an alternative to the longer route over the Forcellina K28 and Septimer K32 passes.

K28 FORCELLINA PASS 2672M
D (51) +++

LK 1:100K map 44 (tourist 109); 1:50K map 268 (tourist 5013), grid ref. 767143 (M218 fold 14)

From the Septimer Pass summit K32 to Juf (see K24).

There is a jeep road from Bivio (excellent haybarn nearby) to the top of the Septimer Pass, rideable where the gradient permits. A signpost at the top points W-wards to a faint path striking up through rocks, hummocks, snow patches and boggy stretches; this is hard going. After the top (of the Forcellina Pass), the path is steep and rocky for a short distance, but then levels out and contours the W slopes of the ridge to the N, even climbing slowly back towards the ridge. An ibex was seen near here in 1995. Eventually you meet a path coming over the next col in the ridge, which zigzags steeply down to the valley. This path is very narrow and boulder-strewn throughout the 300m descent.

Then there is a smooth easy descent on a good path down to Juf, which at 2126m is claimed to be the highest permanently inhabited village in Europe.

Allow at least 5 hours from the Septimer Pass to Juf. Not advisable before mid-July.

(A. J. Howarth, 1956; F. Wright, 22.7.86; P. Hinton, 1995)

K32 SEPTIMER PASS 2310M
D ++

LK 1:100K map 44 (tourist 109); 1:50K map 268 (tourist 5013), grid ref. 769143 (M218 folds 14 & 15)

From Casaccia, on the main road just W of the Maloja Pass, to Bivio, 6km W of the Julier Pass.

This pass was known to the Romans, and there was a hospice on the summit mentioned in A.D. 831. Until the 13th century it was the only pass across the main watershed between the Simplon and the Reschen passes. In 1387 Jacob von Castelmur, a church official, built a cart track across the pass, which survives in parts.

Strike N from Casaccia up a good zigzag road. After about 1km this turns E-wards up through the woods, and becomes very steep indeed, paved with huge round worn stones. After an hour's climb, you enter a hanging valley. In 1956 the waymarked route climbed diagonally across a wide steep rocky slope facing S. This path was badly obstructed with vast recently fallen boulders, and the alternative was to continue along the valley floor to some mountain farm huts, then strike directly (N) up a minor ridge (path). Higher up this side valley, the main path crosses to the W side of its stream, so if the minor ridge goes N up the W side of this stream, you will not have to cross it later on. Another report mentions going up a very steep grassy hillside, with streams to wade, and double carrying necessary.

At the top of this steep slope, the path continues less steeply over open country, with some traces of the old paved way, and superb views to the S. Later the path winds up a minor gorge to reach an open saddle with a group of locked huts on the summit of the pass. From here the Lunghin Pass goes E to the Maloja (no details, probably tough going), and the Forcellina Pass K28 goes W over to Juf. The continuation of the Septimer Pass N-wards is by a rough jeep road down to Bivio, mostly rideable.

Allow 5 hours up, 1 down.

(Mostly A. J. Howarth, 1956; also R. Kemp, 1971)

K36 FUORCLA SURLEJ 2755M

E SIDE M. W SIDE E +++

*LK 1:100K map 44 (tourist 109); 1:50K map 268 (tourist 5013), grid ref.
784144 (M218 fold 15)*

From Pontresina, just E of St Moritz, on the road over
the Bernina Pass, to Silvaplana on the lake of the same name,
just SW of St Moritz; 10km r/s. A very fine route, commanding superb views of the Bernina Alps during the ascent. From
the youth hostel at Pontresina (which is next to the railway
station), take a small road signposted Val Roseg. This very
soon becomes unsurfaced but rideable, with a mostly gentle
slope. It goes among trees, never far from the river. It is out
of bounds to motor traffic. It follows the L bank for 4km,
then the R for 3 more, and finally recrosses the river to end
at a *Gasthaus* (restaurant). From here a rocky path climbs
up the hillside. The path is quite broad and clearly defined,
though not marked by paint, but rough enough to call for
some lifting and carrying—not much of the latter.

After about 50 minutes, at the top of the trees, you come
to a piece of flat ground with a cowshed and a herdsman's
hut on it. Bear R here. The path continues, clearly defined
and not too difficult, to the pass, providing majestic views of
the Bernina group. There is a restaurant at the pass.

The mountains of the Engadine, on the other side, are
less glaciated and less magnificent. On this side there are
several alternative paths leading down to the valley, but
only one main track, which could probably be ridden with a
mountain bike for its entire length, up or down. Large parts
of it could also be ridden with a touring bike. It ends at a
tarmac road just above Surlej.

Times: from restaurant in Val Roseg to pass, 3 hours;
from pass to Surlej (walking along the track), 2½ hours.

(M. A. Stephens, 1969; F. Wright, 24.7.94)

K40 PASS SUVRETTA 2615M

M? +++

*LK 1:100K map 44 (tourist 109); 1:50K map 268 (tourist 5013), grid ref.
778153 (M218 fold 15)*

On a circular route from St Moritz, N to the Val Bever,
then back via Bever in the main valley. Probably fairly easy
for its height; would make a good day trip from the St Moritz
area, travelling light.

K43 BUFFALORA PASS 2340M

E ++

*LK 1:100K map 39 (tourist 109); 1:50K map 259 (tourist 5017), grid ref.
816166 (M218 fold 17)*

From Buffalora Alp, just W of the Ofenpass, to Santa
Maria in the Val Müstair, 21km r/s. This is a southerly variation to the main Ofen Pass road. The middle section is very
remote, lying in effect between two separate passes. A fine
series of peaks on the Italian border lie just S of the route.
Most of it is rideable. Most of the route also lies within
the Swiss National Park, which means that all camping is
strictly forbidden; there is a camping site at Tschierv, on the
E side of the Ofenpass.

A cart track to Alp Buffalora leaves the Ofen Pass road
about 2½km W of the top of the pass. Just above the alp
buildings, a well marked track winds steeply upwards
through the pines, and after climbing about 100m levels
off, passing a couple of cowsheds. Then, turning S, it continues to a house (probably a customs post). Much of this
track is muddy and often unrideable. The fine peak in front
is Piz Murtaröl, and a narrow path across grassland makes
straight towards it. Soon after the top, the path steepens and
worsens, till it crosses a stream. Here the path improves and
becomes rideable down to Alp Mora, from where there is a
good rideable cart track. This soon joins another coming up
from the Fraele reservoir (the Lago di San Giacomo), which
is described below (be careful to fork R here if going W). The
track climbs gradually again through this wild valley with
stumpy pine trees, and 5½km beyond Alp Mora reaches a
second col, Döss Radond.

A very steep and somewhat rougher descent of about
850m takes you down to the main Ofen Pass road between
Valchava and Santa Maria. This is sometimes unrideable
owing to the gradient, or to the stones strewn onto it by the
river when in flood. There are one or two fine waterfalls on
this section.

It is possible to join this route from the N end of the Lago
di San Giacomo, on the Val Alpisella route **L76**. A rideable
track goes over one almost imperceptible pass, the Passo di
Fraele (1952m), to another, the Passo Val Mora (1934m). It
then becomes a path, difficult for the first 3km, then flat and
easy, and joins the main track 8km from the lake.

Allow 1½ hours from Alp Buffalora to the summit;
3 hours thence to the Ofen Pass road. Of the 21km, 16km
are rideable.

*(E. D. Clements, 1956; for the stretch from the Lago di San
Giacomo, W. G. Stoll, undated)*

K46 PASS DA COSTAINAS 2251M

E +

*LK 1:100K map 39 (tourist 109); 1:50K map 259 (tourist 5017), grid
ref. 824170 (M 218 folds 7 & 17)*

From Santa Maria in the Val Müstair, 11km ESE of the
Ofen Pass, to S-charl (the hyphen indicates that the *ch* is
to be pronounced as in Scottish loch) and then Scuol (the
latter in the Lower Engadine): 12km r/s. This is a well-used
route of easy gradients (except for one short stretch), rideable for the most part, but it does not pass through very
interesting scenery in its upper regions. Leave the Ofen Pass
road just E of Fuldera (the turning is signposted), and take
a good tarmac zigzag road to Lüsai and Lü; then continue
straight on up a good unsurfaced road to Alp Champatsch.
About 400m short of the buildings, at the top of a rise, fork
R (signpost 'Pass da Costainas' and follow a track for 200m,
turning L off it to follow a fence, after which there is a rough
path up the last steep pull to the pass. It winds first N, then
SE, then N again where it flattens out just before the top.
This steep 120m climb is the only unrideable stretch of any

length on the whole route, and the way hereabouts is marked by red and white stripes on rocks. The gradual descent to the Alp Astras-Dadaint is mostly rideable in this direction, a slightly stony mule path. (If you are going S, a fingerpost at the Alp points in the general direction of the pass, but you strike uphill for about 100m above the farm to find the good mule path; it is indistinct near the farm.)

A good track, rather muddy in a few places at times, leads on down, being nearly always rideable; after crossing the main stream it becomes a narrow gravel road to S-charl. There are one or two Pension Restaurants here, and a fair road (tarmac for the last 8km) through the fine gorge to Scuol.

Allow 5–6 hours excluding stops; the whole trip is 32km, of which 29km are rideable.

(E. D. Clements, 1956; F. Wright, 5.8.96)

K49 CRUSCHETTA PASS   2296M
M ++

LK 1:100K map 39 (tourist 109); 1:50K map 259 (tourist 5017), grid ref. 826175 (M218 fold 7 bottom)

From Scuol in the Lower Engadine, to Tubre (which Michelin calls Turbe, or Taufers im Müstair), just inside Italy and 7km WSW of Glorenza (Glurns). This is a harder and more exciting route than its near neighbour the Pass da Costainas **K46**, involving some lifting and carrying for about 1½km near the summit, which is rewarded by some fine views of the Ortler massif during the descent into Italy. By omitting the section through the gorge from Scuol to S-charl, this route can be combined with the Pass da Costainas to give a grand circular r/s route from Santa Maria.

A narrow unsurfaced road leads up the gorge from Scuol to S-charl, where there are one or two *Pension Restaurants*. Continuing up the main valley road for about 3km beyond S-charl, you will see a fingerpost pointing up a rather inferior cart track heading due E up a subsidiary valley. This track passes almost immediately through a short stretch of woodland, and continues to the Alp Plazer, about 1km from the fork. Here all trace of a path vanishes; you make a beeline up the valley, and regain the path at the end of the meadows. For a short while the path is quite fair, but it soon becomes very boulder-strewn and reminiscent of the Lairig Ghru in character and difficulty. The summit of the pass, at the Italian border, is marked by a little crucifix, erected in 1953.

The descent into Italy is steep and, for somewhat less than 1km, still rough and boulder-strewn, involving some carrying. Soon you emerge onto a high meadow. An improving path and track, steep but nearly always rideable, leads on down to Tubre.

Allow about 6 hours for the 30km, of which about 25km are rideable.

(E. D. Clements, 1956)

K52 SCALETTA PASS   2606M
D (59) +++

LK 1:100K map 39 (tourist 109); 1:50K map 258 (tourist 5002, part of route), grid ref. 789174 (M218 folds 5 & 6)

From a point on the main road up the Engadine, 10km SW of Zernez, to Davos; 14km r/s. This is a rewarding route, with good glacier views on a fine day. There is a very good track up the Val Susauna, following the river all the way, and becoming fairly steep and rough on the final 1½km to Alp Funtauna. About 400m before a cowshed you cross a stream by a wooden bridge; 50m after the bridge turn R and you will see a path across the grass. (There ought to be a signpost here, but this side of the pass is generally not well maintained.) The path soon starts to zigzag up the W side of a stream coming down from the N, by grassy slopes at first; later the path becomes stony, narrow, full of projecting rocks (so that quite a lot of carrying is needed) and with numerous streams running across it and down it. Some snowdrifts were met on the way up in 1994, but these merely provided firm and easy intervals between the stones. The N side is much better, being 2m wide for much of the way and descending at a steady, not too steep, slope. There is a Gasthaus at Dürrboden, and a tarmac road from there down to Davos.

Allow 5 hours up from the main road, 2 hours down to Dürrboden.

(F. Wright, 23.7.94)

K55 SERTIG PASS   2739M
D? ++

LK 1:100K map 39 (tourist 109); 1:50K map 258 (tourist 5002, part of route), grid ref. 787172 (M218 fold 5)

From Davos to Bergün, on the N side of the Albula Pass. There is a road as far as Sand (1859m). Here fork L and take a track up the Chüealptal to a large hut (the LK shows a mule track up to 2500m), then a footpath, following the stream, to a small lake (the Grünsee). The path is well signposted and goes over scree to the pass, from which there is an extensive view. On the far side you pass between two lakes and then reach a shelter for emergencies near the head of the Val da Ravais-ch. A mule path leads down this valley, and lower down, at Chants (1822m), where three valleys meet to form the Val Tuors, there is a hotel. From here a private unsurfaced road leads down to Bergün.

(Leaflet by Swiss Youth Hostels, amended from the LK)

K58 LANDWASSER (WIESENER) VIADUCT   E +

LK 1:100K map 39 (tourist 109); 1:50K map 258 (tourist 5002), grid ref. 773173 (M218 fold 5)

In this neighbourhood there are two railway viaducts over the Landwasser; the one intended here is the upstream one, near Wiesen. This is a short cut for those who are travelling from Davos to the Albula Pass or the other way, and a quiet and very interesting route. It avoids going down the

Landwasser valley through Wiesen, Schmitten and Alvaneu, and then up the Albula valley to Filisur. There are about 5km r/s. The viaduct takes the Rhätische Bahn (Rhaetian Railway) over the River Landwasser, which comes down SW from Davos. Leave the road from Davos at the point where it leaves the river to climb up to Wiesen (apparently at the W end of a tunnel on the new road), and take a narrow path signposted to the railway station, forking L from the road. This winds gently down to the railway for 1km. The path continues on a gantry over the viaduct, which rests on some of the longest and highest masonry arches in the world. The view of the river below, through gaps in the planking, is paralysing. The track continues through woods up and down to Filisur station, and is rideable for the last part.

Allow about an hour.

(A. J. Howarth, 1956, M. A. Stephens, 1969)

K61 MAIENFELDER FURKA   2440M
                                             M ++

LK 1:100K map 39 (tourist 109); 1:50K map 248 (tourist 5002), grid ref. 775182 (M218 fold 5)

From Arosa, 14km SE of Chur, to Frauenkirch, on the Landwasser valley road, just SW of Davos; 11km r/s. This pass was crossed on skis by Arthur Conan Doyle and two Swiss ski pioneers on 23 March 1894. He was perhaps the first Englishman to ski in Switzerland.

Descend from Arosa to the Stausee, the lowest of the three lakes just E of the village. A track crosses the main river at the lake's SW corner, and the Furkabach at its SE corner; it then continues steeply up through the woods, and becomes a steep path, going through the gap in the hills carved out by the Furkabach, to the col. The descent is very gradual at first, hardly dropping much for nearly 3km; then it bends round to the NE across the broad ridge of the Tiejerfluh, to drop down to Stafelalp; here it is rather ill defined. From the small collection of buildings at Stafelalp, there is a rough but rideable road down to Frauenkirch.

Allow 6–7 hours either way.

(M. A. Stephens 1969, amended from the LK)

K64 STRELA PASS   2350M
                                             M ++

LK 1:100K map 39 (tourist 109); 1:50K map 248 (tourist 5002), grid ref. 779187 (M218 fold 5)

From Langwies, 14km ESE of Chur, to Davos; 6km r/s. There is a good, narrow, unsurfaced road, very steep in parts, through Kupfen. About ½km beyond Kupfen there is a good Gasthaus, and 1km beyond this you fork R off the road. The going is easy for a further 1km before the final rocky path zigzags steeply up the 300m climb to the col. Do not try any short cuts; snow may prove a problem here. A path, good at first, then rough and stony, ascends the Weissfluh, a fine viewpoint. There is a *Pension Restaurant* on the col, at the top of the disused chairlift from Schatzalp, of which only the pylons and wires remain. This chairlift serves as a guide,

if needed, to the way down, which is a jeep track, found by some to be 'mostly rideable' and by others to be too steep, rough and full of loose gravel. From Schatzalp, two roads lead down to Davos. There is a huge hotel at Schatzalp.

Allow 4 hours from Kupfen to Schatzalp.

(E. D. Clements, 1956; G. Newey, 1980; F. Wright, 22.7.94)

K67 DURANNA PASS   2117M
                                             E ++

LK 1:100K map 39 (tourist 109); 1:50K map 248 (tourist 5002), grid ref. 778192 (M218 fold 5)

From Küblis in the Prättigau, 20km ENE of Chur, to Langwies, 14km ESE of Chur. From Küblis take the tarmac road to Conters im Prättigau (1110m), then a steep unsurfaced road. This soon branches in two; take the R branch (signpost Conterser Duranna). This road climbs, not very steeply, with little variation in quality, first through hayfields, then through tall conifers, then over grassy slopes. At about 1800m fork L (signpost 'Fideriser Duranna, Durannapass'). The road ends at a farm called Duranna Obersäss, 2053m. From the farm a broad and gently sloping track leads to the pass. On the other side the path descends over gentle grassy slopes, and it is sometimes easier to follow the jeep marks on the grass. At Sattel (1970m) a jeep track begins, stonier and less rideable than the one on the other side at first, though it improves later.

There is a restaurant at the small village of Strassberg, 1919m. Chalets and farm buildings, forming the scattered settlement of Fondei, are dotted all over the grassy slopes. At about 1750m the road enters a forest. There is a short stretch of tarmac at 1700m, but continuous tarmac is not reached till just below 1500m, a short way above Langwies.

If coming the other way, leave the main road at Langwies, near the church (signpost 'Pirigen, Fondei').

Times: from Conters to the pass, 4 hours (less if you ride all or part of the way); from the pass to Langwies, 2½ hours (again, less if you ride).

(F. Wright, 19.7.94)

K70 OCHSENALP   2010M
                                             E +

LK 1:100K map 39 (tourist 109); 1:50K map 248 (tourist 5002), grid ref. 771186 (M218 folds 4 & 5)

From Chur via Tschiertschen to Arosa. The climb out of Tschiertschen is steep. On reaching the treeline near the cliffs of the Ochsenstein, at about 1700m, you turn N and then go E, on a fairly level path, near the treeline, to Ochsenalp (1936m). Continue E, now on a track and still fairly level, to Rot Tritt (2006m), a good viewpoint. The track now goes SE and then, joining a small road, SW, past two lakes (the Prätschseen). The road then leads S down to Arosa (about 1800m).

(K. Watts, written up in CC 25, 1981/82; and leaflet by Swiss Youth Hostels)

K73 KUNKELSPASS

1357M
E +

LK 1:100K map 38 (tourist 110); 1:50K map 247 (tourist 5002), grid ref. 750191 (M218 fold 4)

From Tamins, 9km WSW of Chur, to Vättis in the Taminatal, 8km to the NNE. This is an easily rideable unsurfaced road. The S side is steep and spectacular, with tunnels.

(K. Watts, written up in CC 25, 1981/82)

K76 CAVELL JOCH

2239M
D ++

LK 1:100K map 34 (tourist 109); 1:50K map 238 (tourist 5012), grid ref. 775212 (M218 fold 5, top)

From Schiers, 10km E of Landquart, to Bludenz in Austria. (According to Michelin it is also possible to start at Grusch, 7km E of Landquart.) There is a road to Schuders, then a rideable track, which becomes stony higher up, to Tamunt. Before you reach the rocky notch, seemingly uncrossable, of the Schweizertor (2139m), a path turns W, below the frontier ridge, to a small col, from which a faint path strikes NE to the Cavell Joch. There is an easy path down to the Lünersee, then a steep and rough one from the N end of the lake to the roadhead.

Seems sometimes to be written Gafall Joch or Gafalljoch.

K79 SCHLAPPINER JOCH

2202M
M ++

LK 1:100K map 39 (tourist 109); 1:50K map 248 (tourist 5002), grid ref. 788200 (M218 fold 5)

From Klosters Dorf to Gargellen in Austria; 11km r/s. A fine route. Leave Klosters Dorf opposite the railway station by a well-surfaced but often steep track to Schlappin. The main valley bends round to the R here; take a path uphill from the hamlet in a NNE direction.

There are no problems in getting to the col, but if coming down this side from Austria be careful to bear L soon after the col; the R-hand path leads to the Zügenhüttli (a hut, also known as the Madrisahütte?). A steep, fairly rough path, with boulders and many zigzags, but not too hard, descends about 350m from the col to meet a good surfaced track running down the E side of the valley. After about 3km, bear L, on a metalled road, into Gargellen.

If going the other way, follow the road above Gargellen (1423m) for a few hundred metres till you come to a bridge; then before crossing the bridge turn R up the L bank of a small river along a signposted track with a good surface, which is, however, mostly too steep to ride. After about 3km on the track turn R across a stream and start climbing up a steep hillside by a zigzagging path. There are fine views from the top to the S and the SE.

Times; 3 hours from Klosters Dorf to the pass, 2½ from there to Gargellen.

(A. J. Howarth, 1967; M. A. Stephens 1977; F. Wright, 20.8.85)

K82 PASS FÜTSCHOL

2768M
S +++

F&B 374; LK 1:100K map 39 (tourist 109); 1:50K map 249 (tourist 5017), grid ref. 811194 (M218 folds 6, 7; Mair 8, 6E bottom; M C8)

From Galtür, 9km NE of the pass on the Silvretta road [Silvretta Hochalpenstrasse] in Austria, to Ardez, 7½km WSW of Scuol in the lower Engadine: 10km r/s and 16km rough road. A rough road goes due S from Galtür up the Jamtal, becoming a jeep road to the Jamtal hut (2165m), with a gradual climb until the last 1½km. Just before the hut, a path forks off to the L and keeps to the R (N) bank of the Breites Wasser. This is steep and stony over the pass, and especially so down the S side to Urschai (2106m); from here a jeep road goes down the E side of the Val Tasna.

K85 ZEBLAS (OR SAMNAUNER) JOCH

2539M
D ++

LK 1:100K map 39 (tourist 109); 1:50K map 249 (tourist 5017), grid ref. 818202 (M218 fold 7)

From Vinadi, near where the road down the Lower Engadine crosses the Austrian frontier, to Ischgl in the Paznauntal, in Austria, 13km r/s. From Vinadi, an unusually busy road goes up to Samnaun, with four unlit tunnels on bends. Bear R (W-wards) in the centre of the village up an easy rideable track for 1km; the track becomes steeper and looser after crossing a side valley. At a fork of tracks, ignore the best one (a dead end) and keep N of the stream on a very steep, soft path. It is easier going again once the original path is regained, but very steep up the side of a waterfall to the derelict farm buildings of Pischa.

From there the going is easy enough to the top and for about 2½km down the W side. Just below a hut there is a fork of paths, where (see note below) the waymarked path turns L across the stream. Our correspondent followed the R-hand path, as marked on the 1:50K map. This keeps N of the stream, and is rather steep, rocky and narrow at first, but becomes easier for a while across a flower-covered pasture as far as a crucifix. After that it is very steep, rocky and overgrown with shrubs, unpleasant to descend, let alone go up in reverse. At the bottom, turn L onto a cart track passing S of the farm at Gampenalp, then R onto the main track down the Fimbertal, which is rideable all the way down to Ischgl, where there are plenty of shops, cafés, etc.

Note: the 1:50K map shows that on the descent the waymarked path which turns L across the stream descends to Gampenalp and the main track; it is probably waymarked and may be easier than the route used by our correspondent (which is not shown at all on the 1:100K map).

Allow 6 or 7 hours from Vinadi.

(G. Newey, 1980)

K88 ZEINISJOCH

1842M
E +++

LK 1:100K maps 34 and 39 (tourist 109); 1:50K maps 239 and 249 (tourist 5017), grid ref. 805206 (M218 fold 6; Mair 8, 5E top; M C8 top;

F&B 372 or 373)

From Partenen, at 1051m on the Silvretta Hochalpen-
strasse, 6km NW of the Bieler Höhe, to Galtür, on the
same road, 9km NE of the Bieler Höhe; 5km rough road.
This is a short cut which avoids the higher part of the
main road and is more interesting. Leave the main road
1½km up from Partenen, going L at the first hairpin on a
steep narrow metalled road. After a short level stretch and
easy climb, there are steep zigzags up the final pull to the
dam of the Speicher Kops (or Stausee Kops). The old path
is to the L of the zigzags. The latter were being made up
in 1967.

(A. J. Howarth, 1967)

K91　VERBELLNER TO WINTERJÖCHLE　2320M

M. SOME D ++++

LK 1:100K map 34 (tourist 109); 1:50K map 239, grid ref. 805209
(M218 fold 6; Mair 8, 5D bottom, 6D; M C7 bottom; F&B 372 or 373)

From the Zeinisjoch **K88** to St Anton on the main road
over the Arlberg Pass, just E of the summit: 11km r/s and
13km rough road. Opposite the inn on the Zeinisjoch, take
a rough track starting NW-wards, winding at first, but soon
edging round to the N and gently dropping to the Verbella
Alm. (A cart track is shown on F&B and the 1:100Kmap,
going N from the W end of the Stausee Kops to the Verbella
Alm.) There is a short steep section above Verbella, then
it is easy going but hummocky for 1½km before the final
steep pull to the pass. Just above is the Neue Heilbronner
hut, a good place to eat. The pass is a wide grassy saddle,
soon descending easily to the NE. There are some muddy
bits, trampled by cows, but mostly it is a rough, stony, boulder-strewn path for about 3½km, after which a new gravel
road drops gently down a deserted valley with fine views
of the shapely Patteriol (3056m) to the E. Eventually you
reach an inn, and 5km later the old Arlberg road, just above
St Anton.

Time: at least 5 hours.

(A. J. Howarth, 1967, amended from the map)

K94　RAUHES JOCH AND　1934M
GMEINE WEIDE　2014M

S SIDE M. N SIDE E ++

*LK 1:100K map 34; 1:50K map 238, grid ref. 791228 (Mair 8, 4D top; M
B7, C7; F&B 371 edge)*

From Dalaas, on the main road over the Arlberg Pass
and 16km W of the summit, to Lech, 10km NNW of the
Arlberg Pass (6½km r/s and 13km rough road), or Raggal,
6km N of Bludenz (11km r/s, 10km rough road). Take the
middle of three paths from the NW end of Dalaas station,
and after 1km turn R (N-wards) up a steep mule path to the
pass; the Freiburger hut is nearby. Pass to the L of the lake
(the Formarinsee) and about 1km after the hut come to a
fork. Then:

(i) For Lech, fork R to join, after a short distance, a
rough road which descends to Zug, for Lech

(ii) For Raggal, fork L, climb to the pass and descend
fairly easily to Laguz Alp

Combining the northern parts of the two routes, from
Lech to Raggal, would give an alternative to the W side of
the road over the Arlberg Pass. Yet another possibility would
be to climb from Klösterle or Innerwald, on the main road E
of Dalaas; the paths up from these places are very steep, but
they lead past the Spuller See to a fairly easily graded mule
path which goes over the Stierloch Joch (2009m) to Zug.

K97　GEMSTELPASS　2009M

M ++

LK 1:100K map 34, grid ref. 804240 (Mair 8, 5C; M C7 top; F&B 364)

From Mittelberg in the Kleinwalsertal, 31km NE of
Bludenz, to the Hochtannberg Pass, between Schröcken and
Warth; 7km r/s. At the SW end of Mittelberg, take the track
to the L, an easy mule path, sometimes rideable, to Hintere
Gemstel Alm, 1321m. From the hut here, a steep but not
dangerous path embarks on a 300m climb, then levels off
but soon climbs again amongst the pastures of Obergemstel
Alm (1694m) in a SW-ly direction, fairly steeply at times,
to the pass. Bear R to the Widderstein hut (2009m), where
the steep descent to the Hochtannberg Pass, visible 300m
below, begins.

A little further W, another pass (the Hochalp, 1921m)
connects Baad and the Hochtannberg Pass, presumably over
similar terrain.

Time: a crossing the other way took 4 hours.

(R. Perrodin, c. 1970)

12.8.90 Madritscher Joch, E side; a level basin just above
the Zufallhütte

9.8.90 Eisjöchl, top, looking into the Pfelderertal;
Stettiner Hütte and military road in the foreground

20.8.90 Hochjoch, N side, not far from the Hütte

20.8.90 Hochjoch, N side; a hard bit on the climb to the
Hochjoch Hospiz

10.7.94 St Gotthard pass, S side; Airolo below

17.8.90 Old military road on the E side of the Val Alpisella
17.8.90 Looking ahead (W) from the top of the Val Alpisella

5.8.90 Haybarn at Vent, where I spent 3 nights in all
6.8.90 Jeep track from Vent up to the Martin Busch Hütte

On the N side of the Parpaillon

Ladder on the Pas de Chèvres

19.8.90 The Schöne Aussicht Hütte on the Hochjoch, looking towards the glacier

23.8.90 Pitztaler Jöchl, top, looking back to the E

25.7.94 Muretto pass, N side, approaching the top of the
first section
10.8.89 The people who gave me grappa at the dam by the
Lago di Cingino

9.8.89 Byre where I spent the night, at the entrance to the
Furggtal, on the climb to the Antrona pass

25.7.94 The true Muretto pass, from the top, looking back
(note path at left, which I failed to find)

15.8.91 The Col de Balme, N side — rock staircase below
Les Grands Dessus
14.8.91 The lake at the Great St Bernard pass

9.8.93 At the Fenêtre de Ferret

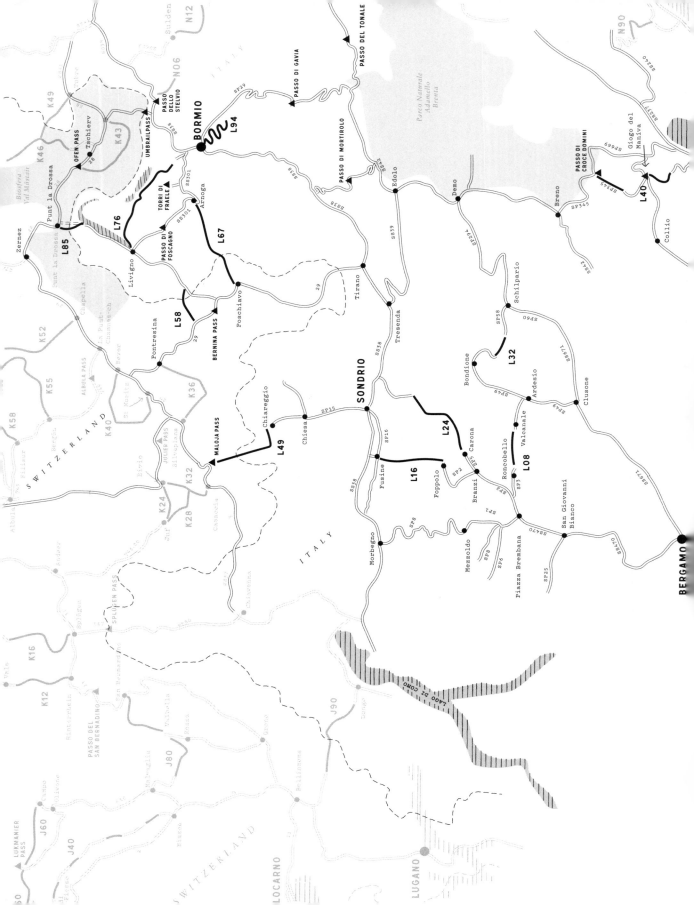

L. **LOMBARDY**

L08   **PASSO BRANCHINO**   1847M
                                                 E +

Kompass map 104

From Clusone, 32km SSE of Sondrio (in the Valtellina), to Piazza Brembana, 29km SW of Sondrio, via Valcanale and Roncobello. Fairly easy; liable to be muddy for 1½km or so near the top of the W side. There are also one or two tricky and steep bits on this side.

L16   **PASSO DI DORDONA**   2080M
                                                 M? +++

Kompass map 104

From Sondrio, in the Valtellina, to Piazza Brembana, 29km to the SW, via Val Madre and Foppolo (leave the main road at Fusine, 10km W of Sondrio). This is only one of several passes from the Valtellina to Piazza Brembana. There is also the San Marco, a road pass, and the following r/s ones, in order from W to E, of which we have no reports: Passo di Salmurano, 2026m, Morbegno to Ornica; Passo di Tartano, 2122m, Tartano and Masino to Branzi; Passo di Publino, 2351m, Sondrio to Carona.

L24   **PASSO DI VENINA**   2433M
                                                 VS?

Kompass map 104

From Sondrio to Carona, 18km to the SSW. Said to be long, hard and sometimes dangerous, and therefore not recommended.

L32   **PASSO DI MANINA**   1799M
                                                 E +

Kompass map 104

From Schilpario, 28km SE of Sondrio, to Valbondione, 12km to the WNW. Mostly a fairly easy track, with one or two tricky spots on the W side.

L40   **GIOGO DELLA BALA**   2129M
                                                 E +++

Kompass map 104

From the Croce Domini road pass (i.e. about 1½km W of the summit of the road at the Goletto di Cadino) to Anfo on the Lago d'Idro. This is a mostly unsurfaced ridge road. For the first km or so the steepness and roughness combined make the road almost unrideable in places; after that the slope lessens and the surface improves. There are fine views to the W over the Val Camonica. About 6½km from the start you come to the bottom of a steep zigzagging section, which again is only just rideable, and which brings you to the Giogo di Bala. From here you can see, a short way further on, the bowl-shaped antennae of an American radar

station on an isolated prominence (the Dosso dei Galli), and just over 1km later you come to a tarmac road (said to have been built by the Americans), which leads down to Collio. After 7km on this road, along the ridge (a slight dip in which marks the Goletto delle Crocette, 2071m), you come to the Rifugio Bonardi al Maniva (1744m), and 1.3km later, at the Giogo del Maniva (1664m), you turn L off the road, pass a restaurant, and continue on an unsurfaced road along the W side of a hill. After 2.2km of mostly gentle climbing the road crosses to the E side of the ridge and then goes along just below the top of another ridge, with spectacular views down the steep slopes, before climbing through four short tunnels and then descending a few km to a kind of holiday camp. Along the ridge there are several small passes, whose names and heights, according to Denzel, are: Passo del Dosso Alto, 1725m; Passo della Berga, 1527m; Passo della Spina, 1521m. At the holiday camp the tarmac reappears, and the real descent, a long one full of twists and hairpins, begins. It ends near Anfo.

(F. Wright, 9.8.85, supplemented from Denzel)

L49   **PASSO MURETTO**   2562M
                                                 S (59) +++

LK 1:100K map 44 (tourist 109); 1:50K map 268 (tourist 5013, part of route), grid ref. 776135 (M218 fold 15)

From the Maloja Pass in Switzerland to Chiesa, at the head of the Val Malenco, 10km N of Sondrio in the Valtellina. As you descend from the Maloja Pass towards Chiavenna, the first traverse downhill is to the R, the second to the L. At the end of the second take an unsurfaced road which leads to the L. This shortly comes to a car park, beyond which cars are not allowed, but continues for 3½km (from the main road). It is rideable, as far as the surface is concerned, but sometimes steep. It ends at a farmhouse, just after a small lake (the Lägh da Cavloc) and a restaurant (1907m). There is then a moderately difficult path for perhaps 1½km. After an awkward rocky section, like a rock staircase, you come to a stone building on the R; this is a disused customs post (the pass was used by smugglers). Just after this the path forks; the R fork (and most of the walkers) go up the upper Val di Forno to the Capanna di Forno. The L fork descends by a flight of wooden steps to a bridge across the river; both before and after the bridge there are short difficult stretches where double carrying may be needed.

The slope which now lies ahead, with a stream flowing among patches of snow, leads to a gap in the hills which may be thought, wrongly, to be the pass. The path up this slope is steep in the middle part, less so towards the top.

Passing through the gap, you find yourself in a little valley, with a flat bottom full of snow and steep slopes of rock and scree on all sides. The valley bends to the R as you look up it.

The path, which our correspondent was unable to find

but parts of which he saw later from above, is thought to climb the scree to the L, follow the top edge of the scree for some way and then climb again towards the nearer of two dips in the skyline (the further, at the head of the valley, has a tongue of snow leading up to it).

Just on the other side of the pass, on a rise to the R, is a stone building which might serve as a bivouac. The Italian side is easier than the Swiss, and the path is clear to see. There are good views of the rarely seen Monte Disgrazia (3678m). At first there were found to be some short stretches of snow. Lower down evidence of careful construction appears, and the path could be described as a mule track. Lower down still, the large and elaborate revetments show that this is an old military road of a kind found elsewhere in the Italian Alps, e.g. Mont Malamot **C08**, Eisjöchl **N30** (our correspondent was told it had been built during the first World War). In these lower parts, jeeps, and perhaps mountain bikes, could use the road, but tarmac is not reached till Chiareggio.

Times: from old customs post to pass, 3½ hours; from pass to Chiareggio, 3 hours.

(F. Wright, 25.7.94)

L58 PASS LA STRETTA   2476M
                                          M ++

LK 1:100K map 44 (tourist 109); 1:50K map 269 (tourist 5013), grid ref. 800148 (M218 fold 16)

From Pontresina, 6km E of St Moritz in Switzerland, to Livigno in Italy, 18km to the ENE. This is an obvious link. It is a beautiful and fairly gentle climb, with a very steep 300m descent on the Italian side. Our correspondent was startled to have a marmot run between his bike and his legs.

(W. G. Stoll, undated)

L67 PASS DA VAL VIOLA   2528M (SEE BELOW)
                        W SIDE S. E SIDE E (61) +++

LK 1:100K map 44 (tourist 109); 1:50K map 269, grid ref. 808143 (M218 fold 16)

From Poschiavo, on the S but still Swiss side of the Bernina Pass, to Arnoga in Italy, on the E side of the Passo di Foscagno (i.e. on the road from Bormio to Livigno). From Poschiavo follow the main road N, climbing, for 8km, and at about 1600m turn off it, R, at a sign 'Val da Camp', to follow an unsurfaced road. After ½km there is a signpost, one of whose arrows reads 'Pass da Val Viola'. Ignore this (it is probably for walkers), and keep to the track on the N side of the valley. This continues for about 5km to (and beyond) a Swiss Alpine Club hut at Lungacqua, 1986m. Food and accommodation are available here. From the hut there is a stony and irregularly surfaced, but not very steep, path to the Lagh da Val Viola.

On the open ground to the L of the lake the path forks. There is a signpost but it only has one arrow, pointing L and saying 'Pass da Val Viola'. Follow this arrow (the other path, with the more numerous paint marks, seems to be a circuit of the lake).

The path continues stony and hard. There is one stretch where the steepness and awkwardness force you to double-carry. After that it is easier. At one point, just below the top, although the paint marks show the main path going R, a lower pass is visible to the L. In fact there are three passes here, close together. The pass to the L can be reached by a faint path, and from it a better path leads on to the third pass, whose height, according to the sign, is 2528m. From the third pass a path leads back down into Switzerland, but we have no report of its start in Switzerland. There are fine views, in various directions, of the Bernina group and other mountains.

The third pass is the start of an old Italian military road running down into Italy, which was built (our correspondent was told) during the first World War, partly in connection with the loss of the Stelvio by the Italians. At present it is rough to start with, but much easier than the Swiss path; the whole distance on this side, up to the pass, is rideable on a mountain bike. After 1½km there is a refuge, the Rifugio Viola, on the R, and the surface improves. The road is popular with walkers, as well as cyclists on mountain bikes. Two hours from the pass you come to a car park, where many people leave their cars, and half an hour later to another car park. The surface improves again, and it is only a short distance to the main road at 1900m, about 7km from the summit of the Passo di Foscagno.

Times: main road to Lungacqua hut, 1¼ hours; on to Lagh da Val Viola, ¾ hour; on to pass, 1¾ hours; on to beginning of tarmac, 3 hours (less if you ride part of the way).

(F. Wright, 4.8.96)

L76 VALLE ALPISELLA   2285M
                                          E ++

LK 1:100K map 39 (tourist 109); 1:50K map 259 (tourist 5017), grid ref. 812159 (M218 fold 16)

From the Lago di San Giacomo, 12km NW of Bormio, to Livigno, 8km due W. This is a rough but mostly rideable jeep track, which has the look of another old military road, especially on the E side, where it is better preserved. To reach the Lago di San Giacomo from Bormio, take the road that leads to Livigno, and at Premadio turn R (signpost 'Torri di Fraele'). Climb on an unsurfaced road in a series of close-packed hairpins (the Scale di Fraele), and at the top pass some ruined towers (the Torri di Fraele). The road now follows the R (S) side of the Lago di Cancano and soon comes to the Lago di San Giacomo.

The pass has a long flattish top (sloping gently uphill from the E), in the course of which it passes two small lakes, both without outlet; the second of these has a notice by it saying 'Sorgenti dell'Adda mt. 2239' (query: how can it be the source of a river without having an outlet?). On the W side the road is more like a path, being narrower and less well preserved, though mostly still easy enough going. It passes first down the L and then down the R side of a steep-sided pine-covered valley, which ends at the Lago di Livigno (or Lago di Gallo).

(F. Wright, 17.8.90)

L85 __PUNT LA DROSSA__ TO __LIVIGNO__   E +

LK 1:100K map 39 (tourist 109); 1:50K map 259 (tourist 5017), grid ref.
809170 (M218 folds 6 & 16)

From Punt la Drossa, which is in Switzerland, on the
main road 8km W of the Ofen Pass (and at the N end of the
tunnel leading to Livigno), to Livigno. There used to be a
good rideable path through the forest, which should bypass
the tunnel on the new road. The last report we have of this is
from the time when the dam was being built, when the bike
had to be hauled up a steep slope of rubble at the frontier.
Up-to-date information would be welcome (the path through
the forest appears, from the map, to link up to the service
road to the bottom of the dam). The tunnel is of course a
quick way through, has a good surface (1996) and is well lit,
but it is not a particularly pleasant experience; the N end of
the tunnel, at 1700m, is 100m lower than the S end; even if
you start at the S end, the distance of 3½km takes several
minutes, long enough for the traffic to overtake you after the
traffic light has gone green behind you. The tunnel closes
at 8 p.m.

L94 __CIMA BIANCA__   3018M
                                                   E +++

LK 1:100K map 44 (tourist 109); 1:50K map 269, grid ref. 828145
(M218 fold 17)

A cul-de-sac just SE of Bormio. From Bormio there is a
tarmac road up to San Pietro, 1492m (two hotels and a few
houses), then a wide, unsurfaced road for 5½km leading to
Bormio 2000. This road can be ridden, though sometimes
with difficulty. Its average gradient is 9.2%. Bormio 2000
consists of the top end of one cable way, the bottom end of
another and a restaurant. The road here becomes narrower
and steeper (the average gradient from here to the top is
13.6%, the distance is 7.4km), but it is still used by a few
cars, motorbikes and mountain bikes. The last of these might
be able to make it to the top, though the slope is sometimes
steep. The road forks once or twice, and is not well signposted (there are some red-and-white paint marks, one with
the number 41), but provided you keep to what looks like the
main road, and when in doubt go uphill, you should be all
right. There is not much water en route, but there is a pipe
and trough at San Pietro. There is a restaurant, the Chalet
dei Rododendri, 2km above Bormio 2000, and a bar at the
summit (not tried). There is an extensive view from the top,
through over 270°, taking in the Val Furva, the Ortler range,
the hills around Livigno and far to the W and NW.

Times (assuming you ride to Bormio 2000, then walk):
San Pietro to Bormio 2000, 1 hour; from Bormio 2000 to
summit, 2½ hours; slightly less in descent.

(F. Wright, 16.8.90)

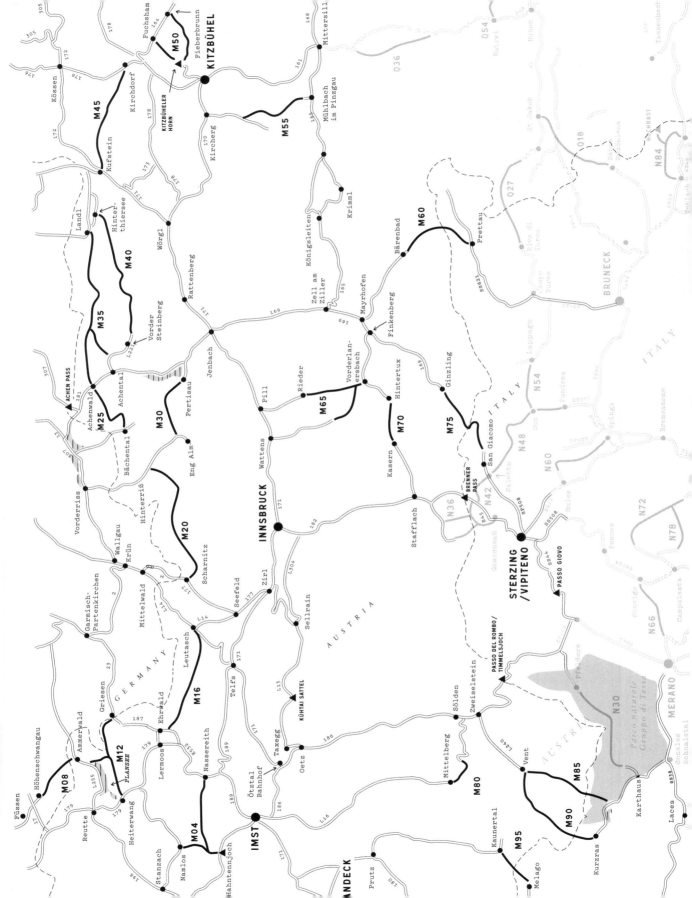

M. **TIROL**

M04 **STEINJÖCHL** AND   2198M
HINTERBERG JOCH   2202M
         D ++

F&B map 352, folds D and E4; ÖK map 115 (Mair 8, 8C, 9C top; M E7 top)

From the Hahntennjoch, 8km NW of Imst, 10km r/s, 10km rough road, either:

(i) To Namlos, 14km NNW of Imst, or
(ii) To Nassereith, 11km NE of Imst

The route is part of the long-distance path Alpin 4, shown as a path over both passes on the F&B map. There is a steep 300m climb to the Steinjöchl, then a descent to the Anhalter hut (2038m). From here (i) a path descends the valley N-wards to Namlos; (ii) remaining on Alpin 4, you climb ENE past Kromsattel (2137m) to the Hinterberg Joch (2202m), descend fairly steeply to the Hintere Tarrenton Alm (1519m), climb gradually on a jeep road to yet another pass, the low Schweinstein Joch (1564m), and finally descend the Tegestal to Nassereith.

M08 **HÖHENSCHWANGAU** TO **AMMERWALD**   1431M
         E ++

F&B map 352, fold F1 (Mair 8, 9A; M E6)

From Höhenschwangau in Germany, 3km E of Füssen (which is itself 32km WNW of Garmisch-Partenkirchen) to Ammerwald, on the frontier with Austria, 12km ESE of Füssen: 3km r/s, 11km rough road. Soon after the start of the track (on which cycling is strictly forbidden) up to Neuschwanstein Castle, turn R on a good track (a jeep road, on the map, as far as the pass), which is rideable where gradients permit. The steep 300m descent to Ammerwald is shown as a footpath on the F&B map. If you are approaching Höhenschwangau from Austria, there is a good rideable track from Unterpinswang, passing just N of the Alpsee.

Allow 2–3 hours.

(Anon., undated)

M12 **PLANSEE PATHS**   E +++

F&B map 352, folds F2 and G2 (Mair 8, 9B and 10B top; M E6)

From Heiterwang or Reutte, just S of Füssen (see M08) to Plansee, at the NE end of the lake of the same name, and Griesen, 8km to the E, on the frontier with Germany: 10km r/s, 10km rough road, or 21km rough road. There is a good rideable path along the SE shore of the lake, all the way from Heiterwang to the hotels near the NE end of the Plansee. This is much better than the road along the NW shore.

You can continue E from the Plansee over a low pass (1003m) into Germany, and on along the frontier to Griesen; this stretch is shown as a road closed to motor traffic on the 1:300K F&B map, as is a road heading NW from the Plansee hotels, which crosses a low pass (1210m) near Opelhaus,

before contouring the wooded hillsides towards Reutte.

(Anon., undated, for the path along the shore of the lake; no details for the rest)

M16 **EHRWALDER ALM**   1585M
         E +++

F&B map 322, fold B3, or map 352, fold H3 (Mair 8, 10B, 11B; M E6, F6 bottom)

From Ehrwald, 16km SW of Garmisch-Partenkirchen, to Leutasch, 18km to the E; 18km rough road. Like the road E of the Plansee M12, this is a road prohibited to cars, according to the F&B 1:300K map. A steep track climbs from Ehrwald to the Alm (1502m), following near the cable car line, and reaches the pass 1½km further on. From the top, a mostly rideable but rather stony track descends to Tillfussalm (1382m), from where there is a jeep road to Platzl. There are fine views of the Zugspitze, the highest point of Germany, and of the Wetterstein Gebirge.

(R. Perrodin, c. 1970)

M20 **HOCHALMSATTEL** (OR **HOCHALPENSATTEL**)   1803M
         M +++

F&B map 322, folds G2 and G3; ÖK map 118 (Mair 8, 13B; M G6)

From Scharnitz, on the main road from Innsbruck to Germany and on the frontier, to the Risstal, some 18km to the NE; 32km rough road. This is a rough jeep road throughout, prohibited to most traffic. Take the road SE out of Scharnitz, and after 1km turn L up the Karwendeltal. The road is steep at first, but soon levels off, a delightful route through the pine woods which eventually comes out into the open and offers good views. The last stretch to the top is steep (25%). At the top there is a well-defined path, or narrow road, leading to the Karwendelhaus, where accommodation and food are available. Then there is some boggy grassland and a small plateau, with several wooden buildings. There is another 25% gradient at the start of the descent, and the E side is very stony, though it improves lower down. On the way down, go L at any forks, down the W side of the main valley (a spectacular gorge called the Johannestal). Eventually you meet a barrier by the rough (?) road from Germany to the Eng Alm. It is possible to remain in Austria by combining this route with the Plumssattel M30, a combination which can take in the Spieliss and Hohl Joche.

(J. J. Martin, 1960; E. A. Jowett, 1961; R. C. Stephens in RSJ 35, 1990, no. 2)

M25 **ROTWANDL HÜTTE**   1510M
         E ++

F&B map 351, fold C2 (Mair 7, 3B, or Mair 8, 14A; M G6)

From Bächental, 31km NE of Innsbruck, on a small road (apparently barred to motor traffic) which runs up the Dürrachtal from Germany, S of the Sylvensteinsee, to Achenwald, just inside Austria, on the road over the Achenpass: 16km rough road. A jeep road leaves the small road just over 1km inside Austria, continues past Zoten Alm to the Rotwandl Hütte, and descends to the Achenpass road 1½km NW of Achenwald.

M30 PLUMSSATTEL 1649M
M +++

F&B map 351, fold C3; ÖK map 119 (Mair 8, 14B, or Mair 7, 3C; M G6)

From Hinterriss in the Risstal, 15km ENE of Mittenwald, to Pertisau, 8km NW of Jenbach: 8km r/s, 8km rough road. Take the road up the Risstal from Hinterriss, which leads to the Eng Alm nature reserve (where there is a café and huts). About 1km beyond the Hagelhütte, turn L and climb to Plums Alm. From here there is a rough grassy cart track to the pass (food is available at the Plumserjoch Hütte), then a zigzag descent to Gern Alm, which is narrower, rougher and much too steep to ride. From Gern Alm, where there is a large Gasthaus, there is a rideable rough road down to Pertisau.

By turning R off the Hochalmsattel road M20 5km down the E side, just before crossing a main stream, you can take a jeep road up to the Spieliss Joch (1773m), below the nearby Falken hut. From this pass, the long-distance path (Alpin 4) continues with a slight dip to the Hohl Joch (1794m), before descending steeply to Eng Alm. A jeep road also descends from the Hohl Joch to the Hinterriss–Eng Alm road.

Allow 8 hours for the Hochalmsattel plus the Plumssattel (3 hours for the Plumssattel on its own, starting at the Hagelhütte).

(*E. A. Jowett, 1961; R. C. Stephens – Plumssattel only – in RSJ 38, 1993, no. 1; we have no report on the Spieliss and Hohl Joche*)

M35 ASCHENBRENNER HÜTTE (GUFFERTHÜTTE) 1465M
ACKERN ALM 1383M
E ++

F&B map 351, fold E1 (Mair 7, 4B, 5B, or Mair 8, 15A, 16A; M H6)

From Achenwald, on the road over the Achenpass and just inside Austria, 21km NNW of Jenbach, or from Achental, about 6km SE of Achenwald, to Landl, 11km W of Kufstein: 3km r/s, plus 27km rough road from Achenwald, or 22km rough road from Achental. We have no details, apart from the stretch Valepp–Kaiserhaus, a route which crosses and hardly overlaps with the route here; see the next paragraph. The route is marked as a jeep road or cart track on the map, except for about 3km of mule path near the L. Aschenbrenner Hütte (shown on some maps as the Gufferthütte), the highest point of the route and on a low pass. The track from Achenwald is not waymarked; take care to avoid going up the valley heading SSE, about 3km from Achenwald. There is another low pass at Ackern Alm, 1383m, much further E, where the road to Landl begins. If you start from Achental (just N of Achenkirch), you leave the road to Steinberg after about 3km, on a waymarked

route, also a cart track, to the L. Aschenbrenner Hütte. The whole route parallels the German frontier, which is only a few km to the N.

About 1½km before the Erzherzog Johann Klause hut, another cart road follows the L (E) bank of the main river S-wards towards Kaiserhaus, switching to the R (W) bank about 2½km before Kaiserhaus, to negotiate the Kaiserklamm gorge. In 1970 an anonymous contributor took his bike through these gorges from Valepp in Germany (12km SE of the S end of the Tegernsee), S past the Erzherzog Johann Klause hut and on through the Kaiserklamm gorge. It was not really rideable, but well worthwhile. It is said to be quite a sight when the sluice gates are opened at Kaiserhaus to allow logs to go down the river in spring. If you do this route, allow 6–8 hours from the Tegernsee to Rattenberg in the Inn valley.

M40 HINTERBERG TO HINTERTHIERSEE E ++

F&B map 351, folds F2, G2, H2 (Mair 7, 5B bottom, 6B; M H6)

From Hinterberg, 3km E of Steinberg (see M35 – Steinberg is 14km N of Jenbach, on a small road running E from Achenkirch), to Hinterthiersee, 8km W of Kufstein; 32km, or less, rough road. This is a route parallel to, and S of, the Achental–Landl route M35, part of long-distance path Alpin 4, another jeep road or cart track passing W to E, this time through Kaiserhaus.

M45 STRIPSENJOCH 1577M
M +++

F&B map 301, fold D2; ÖK map 90 (Mair 7, 7B, 8B; M I6)

From Kufstein to Kirchdorf, 19km to the E; 8km r/s, 6km rough road. The path (part of long-distance Alpin 4) starts steeply from the NE end of Kufstein, with made steps to Pfandlhof (a Gasthaus), reached in ¾ hour. A good rideable track continues to the Anton Karg and Hans Berger inns, where accommodation and food are available. The climb really begins there; it is a steep well-made path at first, then a mostly stepped path to the hut on the pass. The descent is much steeper, with loose stones and more made steps, slippery after rain, down to the Griesener Alm, from where a good surfaced road leads down to Griesenau. There are superb views of the Wilder Kaiser.

Times: allow 4 hours up, 1½ down.

(*Mrs M. A. Stephens, 1979*)

M50 KITZBÜHELER HORN 1996M
W SIDE E. E SIDE M +++

F&B map 301, fold E3; ÖK map 122 (Mair 7, 8C; M J6)

This summit is 4km NE of Kitzbühel. There is a steep but good metalled road, with gradients of 16%, up to the hotel/restaurant at 1669m, then a narrow tarmac path, with some mud, to the summit, which offers an excellent view of the Hohen Tauern and the Grossvenediger. We have no details of the E side, where there are two alternatives:

(i) A path continues from the hotel up to the Hornköpfl Hütte and down the E side of the mountain, to meet a cart road down to Fuchsham on road no. 164

(ii) A path descends gradually SE-wards from the hotel to the Pfeifer Alm (from where a cart road leads down to Kitzbühel), then climbs again to Lachtal; from here a jeep/cart road descends to the Pletzer hut, and then becomes a rough road leading to Fieberbrunn.

M55 STANGENJOCH
1713M
M ++

ÖK map 121 (Mair 7, 7D; F&B map 381 – probably)

From Kirchberg, 6km W of Kitzbühel, to Mühlbach, on the main road between Krimml and Mittersill, 8km W of the latter. From Kirchberg, take a road to Aschau, where there are three places offering accommodation, then an unsurfaced track. Turn L at a fork onto a good forestry road, which lasts for 6km to Rettensteinalm. After this the track deteriorates and doubles back behind the farm for about 500m. The Stangenjoch path then turns off R to proceed up the valley again. It becomes narrow, rocky and wet, and then very steep up a gully for the last 500m to the top. (There is a slightly easier gully to the R of the waymarked route.) A rough road at the top (bear L) leads to the Stangenalm (a farm), then descends steeply to Baumgartneralm (another farm). Take the L fork here and go down the valley for 7km to Mühlbach.

Allow 3 hours from Aschau to Mühlbach.

(R. C. Stephens in RSJ 36, no 4, 1991)

M60 HUNDSKEHL JOCH (PASSO DEL CANE)
2557M
N SIDE S. S SIDE D (60) +++

F&B map 152, fold G3; ÖK map 150 (Mair 7, 6E; M I7 bottom)

From Bärenbad, at the top of the Zillergrund, 15km ESE of Mayrhofen, to Prettau, near the top end of the Ahrntal (Valle Aurina), 29km NNE of Bruneck in Italy: 13km r/s, 6km rough road. From Mayrhofen a narrow and sometimes steep, but well surfaced, tarmac road leads to the Gasthaus at Bärenbad (1450m), just below the dam. Just before the Gasthaus turn R over the river to follow an unsurfaced road up into the Hundskehlgrund (the top part of the Zillergrund). This road is sometimes rideable where not too steep. It ends at 1840m at the Mitterhütte, a tiny hut, which may be padlocked. From here to the top is a mostly rocky path, which looks as if it was originally a roughly constructed mule track. It is well supplied with red paint marks (occasionally red and white, with the number 516), and it is not difficult to find the way. You must carry the bike more than you push it. From the pass there are fine views, especially of the mountains in Italy.

After ½km of descent the path forks. Here there is a green metal plate with directions. The path to Prettau (the shortest and probably easiest descent) is shown as 16b on the plate, but the rocks are painted with 16a. However, the path

marked 16a (which goes L at the fork) seems to be the right one. It is steep but less rocky than the one on the Austrian side. It brings you to a restaurant at the Waldner Alm (2068m), from where an unsurfaced road takes you down to Prettau (1476m). Tarmac recommences 1km before Prettau.

Times: from the Mitterhütte to the pass, 3¼ hours; from pass to Waldner Alm, 1½ hours.

E. Matthews, 1976; F. Wright, 4.8.95)

M65 GEISEL JOCH
2292M
E +++

F&B map 152, folds C1 and C2; ÖK map 149 (Mair 8, 15C bottom, or 7, 4D bottom; M H7)

From Rieder, a small hamlet 7km ESE of Wattens in the Inn valley, to Vorderlanersbach in the Tuxertal, 8km W of Mayrhofen, 24km rough road. This is shown as a cart/jeep road throughout from the Weidener (Nafing) hut to Vorderlanersbach.

The Torjoch (2386m) and the Klammjoch (2359m, not to be confused with the Klammljoch 027) are inside the military area; the boundary of this is shown on Mair, the F&B 1:300K, the German Reise- und Verkehrsverlag 1:200K and the AA 1:200K, but not on the 1987 Michelin or F&B 1:50K. The Klammjoch is shown as a cart road throughout on its E side; the cart road continues to a hilltop at 2448m, then zigzags down to the Mölstal and Walchen, on the rough road up to Lizum. This provides a short circular tour (18km rough road) from Walchen, if the military area is not in use. The W side of the Klammjoch, also both sides of the Torjoch, are shown as waymarked paths, not particularly steep.

M70 TUXER JOCH
2338M
W SIDE D?. E SIDE M ++

F&B map 152, fold B3; ÖK map 149 (Mair 7, 3E, or Mair 8, 14D; M G7, H7)

From Kasern, at the head of the Schmirntal, 24km SE of Innsbruck, to Hintertux, at the head of the Tuxertal, 15km WSW of Mayrhofen: 3km r/s, 8km rough road. About 2km of rough road up the Kaserer Winkl brings you to the foot of a goods lift. The path goes up near this lift and climbs very steeply for well over 300m, the gradient easing as you approach the pass. A cart road continues to the Tuxer Joch hut, then descends with many zigzags below, first, a chair lift, then a cable car, to the valley road just above Hintertux.

M75 PFITSCHER JOCH (PASSO DI VIZZE)
2251M
N SIDE M. S SIDE E +++

F&B map 152, fold B4; ÖK maps 149 and 176 (Mair 8, 15D and 14E, or Mair 7, 4E and 3F; M G8, H7)

From Ginzling, 8km SW of Mayrhofen, to San Giacomo (Sankt Jakob) in the Italian Val di Vizze (Pfitschertal): 5km r/s, 10km rough road.

The metalled road from Mayrhofen through Ginzling (take lights; there are several tunnels) continues to the end of the short SW arm of the Schlegeisspeicher (reservoir), 1783m. (The dam is 725m long along its top, and 131m high.) Leave the road where it doubles back around the lake, and take a rough road along the R (SE) bank of the river. This soon becomes an unrideable track of sizeable rocks roughly thrown together, and with a reasonable gradient, up the Zamser Grund. A few glaciers can be seen from the top, where there is a hut/restaurant. An unsurfaced road descends to San Giacomo, from where a tarmac road leads to Sterzing (Vipiteno).

It was from Mayrhofen and over this pass that, in August 1912, D. H. Lawrence, his friend and future wife Frieda von Richthofen, and two young Englishmen walked to Sterzing. (Later, at Gargnano on Lake Garda, Lawrence wrote or re-wrote *Sons and Lovers* and other works.)

Times: 2½ hours from reservoir to top, 1½ hours down to San Giacomo.

(*M. Stephens, August 1984; F. Wright, 17.8.85, and others*)

M80 PITZTALER JÖCHL   2996M
VS (55) ++++

F&B map 251, folds D4 and E4; ÖK map 173 (M218 fold 9; Mair 8, 10E; M E8 top)

From Sölden in the Ötztal to Mittelberg at the head of the Pitztal; 8km r/s, 1½km rough road. The Gletscherstrasse from just above Sölden climbs 1400m in 13km, an average gradient of nearly 11%. From the road-head (a large car park) at 2800m, a fair path climbs steeply to the pass, at first over rocks and then across, and up, a glacier. The surface is partly soft snow, partly hard ice; instep crampons make progress easier. There are fine views from the top. On the other side, the path is difficult at first (double carrying may well be necessary), and you soon reach a point where it is necessary to climb down holding the rock face; therefore it is advisable to have straps in order to carry the bike on your back (see Appendix II). The path is then mostly easy down to the Braunschweiger Hütte (there is some scree just before the hut). Below the hut (where a night cost 120 schillings in 1984) there is a long stretch of difficult and steep path, which lasts most of the way down to the bottom of the slope, and includes another short section where it may be necessary to use straps. Soon after reaching fairly level ground, at about 1950m, you come to the bottom of the cable hoist to the hut above, and from here a good jeep track leads past a small restaurant to a tarmac road at Mittelberg (1734m), about 1½km away.

Times: roadhead to pass, 50 minutes; pass to hut, 1½ hours; hut to start of jeep track, 2½ hours (increase all these if you do a lot of double-carrying).

(*P. Hinton, 1984, reported in CC 34, 1985; F. Wright, 23.8.90*)

M85 NIEDERJOCH (GIOGO BASSO)   3018M
D (55) +++

F&B map 251, fold D6; ÖK map 173 (M218 fold 9; Mair (Südtirol) 6B, W edge, or 8, 10F)

From Vent, at the end of the road up the Venter Tal (itself a side valley of the Ötztal, S of Sölden), to the Schnalstal (Val Senales) in Italy. This and the Hochjoch, M90, are the routes by which the Venter Tal was settled from the Schnalstal in the 13th century or earlier. The body of Ötzi the Iceman was found on 19.9.91, near the Hauslabjoch (3280m) at 3210m, at a point about 1km NW of the pass along the frontier ridge (Franz von Hauslab, 1798–1883, was an Austrian general, geographer and historian).

There is a good jeep track from Vent (1893m) up to the Martin Busch hut (2501m), which replaces the Samoar Hütte, built in 1879. Much of the track is fairly level, but the last 1km is steeper. From the hut (where a place in a dormitory cost 120 schillings in 1990), a fairly good path leads to the pass. Some lifting and carrying over the rocks is necessary. Just before the pass you walk over the upper part of a glacier for ¼ hour; the surface is level and firm, and crampons are not needed, nor are there any crevasses; in fact it is more like a snowfield than a glacier. At the pass is a hut, the Similaunhütte.

The path on the S side is better, though steeper, than the one on the N. It zigzags down a steep hillside, and in places is steep itself, but not difficult. Then it descends across grassy slopes for a few km before entering pine woods above the Vernagt Stausee (1664m). From the reservoir a good tarmac road leads down the Schnalstal.

Times: from Vent to the Martin Busch hut, 3 hours; from the hut to the pass, 2½ hours; from the pass to the reservoir, 3 hours.

(*F. Wright, 8.8.90*)

M90 HOCHJOCH (GIOGO ALTO)   2861M
S SIDE D, N SIDE S (55) +++

F&B map 251, fold C6; ÖK map 172 (M218 folds 8, 9; Mair 8, 9F, or (Südtirol) 5B; M E8)

From Kurzras (little more than a hotel) at the head of the Schnalstal (Val Senales) in Italy, to Vent (this and the Niederjoch M85, 5km to the ESE, are alternatives): 18km r/s, 1½km rough road. The road up the Schnalstal is steep, and in August can be noisy and fume-laden, and the 800m climb from the Hotel Kurzras (ultra-modern, probably built for skiers) is a pleasant relief. The path is steep and in places rocky, so that some carrying is needed, but it is clearly visible, quite wide and well constructed all the way to the pass. A place at the Schöne Aussicht Hütte (Rifugio Bellavista) cost 15,000 lire in 1990. (The hut's height is usually given as 2842m, and it is a little above the physical pass; the 2861m on the ÖK 1:25K map is the height of a customs hut.)

The path on the Austrian side is harder, though much less steep. It is also narrower and much less used. At first the way is over rocks, a short way above a glacier to the R, and the only evidence is paint marks. Then for a short distance it is easier, but then there is a long section (which lasts down to about 1km beyond the bottom of the glacier) where the path, though mostly visible and anyhow marked by paint, is narrow and rocky, and carrying is the rule rather than the exception. The carrying makes this part slow and tiring. Height is lost only gradually.

About 1km beyond the end of the glacier the path improves, and pushing, rather than carrying, becomes the norm. The path descends to cross a side valley, then climbs to the Hochjoch Hospiz (2412m, built in 1927). This climb is not long (less than 150m vertically), but it contains the most difficult sections of the route. These, though short, are **vs**, and double carrying is probably advisable. After the Hospiz the path is reasonable and not steep (some carrying is still needed). For about 1km it passes through a gorge, and soon after that comes to the bottom of a cable hoist and some hay-barns, known as Rofenalm. From there a good track leads down for 1½km to Rofenhöfe, where there are hotels, and from there a tarmac road leads for another 1½km to Vent.

Times: Hotel Kurzras to Hütte, 2¾ hours; Hütte to Hochjoch Hospiz, 4 hours; Hospiz to Rofenalm, 2 hours.

(F. Wright, 19–20.8.90)

M95 WEIßSEEJOCH · 2965M
S (61) ++++

F&B map 251, fold B5; ÖK map 172 (M218 fold 8; Mair (Südtirol) 5A, SW corner, or 8, 9E, SW corner)

From the head of the Kaunertal (SSE of Prutz and Landeck) to Melag, at the head of the Langtauferer Tal, in Italy, 12km E of the Reschenpass. This is the most difficult of the three r/s passes between Austria and Italy in this part of the Alps (the others being **M85** and **M90**). Both sides of the pass are difficult, but the Austrian side is shorter (about 450m compared with 1050m on the other side).

The Gletscherstrasse (mostly steep above the lake, the Gepatsch Stausee) has numbered hairpins, starting at no. 29 below the lake. At 2470m (according to the sign) you come to a small muddy lake, the Weißsee. Soon after this you come to *Kehre 4* (hairpin 4), and 100m later there is a small notice pointing to the R, to the Weißseejoch. The path is mostly steep, sometimes very steep, and two stretches will probably call for double carrying. Just below the top there is a small snowfield, not difficult. There are fine views N and S from the pass.

The path on the Italian side starts off quite well, easier than the way up. However, there is a difficult short steep stretch of loose gravel and rocks leading down to a large snowfield (perhaps the remains of a glacier), and lower down the path is often steep and rocky, though later it is interspersed with fairly easy, almost level, stretches. At about 2500m do not take the path which branches off to the R. At about 2200m it is possible to leave the path and take a rough jeep track which later joins a better one. This leads down to a farmhouse at the valley bottom, at the end of the tarmac road coming up through Melag, about 1km up-valley from Melag church.

Times: from the road to the pass, 2¼ hours; from the pass to the valley bottom, 3 hours.

(F. Wright, 29.7.96)

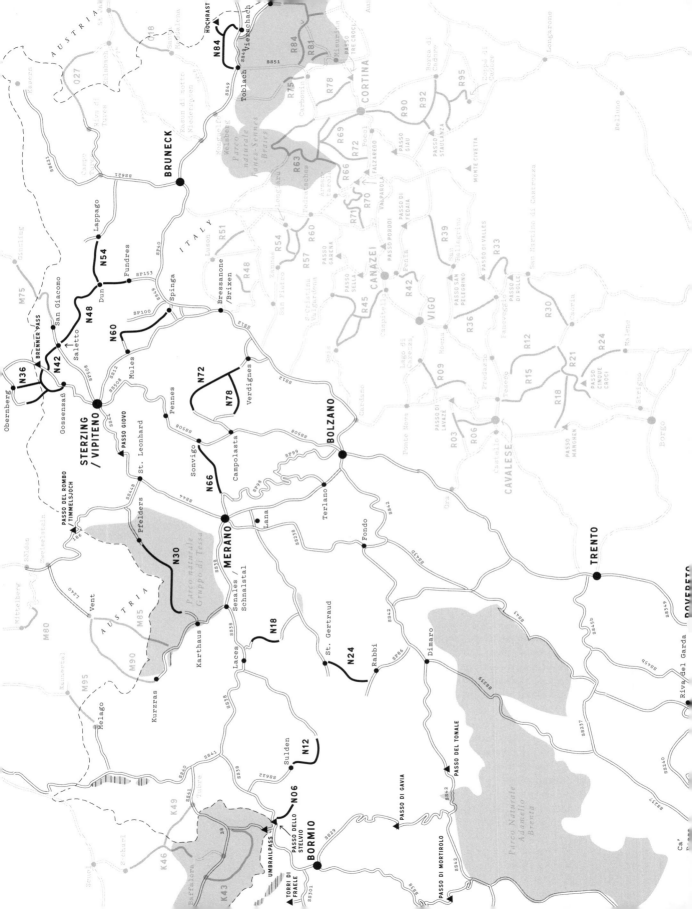

N06 RIFUGIO LIVRIO (LIVRIOHÜTTE)   3174M

M +++

F&B map WK S6, fold A2 (M218 fold 17; Mair (Südtirol) 3C, SE corner)

This is reached from the end of a cul-de-sac rough road, and lies 3km SE of the summit of the Passo dello Stelvio (Stilfser Joch). According to Denzel it is the highest point in the Alps accessible to four-wheel-drive vehicles (they need chains to get across the glacier). There is quite good unsurfaced road as far as the Rifugio Pirovano (3026m); this is steep in places (about 35% according to Denzel); from there to the Rifugio Livrio (which is connected to the Rifugio Pirovano by a cable way) it is a glacier, popular with skiers, with a lot of hard ice (instep crampons may help, but are not essential) and many deep, though narrow and easily avoided, crevasses.

Times (assuming you walk): from Stelvio summit to Rifugio Pirovano, 1 hour; from there to Rifugio Livrio, ½ hour.

(F. Wright, 13.8.90)

N12 MADRITSCHERJOCH   3123M

E SIDE S. W SIDE E (55) ++++

F&B map WK S6 fold C2 (M218 fold 18; Mair (Südtirol) 4D, NE corner)

From the head of the Martelltal (Val Martello), SW of Latsch (Laces – 24km W of Merano), to Sulden (Solda) at the head of the Suldental, 12km E of the Stelvio Pass. An easy track leads from the roadhead in the Martelltal to the Zufallhütte (2264m), where a bed cost 11,500 lire in 1990. A good path starts from the hut, but very soon (after crossing a stream, or sooner if you take the signposted short cut) this degenerates into one that is rocky, irregular and often narrow and rutted, so that quite a lot of lifting and carrying is needed. There are some easier bits later, but there is also a difficult steep section where you keep crossing two wires coming down the slope (probably the remains of a cable hoist); and the last section to the pass, after crossing a stream, is long and steep. From the top there is a good view of the Königsspitze and the Ortler (though a better view is to be had from closer up, lower down at the Schaubachhütte). On the W side, after ½km of easy path, you come to the top of a ski lift, and from then on the going is easy, down a wide and fairly smooth track (probably a ski piste in winter). At 2818m there is a smart new one-storey hut, the Madritscherhütte, opened in November 1989, and lower down, at about 2600m, there is a restaurant which is also the upper end of a cable way from Sulden. Just below this is the Schaubachhütte, where an unsurfaced road (not much of an improvement on the track above) starts, leading down to Sulden.

Times: roadhead to Zufallhütte, 1¼ hours; hut to pass, 4 hours; pass to Sulden, 2 hours.

(F. Wright, 12.8.90)

N18 TARSCHER PASS   2517M

D (61) +++

F&B map WK S6 folds F1 and G2 (M218 fold 19 top; Mair (Südtirol) 6C)

From Tarsch, just above Latsch (Laces, 24km W of Merano), to the Ultental (Val d'Ultimo), which runs SW from Merano. (The Tarscher Joch, 2482m, lies 1km ENE of this pass.) The best approach from Tarsch seems to be up a road whose higher part at least is unsurfaced, and which leads to the Tarscher Alm (1940m). Here food and accommodation (in a cowshed if you prefer it) are available. (Not knowing any better, our correspondent took another road – tarmac ended at 1200m – which led to the Latscher Alm, 1715m, then a path through the woods to the Tarscher Alm.) From here a broad and smooth, though mostly quite steep, track leads to the Zirmruanhütte (2251m), at the top of a ski lift (there is another ski lift which ends just above the Tarscher Alm). There is then a stony footpath, mostly not very steep, but with a steep and tricky bit just below a wooden cross at 2425m, from where there are nice views of the Vinschgau.

The descent, steep and rocky, brings you to an unsurfaced road which leads down to the Kuppelwieser Alm (1950m). Here tarmac recommences.

If going the other way, go through three hairpins on the unsurfaced road, pass some running water and look for a break in the wall on the R (about 300m after the hairpin). Here the number 342 is painted in black on the wall, also a white arrow on red; and a stone nearby, painted red and white, bears the figure 1 (originally 11, but the second 1 is partly obliterated). This is the start of the path. (Another path, about 150m after the third hairpin, climbs to the R towards the Tarscher Joch.)

Times: Tarscher Alm to pass, 2¼ hours; pass to unsurfaced road, 1¼ hours; road to Kuppelwieser Alm, ½ hour (if you walk).

(F. Wright, 31.7.96)

N24 RABBI JOCH (KIRCHBERG JOCH)   2449M

N SIDE E. S SIDE M ++

F&B map WK S6 fold F3 (Mair (Südtirol) 5/6D)

From Sankt Gertraud, near the head of the Ultental (Val d'Ultimo), SW of Merano, to San Bernardo in the Val di Rabbi, NW of Malé in the Val di Sole. The two sides of this pass are quite different. On the N it is a gradual climb of 900m up a valley from Sankt Gertraud, on the S it is a descent of 1300m down a steep hillside to San Bernardo. Nearly all the route can be ridden, N to S, on a mountain bike (part of the S side is probably too steep to climb).

From Sankt Gertraud (1519m) take a steep tarmac road, but after 200m, before crossing a bridge, turn L (signpost Rabbi Joch) up an unsurfaced road. Follow this to its end at the Bärhap Alm (2296m). The Enzianhütte, about an hour from Sankt Gertraud, would provide a bivouac in bad weather.

From the Bärhap Alm a mostly easy path continues to the pass, and just on the other side is a refuge, the Edelweisshütte (Rifugio Stella Alpina). From here there is an easy and gently sloping path for about 1km; then the path becomes steeper, but it is still fairly smooth apart from wooden poles fastened across it to prevent erosion. Loose stones on the path make it slippery.

Not long after entering the woods, you come to an unsurfaced road. To the L it climbs, to the R it apparently goes level. So it is probably best to ignore the road, cross it and continue straight down on the path. This soon brings you to another road, where you turn R. This road has an unpleasant surface of loose gravel. The conifers provide some shade. Eventually tarmac recommences at about 1300m, a short way above San Bernardo.

Times (assuming that you walk): from Sankt Gertraud to Bärhap Alm, 3½ hours; from Alm to pass, ¾ hour; from pass to beginning of tarmac, 2½ hours.

(F. Wright, 1.8.96)

At the time of republishing, summer 2018, there is a Gasthof Enzian in the nearby Martelltal, but not seemingly in the Ultental. However, there is a hut (possible bivouac?) at Bärhap Alm, and the Edelweisshütte (Rifugio Stella Alpina) is still open on the other side.

N30 EISJÖCHL (PASSO GELATO)   2895M
                                                 M ++++

F&B map 251, fold F6; ÖK map 173 (M218 folds 9, 10; Mair (Südtirol) 7B)

From the head of the Pfossental (Val di Fosse), NE of Karthaus (Certosa) in the Schnalstal (20km WNW of Merano), to the head of the Pfelderer Tal (Val di Plan), W of St Leonhard in Passeier (San Leonardo in Passiria). From a point just below Karthaus, at about 1200m, a road branches off which leads up into the Pfossental, with gradients of up to 20%. This ends at Vorderkaser, and there is then a good unsurfaced road, largely almost level, which leads past one or two isolated farms and ends at a farm a little above 2000m. A good track continues, almost level at first but then climbing at the head of the valley. This is part of the Meraner Höhenweg, which goes right round the Texelgruppe. You soon see evidence of construction (in places there is a causeway across the hillside, and elsewhere elaborate stone revetments), and it is highly probable that this is an old military road, built by the Italian army under Mussolini or before his time (cf. the Varaita–Maira ridge **D18**, and the Colle del Turlo **E89**). The slope is mostly easy, and the road on both sides of the pass is mostly in a good state of repair. There are two exceptions. At the very top, for about 50m on each side, the road is missing; an easy alternative path exists on the W side (watch for it at the last bend), but the one on the E side is rougher. The Stettiner Hütte (Rifugio Petrarca) stands

about ½km from, and a little below, the pass, on the E side. At about 2500m on the E side the road goes over the edge of a steep slope and zigzags down to a farm/restaurant on level ground at about 1850m (this is Lazinser Kaser). Some of these zigzags, consisting of stone steps which presumably replace dilapidated sections of road, form the second of the two exceptions mentioned above. From the farm/restaurant a road, unsurfaced but easily rideable with an ordinary bike, leads for 4.3km to just below the village of Pfelders (Plan, 1620m) and a good tarmac road.

Much of this route probably lends itself to a trip on a lightly loaded mountain bike.

Times (assuming that you walk all the way): Vorderkaser to pass, 5½ hours; pass to farm/restaurant, 3 hours.

(D. Purdy, 20.8.89; F. Wright, 9.8.90)

N36 FLACHJOCH   2120M
                                S SIDE E. N SIDE D ++

F&B map 241, fold F4; ÖK map 175 (Mair (Südtirol) 9A top, or no. 8 13E)

From Brennerbad, just SW of the Brenner Pass, to Obernberg in Austria. The road on the Italian side is part of a network of old military roads built in the 1930s, which is well described by Denzel. Another start to the network is at Gossensass (Colle Isarco), from where you climb to the Passo di Santicolo (Sandjöchl, 2165m), a short way SW of the Flachjoch.

From the Silbergasser hotel, on the downhill side of Brennerbad, take a narrow road which goes up the hillside, at first through trees. The climb is through 10 hairpins. The road is tarmac (rather old and worn) to between nos. 3 and 4, and again from between nos. 6 and 7 to no. 9. Then the slope increases and the surface deteriorates, being partly overgrown with grass above no. 10. But about 1km above no. 10, just after a small farm, the slope lessens and the surface improves markedly, being smooth gravel, easily rideable. This remains so as far as the top.

Between nos. 2 and 3 there are four short tunnels, all close together. At no. 9 you are above nearly all the trees, and a small wooden hut is available as a bivouac. At the small farm there is a choice of three roads; take the L-most. Just before the top an abandoned military barracks presents another possible bivouac site.

The pass is a smooth grassy saddle, with no signpost to indicate the path into Austria. Directly below the pass, and not far away, you can see a small farm, the Hochleger (1947m). A very faint path can be made out across the saddle, but it seems to be hardly used, and on the other side it can only be seen with difficulty. According to the map it starts off heading to the R, but there is little to show it; the hillside is covered with knee-high heather-like plants; often there are several paths in parallel, all of them, perhaps, made by cattle, and all descending, if at all, very slowly; each path is narrow and sometimes rutted. It is probably better, or necessary, to abandon the 'path' altogether and force your way down the slope, over and through the heath plants, till you come to grass, where the going is easier. Somehow you arrive at the track which leads to the small farm. This track is rough, but of course much easier than the hillside, and it improves as you go down. A shed with a projecting roof, at about 1800m, provides a bivouac site. After about 2km you come to a grassy level space with some farm buildings on it, the Fraderalm (1619m). The track is then rideable, with care, down as far as Obernberg (1396m).

Times: pushing, with a heavily loaded bike, 3½ hours from main road to pass; from there to farm, 40 minutes; from farm to Obernberg, 1½ hours.

(F. Wright, 7.7.00)

N42 SCHLÜSSELJOCH (COLLE DELLA CHIAVE) **2212M**
E ++

F&B map S4, fold D1 (Mair (Südtirol) 10A or no. 8 14E)

From Gossensass (Colle Isarco), on the S side of the Brenner Pass, to Wieden (Saletto) in the Pfitscher Tal (Val di Vizze), 16km rough road. A rough (formerly military) road leaves the Brenner Pass road (SS12) 1½km SW of Gossensass, immediately beneath the motorway, to zigzag up past the Rifugio Genziana Zirago (Enzianhütte Zirog) over the col and down to Saletto. According to Denzel, the top part of this road, and the whole of the E side, are too rough to be used by cars.

N48 PASSO DI FUNDRES (PFUNDERSJOCH) **2568M**
S +++

F&B map S4, fold E1; ÖK maps 175 and 176 (Mair (Südtirol), 10A or no. 8 14E)

From Saletto (Wieden) in the Pfitscher Tal (Val di Vizze), 10km NE of Vipiteno (Sterzing), to Fundres (Pfunders), 21km E of Vipiteno: 14km r/s, 6km rough road. There is a steep rough road from Saletto to Grossberg Alm (1932m); then the route is shown as a mule path, not always numbered. A rough road starts again at Dun, the start of our **N54**. There should be good views of the Gran Pilastro (Hochfeiler) from the top of the pass.

On republishing in 2018, alternative information was found suggesting mountain bikers might also start in the Pfitscher Tal by turning R onto a forest road (signposted Passo di Fundres) in Fossa Trues.

N54 PASSO PONTE DI GHIACCIO (EISBRUGGJOCH) **2545M**
S ++++

F&B map S4, fold G1; ÖK map 176 (Mair (Südtirol) 11A or no. 8 15E)

From Dun, a little place just NNW of Fundres (Pfunders) in the Val di Fundres (Pfunderer Tal), about 19km N of Bressanone or 21km E of Vipiteno (Sterzing), to Lappago (Lappach) in the Valle Selva dei Molini (Mühlwalder Tal), 8km to the ENE: 10km r/s, 13km rough road. This route is shown as a mule path throughout from Dun to the Lago di Neves, near the head of the Valle Selva dei Molini. The path

is steep (25%), especially lower down the W side, and for much of the E side. The path is no. 13 on the W side, no. 26 on the E side. There is a refuge (Edelrauthütte) at the top of the pass.

You could continue the route and end up in the Ahrntal (Valle Aurina), by taking a steep mule path (no. 24) E-wards from the N end of the Lago di Neves, over the Passo di Neves (Neveserjoch), 2407m, into the Val del Rio Bianco (Weissbachtal). This path becomes a rough road at the Gögen Alm (2050m), nearly 2km E of the pass.

The S-erly alternative to the Passo Ponte di Ghiaccio, the Passenjoch, from Fundres to Campo, is probably not worth the effort; it is steep throughout, and the views are almost certainly inferior.

N60 PASSO DI VALLES (VALSER JOCH) **2032M**
W SIDE M. E SIDE E +++

F&B map S4, fold E2; ÖK maps 175 and 176 (Mair (Südtirol) 10A bottom)

From Mules (Mauls), 8km ESE of Vipiteno (Sterzing), to Spinga (Spinges), at the bottom end of the Valser Tal, 8km N of Bressanone (Brixen): 5km r/s, 14km rough road. There is a rough road up to Ritzail, then a mule path (no. 10) to the pass. This path no. 10 descends steeply E-wards to Valles (Vals); however, there is another path (no. 9), which leads SE-wards from the pass, much less steeply. This becomes a rough road down to Spinga, and should provide better views to the Dolomites.

N66 MISSENSTEINER JOCH **2128M**
N SIDE M. S SIDE E ++

F&B map S4, fold A4 (Mair (Südtirol) 8B)

From Merano (Meran) to Sonvigo (Aberstückl) in the Val di Pennes (Pensertal), 25km N of Bolzano (Bozen); 6km r/s, 13km rough road. There is a metalled road from Merano up to Falzeben, then a cart road up to the Kirchsteiger Alm (1935m, which is marked as S. Osvaldo on the TCI map). This is the terminus of the cable car (ski lifts go higher). There are paths from here to the pass, then a path (no. 13) NE-wards; fairly soon, after a steep section, this becomes a mule path to Sonvigo, with an alternative forestry road from 1650m down to the main valley. Views of the Dolomites may well be improved by a short climb from the pass to one of the neighbouring viewpoints.

N72 FORTSCHELLSCHARTE **2299M**
D ++

F&B map S4, fold D4 (Mair (Südtirol) 9B & 10B)

From Valdurna (Durnholz) at the head of the Valdurna (Durnholzertal), 28km NNE of Bolzano (Bozen), to Verdignes (Verdings) and Chiusa (Klausen), 24km NE of Bolzano: 13km r/s, 10km rough road. This is shown as a mule path throughout, with fairly easy gradients over the top to the Rifugio Chiusa al Campaccio (Klausener Hütte).

The direct descent S-wards from here (on path no. 2) is very steep, so it would probably be easier to follow the gradually descending mule path no. 17 E-wards; after 3km this becomes a cart road down to Verdignes.

On the way up to the Fortschellscharte, another mule path (no. 4) forks L up to the Schalderer Scharte (2324m). However, the E side of this pass is continuously steep, and unlikely to give worthwhile views.

N78 PASSO SAN CROCE DI LAZFONS 2378M
D ++

F&B map S4, fold D4; (Mair (Südtirol) 9B & 10B)

From San Martino (Reinswald), 22km NNE of Bolzano (Bozen), to Verdignes (Verdings) and Chiusa (Klausen), 24km NE of Bolzano: 16km r/s, 6km rough road. This is another fairly easily graded but long route, path no. 7. It is a mule path except for the last 3km up the W side from a point at 2083m to the Rifugio San Croce di Lazfons (Schutzhaus Latzfonserkreuz) at 2302m. This route joins that from the Fortschellscharte **N72** before the Rifugio Chiusa. The E side of both these passes should give fine views of the Dolomites.

N84 MARKINKELE (MARCHGINGGELE) 2505M
M +++

F&B S3, fold G2 bottom, also folds F3 and G3, top (Mair (Südtirol) 14/15B)

This is on an old military road which runs ENE, up to the Austrian frontier, from Dobbiaco (Toblach), at the head of the Val Pusteria (Pustertal), about 70km ENE of Bolzano (Bozen). The route can also be approached from Vierschach (Versciaco), on the main road 8km E of Dobbiaco. It is a long day trip for a lightly loaded cyclist based at Toblach. It is advisable to get a map of the town from the tourist office (just below the crossroads on the main road), and to take plenty of water.

There are three choices for the lower part of the route. The description which follows is of Route A (going up) and Route B (coming down). We have no reports of Route C, which runs to the S of Route A. All three routes meet at, or near, a ruined building at 1795m (this place is called Bodeneck, according to Denzel), from where there is only one road to the top.

Route A. Go L round the main church in Toblach and take the Herbstenburgstraße, which after crossing the road leading to Wahlen becomes the Ehrenbergstrasse. This is narrow and well surfaced and climbs through woods to 1660m, just before a little house called the Lachwiesenalm (or Lachwiesenhütte). From here the road is unsurfaced but fairly smooth and often rideable (with a lightly loaded bike). It climbs to the top of a ridge, all in trees, at 1911m, then descends to the ruined building.

Route B (described as a descent). Just before the ruined building, turn R and go roughly level, at about 1800m, along a road of variable surface and gradient. After about 1km this goes L, crosses a substantial stream, passes through a grassy area where there are cattle and then descends along the valley, never very far from the stream (the Silvesterbach). The surface is fairly smooth at first, but deteriorates, and you may have to push quite a lot. At 1391m tarmac recommences, and progress is much quicker, though transverse channels cut in the surface give you a jolt from time to time. The road goes past the Enzianhütte (Rifugio Genziana) [*now a restaurant*], and past the village of Wahlen, a short way above Toblach.

On the climb from the ruined building, the road becomes much rougher and stonier, and you may have to push nearly all the way to the top. The road goes through eleven hairpins, the last of which is near the top. There is no water, apart from a few trickles before the first hairpin and a slow-running water pipe at the seventh. There is hardly any traffic, just the occasional motorbike or mountain bike. At the top the road crosses the frontier ridge through a slight gap, runs along the other side for a short way and then descends along the S side gradually for about 1½km to a point at 2436m called Hochrast (we have no reports of the road after it has reached the ridge). From where you reach the ridge, a short path leads to the summit of the hill, which is crowned with a wooden cross. From here there are good views in nearly every direction—snowy peaks to the N, the Dolomites to the S.

Times: with a lightly loaded touring bike, say 4½ hours for the climb and 3½ for the descent; with a mountain bike, less.
(F. Wright, 6.7.00)

Also known as the **CORNETTO DI CONFINE**.

N90 PASSO DI TREMALZO AND 1694M
BOCCA DI VAL MARZA 1863M
M +++

Kompass 1:50K map 10

From the Val d'Ampola, 16km W of Riva del Garda (at the N end of Lake Garda), to any one of several possible places on the W shore of the lake, about 13km to the SE. Those who like their rough roads rough should enjoy the stretch from the Bocca di Val Marza to the Passo Nota, and in any case this stretch, which is perhaps an even more surprising piece of roadbuilding than the Pasubio **R27**, will be one of the highlights of any tour in this area.

The climb from Storo (388m) in the W, to the Passo Tremalzo, is on tarmac and is worth doing if only for the initial interesting climb through the gorge of the Val d'Ampola. From the pass, which is on a narrow ridge, there are fine views to E and W. There is also a *rifugio* and a restaurant.

Here you have a choice of two roads, neither tarmac, for the descent. One, which turns R at the pass and goes down the far side of the ridge into the Val di San Michele, is shown on the TCI map as a private road, but it seems that no objection is raised if cyclists use it. It has a much better surface than the other. We have no reports on it.

The other road goes ahead at the pass, climbing uphill along the far side of the ridge. At first the surface is reasonable, but when the slope increases the surface becomes much rougher. At the top (the Bocca di Val Marza) there is a short tunnel, preceded by a cave which would serve as a bivouac. On the other side the road (built by the military in the first world war) becomes very rough indeed, and if you have an ordinary touring bike, well loaded, you have to go very slowly and carefully. Mountain bikes, however, can be ridden uphill, with difficulty, and downhill at some speed.

Not far below the summit tunnel there is another short tunnel, and lower down there are one or two more. From time to time there are little caves, thoughtfully cut in the rock by the roadbuilders to provide shelter from storms. But there is no running water till just below the Passo Nota (1240m), a long way below. The road is cut out of a steep and rocky hillside, with good views, from time to time, of Lake Garda.

Just before the Passo Nota there is a short stretch (about 400m) of old tarmac, and at the pass there is a *rifugio* (Rifugio degli Alpini). The road does not cross this pass but keeps to the R of it, and there is a fork. For the route described here, take the R fork (sign 'Tremosine'); you soon come to a water pipe and trough, and a long stretch of tarmac, which lasts for the steep part of the descent into the Val di Bondo. At about 750m, now on a fairly level stretch in the valley, there is a little more than 1km of unsurfaced road, presumably left there to preserve the rustic quality of the valley. Then tarmac resumes, at a gentle slope, and takes you to Vesio (626m), where you have a choice of roads descending to Lake Garda. (If you are heading S, be warned that the tempting-looking road through Tignale involves two gorges and a good 300m of climbing, much of it at 10–12%.)

Times: if you have an ordinary touring bike and are well loaded, allow ¾ hour from the Passo Tremalzo to the Bocca di Val Marza, and 2½ hours from there to the Passo Nota.

(F. Wright, 16.7.00)

P14   GERLOS PASS OLD ROAD

1507M
E +

F&B map 152, fold H1 (Mair 7, 6D, 7D; M I7)

This is an easy alternative to the higher new road over the pass, which is 22km ENE of Mayrhofen, between the Zillertal and Krimml: 8km rough road.

P28   BIRNLÜCKE (FORCELLA DEL PICCO)

2667M
S (50) ++++

F&B map 152, fold J3; ÖK map 151 (Mair 7, 7E; M I7)

From Kasern in Italy, near the head of the Ahrntal (Valle Aurina), 30km NNE of Bruneck (Brunico), to Krimml, 24km E of Mayrhofen: 11km r/s, 16km rough road. The road up the Ahrntal continues past Prettau and Kasern to end at Trinkstein, 3km further up (there are some interesting miniature churches hereabouts). The path is easy enough for perhaps a bit over 1km, but then becomes steep, with many zigzags, rocks and boulders, on its 1000m climb to the pass. There are views of the Dreiherrnspitze. From the Birnlücke hut at 2441m, the path goes up a ridge; so it is advisable to fill up with water before going on.

The descent into Austria is, if anything, steeper and rougher, again with many zigzags, but the path is well marked and unmistakable on both sides of the pass, at least when there is little snow about. The Ahrntal is well populated, but on the other side the Krimmler Achental has only a few farms and a sawmill. The head of the valley is ringed in by high mountains, some with glaciers, and there are views of the Grossvenediger. An almost level unsurfaced road leads down the valley to the top of the famous series of waterfalls above Krimml, whose total height is 380m. Near the Gasthof Schönangerl above the main middle fall, the track splits; go R for Krimml, L for the Gerlos Pass.

Allow probably 8 hours for the footpath section alone, another 3 for the descent to the main road.

(F. Wright, 15.8.85)

P42   RAMMERN SATTEL

1202M
E +

F&B (who call it Römer Sattel) map 393 (Mair 7, 9C, 10B; M J6, K6; fold B4)

From Hochfilzen, 18km E of Kitzbühel, to Lofer, 14km to the NNE: 3km r/s, 10km rough road. This is a very easy route, which crosses an army firing range near its SW end, so you have to wait if firing is in progress. There is a good track up to the pass, and a narrower one down the NE side, which is mostly rideable where gradients permit. Later you meet a rough road; this joins road no. 311 about 6km SE of Lofer. (If you turn R at the road and follow it for 3km, you come to Weissbach, the start of the Hirschbichl road pass, which leads to Berchtesgaden in Germany.)

(Anon., undated)

P56   SCHANZEL (SPIELBERG HUT)

1332M
E ++

F&B map 382, fold D1 (Mair 7, 9C; M J6)

From Fieberbrunn, 12km ENE of Kitzbühel, to Saalbach, 20km ESE of Kitzbühel, 11km rough road. This is presumably a very easy low pass. A rough road goes up past Trixlegg to Burgeralm; then there is a cart road over the pass (where the Spielberg hut is) to Saalbach. The route is marked on Mair and on the F&B 1:300K map as an almost straight connecting link.

P70   OBERHÜTTEN SATTEL

1866M
E +

F&B map 202, fold D1 (Mair 7, 15D, or Mair 4; M M7 top)

From Forstau, on a small road 7km E of Radstadt and 10km W of Schladming, to Hinterweisspriach, 23km to the SSE; this pass, like the Znach Sattel P84, is an alternative to the road over the Radstädter Tauern Pass: 3km r/s, up to 24km rough road. There is apparently a jeep road from above Forstau to the Oberhütte am See (by the lake) on top of the pass. A path goes down to the head of the Weisspriachtal; from there a rough road, shown as metalled after Hinterweisspriach, goes on down the valley.

P84   ZNACH SATTEL

2059M
E ++

F&B map 202, fold E1 (Mair 4; M M7 top)

From Pichl Preunegg, 6km WSW of Schladming, to Hinterweisspriach, 20km to the SSE. This pass, like the Oberhütten Sattel P70, is an alternative to the road over the Radstädter Tauern Pass: 6km r/s, up to 19km rough road (?). The route is shown as a rough road on Michelin and F&B up to Ursprung Alm, then as a jeep road up to the Giglachsee hut, a little below the pass; a path continues over the top and down to Greimeister Alm, with fairly easy gradients, and is followed by an equally easily graded mule path down to the Weisspriachtal.

Q. OSTTIROL & KÄRNTEN (CARINTHIA)

The Hohe Tauern and Radstädter Tauern, which border this area in the N, are crossed or tunnelled through by a succession of roads, railways and r/s passes. From W to E these are: the Felber Tauern 036 (and road tunnel), the Kalser Tauern 045, the Grossglockner (road pass), the Mallnitzer Tauern 081 (and Tauerntunnel railway tunnel), the Arlscharte 090, the Tauerntunnel (motorway tunnel, not to be confused with the railway tunnel) and the Radstädter Tauern (road pass). The Bockhart Scharte 072 is in the Salzburger Land, but is included here because of its closeness to some of the routes in this section.

Q09   MEL È DIS (OR MELÈDIS)   1578M
                                          M ++

F&B 223 (Mair 6, 7E; M L9)

From Stranig, 37km SE of Lienz (or 13km ESE of Kötschach, or 16km W of Hermagor), to Paularo in Italy, 16km NE of Tolmezzo: 4km r/s,10km rough road. The pass lies about midway between two road passes, the Plöcken Pass to the W and the Nassfeld Pass (Passo di Pramollo) to the E. The route begins as a stony track without a sign to the pass. It continues similarly and is rideable. There is a café just before the top, and a few cars use the route. The TCI map is wrong in showing the track continuing up and over the pass. The main track continues to Waidegger, to the W, still inside Austria.

Just past the café there is a turning to the L. Take this, pass a large area of grass on the R, turn off the track and follow the edge of a wood. Shortly after, turn into the wood following what looks like a stream bed, and the path becomes more distinct. Down the S side, the path soon becomes rideable. There is a short steep rise and then a very steep track down to the road to Paularo. The road also descends steeply, and then rises by a deep gorge, and there is a final narrow stretch of road down to the town.

Q18   GSIESER TÖRL   2209M
                                          M ++

ÖK map 177 (Mair 6, 2C bottom; Mair (Südtirol) 14A bottom; M 18;
F&B map S3, fold F1)

From St Jakob in Defereggen, 34km WNW of Lienz, to Santa Maddalena Vallalta (St Magdalena in Gsies), 23km ENE of Brunico (Bruneck), in Italy: 8km r/s, 3km rough road. This is an E-ly alternative to the road over the Staller Sattel. As you go up the Defereggental, turn off this road at Mariahilf, cross the main stream, and follow a path on the R (SE) bank of a side stream (the Lapp Bach) for about 500m before crossing the stream and climbing steeply through the forest to Lappach Alm (1910m). From here onwards the route is shown as a mule path, with easier gradients to the col, but still fairly steep on the descent into Italy.

Q27   KLAMMLJOCH (PASSO DI GOLA)   2298M
                                          E +++

F&B map 152, fold H4 (Mair (Südtirol), 13A, 14A; M 18 top)

From Riva di Tures (Rain in Taufers), 19km NE of Brunico (Bruneck) in the Italian Val Pusteria (Pustertal), to the head of the Austrian Defereggental: 21km rough road. The metalled road up the Val di Riva ends at a car park 1km beyond Rain. The rough road to the top is a 6km push, rideable slowly downhill, and just negotiable by cars. There is a restaurant on the way up, and quite pretty views, also some deserted buildings just before the top which would provide shelter in wet weather. If you don't mind ignoring the official notices at the top, you can continue down on a road to the Defereggental (9km down to Oberhaus Alm, another 6 down to Erlsbach, probably easy enough going).

(F. Wright, W side only, 14.8.85)

Q36   FELBER TAUERN   2481M
                                          S +++

F&B map 121 or 382, fold B4; ÖK map 152 (Mair 6, 3B, 4B top, or 7,
8D, 8E; M J7)

From Matrei, 26km NW of Lienz, to Mittersill, 20km SSE of Kitzbühel: 14km r/s, 5km rough road (or 24km if you avoid the main road). The very busy main road, with about ten tunnels, up to Matreier Tauernhaus (at the S end of the tunnel, a good place to stay), can be avoided by tracks, old road and footpaths to the W of the new road. From there, a chair lift, which takes bikes, goes up to a hut at 1985m, and a good easy path contours the hillside to join the original path, now little used. (This little-used path roughly follows the line of the chair lift, for those who don't want to use the lift.) A grass road continues up the main valley in hairpins, obviously made when the new pylons were put in, since it stops at the last one before the top. (There was a pylon line over the top in 1953.) You have to cross onto the old path – there is a small snowfield, which is not a problem.

The descent to the Hintersee is long and steep, with a short easier section in the middle. Much carrying is needed. About 2½km from the top, a path forks L, which should be avoided because it is precipitous lower down. So keep R here, over a slight bluff, before the interminable descent to the Hintersee continues. There are fine views of the Freiwand opposite. A rough road continues down to the main road, just before a tunnel. No bypass to this tunnel is shown on the large-scale map, but just beyond it a small road is shown just W of the main road, right down to Mittersill.

(R. Sauvaget, 1957; Mrs M. A. Stephens, August 1984)

Q45   KALSER TAUERN   2518M
                                          VS +++

F&B map 122; ÖK map 153 (Mair 6, 4B top, or 7, 9E top; M J7)

From Uttern dorf, 18km WSW of Zell am See, or 7km

E of Mittersill, to Kals, 21km NNW of Lienz; this pass lies between the r/s Felber Tauern pass **036** on the W, and the road pass over the Grossglockner on the E: 13km r/s, 16km rough road. There is a metalled road to Enzinger Boden, then an 8km climb on a rough (or by now perhaps metalled) road to the Tauernmoossee; or you can take the fairly easy, sometimes boggy, path below the cable car lift to the lake. The path along the W side of the lake is rideable to a fork of paths just over 1km from the top station of the cable car. Our correspondent missed this fork, and kept on the L-hand path, which soon became rough and boggy, with many boulders, calling for carrying. The 'Stiege' (staircase) marked on the map is a very steep 'rake' slanting across a 60m cliff, and needs a double carry and great caution; but for it the route would count as S, not VS. The Rudolfshütte (café, etc.) is just over the top of this. Our correspondent met many snowdrifts on the final easier ascent to the pass.

The first 300m or so of the descent is very awkward; there is no path, just paint marks on the rocks. There is a short cliff, followed by a scree slope, then a narrow path to the top of Erdiges Eck. Here there are fine views, and the path improves, but still you occasionally need to carry across a rock landslide. By the Dorfer See you have to carry across a mass of boulders that made a dam to form the lake. After this you can ride most of the way to Kalser Tauernhaus, whence a jeep road leads to Kals.

No time was given, but it must be a long day.

(R. Sauvaget, 1957)

054 KALS-MATREIER TÖRL
2207M

M ++

F&B map 181, fold B1; ÖK, on corner of four maps (Mair 6, 4B, 4C, or Mair 7, 9E, 9F; M J7, J8)

From Kals, 21km NNW of Lienz, to Matrei, 8km to the W and on the main road from Lienz up the Iseltal: 6km r/s, 5km rough road. From Grossdorf, near Kals, go up to the last houses and into the valley on the R. It is a good forest track, almost level at first, then climbing very steeply to the L below the meadows. The track is less steep, but narrow and rather overgrown, through these scrubby meadows; then it goes straight up to the pass through open grassland. Allow at least 3 hours to the top from Grossdorf.

The meadow track down from the pass is too steep and stony to ride, but after an hour or so you reach the forest, where a better track allows you to ride down to Matrei.

(R. Perrodin, c. 1970)

063 BERGERTÖRL
2651M

M, SOME D ++++

F&B map 181, folds C1 and D1; ÖK map 153 (Mair 6, 5B bottom, or Mair 7, 10E; M K7 bottom)

From Kals, 21km NNW of Lienz, to Heiligenblut, on the S side of the Grossglockner road pass, 24km NNE of Lienz; or to the road leading to the Franz-Josefs-Höhe from the S side of the Grossglockner pass: 10km r/s, 3km rough

road. There is a metalled road from Kals to the Lucknerhaus (restaurant, etc.). A jeep road strikes off to the R, about 250m before the hut, becoming a narrow path to the pass after about 1½km; the route follows the line of the cableway which takes provisions up to the Glorer hut. You can stay the night here, in season, at the pass. An easy path leads down to and along the Leitertal; about 6km from the pass and just above the Leiter falls, the main path crosses to the R side of the river and continues down to Heiligenblut, joining a cart road from Wirtsbauer Alm 3km before the village. Just before crossing the river (the Leiter) above the falls, a path goes off to the L (the N). This path is hard going, very steep in places, with a lot of undergrowth. It climbs to a dam, where there is a good view of the Grossglockner, and a gravel road continues to join the metalled road to the Franz Josefs Höhe (this road, too, gives good views of the Grossglockner and of the Pasterzen glacier). Above the hotel at the Franz Josefs Höhe, a good track continues up the valley past the Hofmanns hut, again with fine views, but it is a dead end.

Two correspondents, trying this route in late June, got over the pass without much difficulty, despite some snow, and followed the path down the Leitertal, but found that the bridge over the river had been dismantled (possibly for the winter, though this is not clear). They had to return over the pass, where they spent a good night at the Glorer hut.

(J. Haigh, July 1982; E. and S. Wagstaff, 25.6.94)

072 BOCKHART SCHARTE
2226M

M, SOME D ++

F&B map 191, folds A5 and B5; ÖK map 154 (Mair 6, 6B, 7B, or Mair 7, 11E, 12E; M K7, L7 bottom)

From Kolm Saigurn, at the head of the Hüttwinkltal, 12km ENE of Heiligenblut, to Sportgastein, 6km to the E, in the Nassfelder Tal; this pass lies between the road pass over the Grossglockner on the W and the r/s Mallnitzer Tauern pass **081** on the E: 8km r/s, 1½km rough road. From the Hotel Ammererhof (1628m), at the head of the Hüttwinkltal, a mule track climbs easily to Filzen Alm. Thereafter there is a fairly steep path over the pass and down to the Ober Bockhart See; then the path is easily graded as far as the Bockhart See hut (1917m), and steep again till it meets a rough road leading down to Sportgastein.

081 MALLNITZER (OR NIEDERER) TAUERN
2446M

S +++

F&B map 191, fold B6; ÖK map 155 (Mair 6, 7B, or Mair 7, 12E; M L7 bottom)

From Böckstein, 39km NE of Lienz (or just S of Badgastein at the head of the Gastein Tal), to Mallnitz, 12km to the SSE: 10km r/s, 16km rough road, if you avoid the tunnels. As a means of getting from A to B, this route is equivalent to the (railway) Tauerntunnel between Böckstein and Mallnitz; it lies between the Grossglockner road on the W and the (motorway) Tauerntunnel on the E. It is also an alternative to the Arlscharte **090**, a few km to the E.

A Roman road called the *Via Aurea* (on account of the gold mined in this area) led over this pass, and it is said to have been the highest vehicle road in the Roman Empire. Parts still survive, though not mentioned by our correspondent. Silver coins were found on the pass in 1998, and a museum devoted to the Roman road is planned.

At the SW end of Böckstein, fork L on a narrow steep rough road to avoid the three long tunnels on the new road up to Sportgastein. Turn L at Sportgastein, to the S, on an almost level rideable road across the meadows; this track ends at Veit Alm, where a very steep path, narrow at times, climbs with many zigzags between two branches of the stream. The gradient eases at the top of this section, and the path crosses the stony western slopes of a low ridge running N from the pass. The Hagener hut stands on the pass, above a last steep rocky slope.

Descend almost due S; below 2300m the path is shown as a mule track, again zigzagging between two parallel streams. Lower down it becomes a jeep track, unrideable, across the meadows. Eventually you reach the Jamnig hut, useful for a meal. A better road, but one that is still too stony to ride, continues down from the hut, and meets a rideable road about 3km above Mallnitz.

Allow at least 4 hours up, 2½ hours down.

(R. Perrodin, c. 1970)

090 **ARLSCHARTE**

2259M

S SIDE D. N SIDE VS ++

F&B map 191, fold E5; ÖK map 155 (Mair 6, 8B, E edge)

From the head of the Maltatal, which runs NW from Gmünd (40km NW of Villach) on the main road over the Katschberg Höhe, to the head of the Grossarltal, which lies E of Bad Hofgastein. The road up the Maltatal, which starts climbing at about 900m, just after the toll station, goes through six tunnels, all unlit; in most of these, pedestrians are not allowed, and in at least one a part of the tunnel is out of sight of either entrance. Both the Maltatal and the Schödertal (the upper part of the Grossarltal) are parts of the Hohe Tauern national park. There are several hotels and restaurants on the way up.

From the Sporthotel, just above the dam, follow an unsurfaced road along the N shore of the reservoir for about 1½km, to just after a small promontory. Here a sign points up the hillside to the Arlscharte. A short but steep carry brings you to some scree, where the path forks and is not easy to see. Resist the temptation to head for the Jägersteiger Hütte, visible a short way off, and keep to the L, heading up the grassy slope. Once found, the path is easy to follow, being marked with red and white paint and occasionally the number 512. It is, however, steep and difficult.

The path descends briefly on the other side before climbing to the L, more than regaining the height lost, in order to avoid a cliff overlooking a small lake. After a fairly easy stretch there is a steep and difficult scree-filled gully, which leads to a wooden hut (1835m) visible from far above. The path remains steep and difficult after the hut. It soon goes

down into a long steep rocky gully, which is also the bed of a torrent. It follows the torrent down to a level grassy space (1440m), which used to be a lake, but (at least at the time of our correspondent's visit) had dried up. Here the slope becomes much easier, but because of the rocky nature of the path carrying, rather than pushing, is still the rule. An unsurfaced road is reached just before a small lake (1068m).

Carrying will probably be needed for more than half of the 6-hour descent.

Times: 1½ hours up from the lake, 6 down to the other lake.

(F. Wright, 30.7.92)

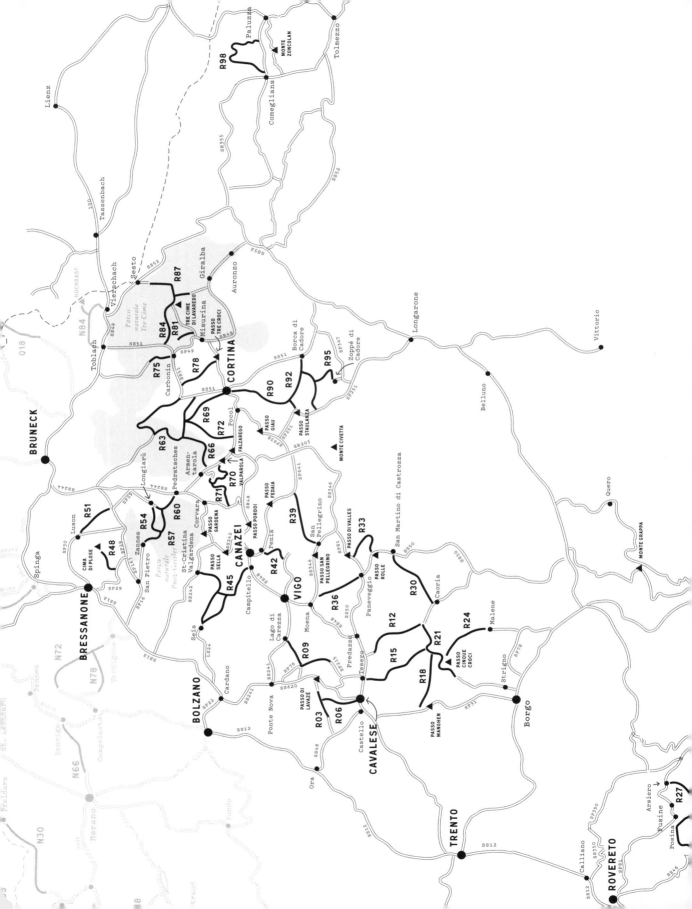

This section includes some routes (Pasubio **R27**, Panoramica delle Vette **R98**) which are rather outside the area usually understood by 'the Dolomites'.

R03   PASSO DI OCLINI (GRIMM JOCH)   1989M
E ++

F&B map S7, fold F3 (Mair (Südtirol) 9D bottom)

From the Passo di Lavazè, 19km SE of Bolzano (Bozen), to the main road (SS48) leading from Predazzo to Ora (Auer): 6km rough road. This was found to be a perfectly easy route on 13.8.95.

R06   PASSO CUGOLA (KUGEL JOCH)   1923M
E ++

F&B map S7, fold F3 (Mair (Südtirol) 9E top)

From Cavalese, 24km SSE of Bolzano (Bozen), to the W side of the (unsurfaced) road over the Passo di Oclini **R03**: 8km rough road. There is a long, steep cart road (path no. 502) from Daiano to the pass. On the N side, a short steep bit of mule path soon becomes a fairly level cart road to meet the W side of the road over the Passo di Oclini at about 1750m. There are many other rough and cart roads all over this area, mostly in the woods.

R09   PASSO DI PAMPEAGO (REITERJOCH)   1996M
E +++

F&B map S7, folds G2 and G3 (Mair (Südtirol) 10D bottom)

From Tesero, 4km E of Cavalese (which is 24km SSE of Bolzano), to San Floriano (Ortner), 10km to the N: 5km r/s, 6km rough road leading to the Lago di Carezza. There is a steep, metalled road up to the Rifugio Pampeago, then a rough road, rideable, over the pass. The road becomes metalled again, soon after the top, and remains so down to Floriano, where turn R for Pievalle (Bewaller), and R again (uphill at first) past the Pension Bewaller along a delightful level track through the woods (path no. 8) to the beautiful Lago di Carezza (Karersee).

The nearby Passo Feodo (Satteljoch), 2121m, is a long, steep, rough road up from Predazzo, then a mule path (no. 504) over the top near the Pampeago col.

Allow 3 or 4 hours (for the Passo di Pampeago).

(M. A. Stephens, 1977)

R12   FORCOLA SADOLE   2066M
N SIDE E. S SIDE D +

F&B map S7, fold H4 (Mair (Südtirol) 10E)

From Ziano di Fiemme, 8km E of Cavalese (which is 24km SSE of Bolzano), to the E side of the Cinque Croci **R21** pass; 8km rough road on N side, then 8km r/s. The rough road up from Ziano leads to the Baita della Madonna

(1817m), 1½km beyond the Rifugio Cauriol; then there is a mule path to the col. There is a long steep descent to the Rifugio Refavaie on the Cinque Croci road. The route is numbered 320 throughout.

R15   FORCOLA DI LAGORAI   2372M
M +

F&B map S7, fold G4 (Mair (Südtirol) 10E)

From Lago, just S of Tesero (see **R09**), to the Cinque Croci **R21** road, near its top; 8km rough road on N side, then 8km r/s. A rough road from the W end of Lago village follows the E bank of the Rivo Lagorai to Lago Lagorai (1870m). There is then a mule path as far as the Laghetti Lagorai (2270m), then a path over the col, with a steep descent to the Malga Val Ciotto Alta (1841m), where the path turns S up to the Cinque Croci road at the Malga Val Cion (1973m), 1½km N of the road's summit. The route is numbered 316 throughout.

R18   FORCOLA VAL SORDA   2256M
W SIDE M. E SIDE E +

F&B map S7, fold G4 (Mair (Südtirol) 10E bottom)

This connects the Passo Manghen, now a surfaced road, 13km S of Cavalese (which is 24km SSE of Bolzano), with the road over the Cinque Croci **R21**: 5km rough road on the W side, then 8km r/s. From Ponte delle Stue on the N side of the Manghen pass, a rough road follows the R (N) bank of the Rivo delle Stue to the Malga Cazzorga (1845m). From here a mule path climbs up to the col. A path descends fairly gradually to the Malga Val Cion (1973m) on the Cinque Croci road, passing a low col, the Passo Val Cion (2076m), on the way. The route is numbered 318 throughout.

R21   PASSO CINQUE CROCI   2018M
M ++

Kompass map 76, fold A5 (Mair (Südtirol) 10E bottom)

From Strigno, 30km E of Trento, to Caoria, 18km to the NE: 22km rough road. From Strigno the road is thought to be tarmac to start with. Our correspondent combined this route with the Manghen, which he crossed from N to S, by turning L 13½km from the summit of the Manghen, and taking a rough road which led down to a quarry (cantiere), across a river and up another valley at a steep slope. This road led him, after 3km in all, to a tarmac road coming up from Strigno and leading to the Cinque Croci Pass. The tarmac only lasted for 2km; then there was 9km of unsurfaced road, largely unrideable, to the top, a grassy saddle on which stands a metal pole supporting five crosses. After the top the road is almost level for ½km, then it descends through pines for 13km before reaching tarmac at the Rifugio Refavaie (1116m).

(F. Wright, 11.8.85)

R24 FORCOLA MAGNA   2117M
W SIDE E. S SIDE D +

Kompass map 76, fold A5 (Mair (Südtirol) 10E bottom, 10F)

From the Passo Cinque Croci **R21** to Pieve Tesino, 36km E of Trento or 16km WNW of Fonzaso: 8km r/s, 5km rough road on S side. A fairly level path (no. 326) leads from the very top of the Cinque Croci road to the col; then there is a very steep descent to the Malga Cima d'Asta (1588m). From here there is a rough road down to Malene, and a metalled one to Pieve Tesino. The nearby Forcola Regana is very long and steep on both sides, and is not recommended.

R27 PASSO PORTE DEL PASUBIO   1934M
M +++

Kompass 1:50K map 101

From the Passo Pian delle Fugazze (1162m), 16km SE of Rovereto (which is 20km S of Trento), to Arsiero, 14km to the ENE. A fine route, very quiet, dramatic in the upper reaches and not difficult (the M merely means that it is toilsome pushing over the gravel; with a mountain bike this route could be ridden).

The start is 200m E of the summit of the road pass of the Pian delle Fugazze. The road on this side of the Porte del Pasubio is known as the **STRADA DEGLI EROI** (Road of the Heroes), because the road was built by the Italian army in 1917, in an area where the Austrians were trying (in vain, as it turned out) to break through. The surface, on this side and the other, is loose gravel, with occasional fairly smooth stretches; on the other side there is tarmac at the hairpin bends. The gradient is moderate to start with, but a bit steeper higher up. On this side there are trees as far as the first tunnel, the Galleria D. Havet, 1797m.

At the Galleria D. Havet there is a metal barrier, which may force you to unload your bike and which probably explains the absence of motorbikes. The tunnel is about 60m long. Once you are through it, the scenery changes. The road goes through several short tunnels (lights not needed) cut in the cliff face; later it is overhung, for its full width, by the rock. To the R there is an almost sheer drop of hundreds of metres. About 1½km after the tunnel you come to a large refuge, the Rifugio Papa (named after one Generale A. Papa). This is 10.4km from the start of the road at the Pian delle Fugazze. You may be able to get water here (there is no running water elsewhere till you get to the Passo Xomo).

At the pass itself, which is just after the *rifugio*, there is a war memorial, and you can tour various relics of the 1917 fighting. On the descent, the road (indicated at the pass by a sign painted on the rock, '377 Val Sorapache') starts along grassy slopes interspersed with rocky outcrops, but then it turns a corner and goes across another rock face, with a tunnel and a gap blasted through the rock. This is followed by a long series of hairpins. There are trees from about 1600m, and tarmac recommences, about 10km after the pass, at the Bocchetta di Campiglia (1216m), shortly after which you come to the Passo Xomo, 1058m. Here there is a water pipe, and five roads meet: one descending from

the Porte del Pasubio, three descending to the SW, S and SE respectively, and one descending to the N, to Posina, Fusine and Arsiero.

Times: if you are pushing, allow 4 hours up, 3 down (to the Bocchetta di Campiglia).

(F. Wright, 26.6.00)

R30 PASSO TOGNOLA   1988M
M +++

Kompass map 76, fold C3 (Mair (Südtirol) 11E)

From Caoria, on the E side of the Passo Cinque Croci **R21**, 27km NW of Feltre, to San Martino di Castrozza, on the S side of the Passo Rolle: 5km r/s, 13km rough road. There is a rough road up the Val Sorda, then a fairly easily graded mule path (no. 352) over the col, meeting another rough road on its way down from Alpe Crei (Alpe Tognola on the TCI map) to San Martino.

R33 PASSO DELLA COSTAZZA (BAITA SEGANTINI) 2174M
E +++

Kompass map 76, fold C2 (Mair (Südtirol) 11E)

From near the top of the Passo Rolle (road pass, 24km E of Cavalese, 1989m) to the road over the Passo di Valles (another road pass, 5km to the N, not the r/s Passo di Valles **N60**); 11km rough road. The road to the *baita* (shepherd's cottage – Segantini was a 19th-century painter of, among other things, Alpine landscapes) starts from just E of the top of the Passo Rolle. As far as the top (the *baita*) it was, in 1985, unsurfaced but rideable; the first 3km on the other side was not rideable, but then the road levelled off (in a small valley called the Valle Venegia) and could be ridden, slowly. In good weather there are wonderful views, from quite close up, of the extraordinary Cimon di Pala and nearby mountains.

(F. Wright, 12.8.85)

R36 PASSO DI LUSIA   2056M
E +++

F&B S5, fold B4 bottom; Kompass map 76, fold B1 (Mair (Südtirol) 11D bottom)

From Moena in the Val di Fassa, 28km ESE of Bolzano (Bozen) or 14km SW of Canazei, to Paneveggio, 10km to the SE, on the W side of the Passo Rolle: 18km rough road. This is a rough road throughout. You can start in Moena, or 1½km up the San Pellegrino road (path no. 621), or higher up that road from Fango (path no. 625). From Paneveggio, you start about ¾km W of the junction of the roads which go over the Rolle and Valles passes. It is known to be a fine route.

R39 PASSO DI FORCA ROSSA   2490M
D ++

F&B map S5, fold D4 (Mair (Südtirol) 12D)

From the Passo di San Pellegrino (road pass, 11km S of

Canazei) to Rocca Pietore, 15km to the ENE, on the E side of the Passo Fedaia: 8km r/s, 8km rough road. There is a rough road to the Rifugio Fuchiade (1972m), then path no. 670 or 694 to the col. There is a mule path (path no. 689) down the NE side, very steep down scree for 300m; this later becomes a rough road down to and through the Sottoguda gorge (very spectacular – there is just room for road and river between the vertical cliffs).

R42 PASSO DI SAN NICOLÒ — 2338M — M +++

F&B map S5, fold C3 (Mair (Südtirol) 11D)

From Penia, 3km SE of Canazei on the road over the Passo di Fedaia, to Ciampiè, 5km to the SSW, at the head of the Val di San Nicolò; 5km r/s, 6km rough road. This is shown as a cart road starting near the cable-car station at Penia, and climbing very steeply at first to the Rifugio Contrin (2016m). From there, take path 608 to the rifugio on the col. (The direct path omitting the Rifugio Contrin is very steep, too.) A mule path goes down the W side of the pass (W at first, then S), becoming a cart road at 2100m down to Ciampiè.

R45 ALPE DI SIUSI (SEISER ALPE) AND MAHLKNECHT JOCH — 1844M / 2188M — E +++

F&B map S5, fold A3 top (Mair (Südtirol) 10C, etc.)

Three ways are detailed here: (i) from Siusi (Seis), 17km ENE of Bolzano (Bozen), to Santa Cristina Valgardena, 12km to the ENE, 6km rough road; (ii) from Campitello, 3km W of Canazei, to Siusi, mostly rough road, some tarmac near Siusi; (iii) from Campitello to Santa Cristina Valgardena, mostly rough road. According to Denzel, this area is the most extensive Hochalm (high pasture) in all the Alps.

(i) There is a metalled road from Siusi to the Alpe di Siusi (Rifugio Bellavista on the TCI map), where there are several hotels. Cars are not allowed beyond this point, though the road is metalled as far as Saltaria or Saltria (Saltner), and buses go that far. Thence it is a rough road (all rideable downhill) to Santa Cristina Valgardena.

(ii) The climb from Campitello (1448m), which takes 3 hours if you walk all the way, falls into three parts. For the whole way it is an unsurfaced road, rideable for unloaded mountain bikes but not for a loaded touring bike. (a) There is a steep, sometimes very steep, climb, with no zigzags, up the narrow wooded valley. About an hour from Campitello the road forks (no signpost). The R fork is the one to take (the L fork brings you in a short distance to the Rifugio Micheluzzi, 1860m). (b) Soon after this the road forks again; take the L fork (sign 'Baita Lino–Brach'). This descends gently to the stream (there are fewer trees now) and then goes along level for about 3km up the Valle di Duron. (c) There is a final climb, probably less steep than part (a), to the Mahlknecht Joch pass.

Soon after the pass you come to the Rifugio Sciliar,

2145m (large, modern). Continue on the unsurfaced road, descending to about 1980m, then take a road which goes to the L, climbing past the Mahlknecht Hütte, 2054m, also known as the Rifugio Molignon, to about 2100m. Then the road stays at roughly the same level, but with some ups and downs. About 1½km after the Mahlknecht Hütte the road becomes tarmac, and remains so all the way to Compatsch, 1870m (shops), from where a winding descent on a good tarmac road takes you to Siusi (Seis). If coming the other way, turn R at Compatsch (sign 'Molignon').

(iii) The climb from Campitello (where there are many places to stay) has already been described. The descent from the Mahlknecht Joch, through Saltaria (good refreshments available), is nearly all rideable; it is also fairly level apart from a short steep bit just after the pass and the last 2½km down to Santa Cristina Valgardena.

(For (i), Mrs M. A. Stephens, August 1984; for (ii), F. Wright, 12.8.95; for (iii) E. and S. Wagstaff, 17.6.94)

R48 CIMA DI PLOSE (PLOSE BÜHEL) — 2486M — E ++++

F&B (who call it Monte Telegrafo) map S4, fold G4 (Mair (Südtirol) 11B)

This is a summit on a cul-de-sac, which can be reached either from Bressanone, 6km to the WNW, or from the road over the Würzjoch, 7km to the ESE. Our report is from someone who approached from the Würzjoch. At Palmschoss, just before Afers, continue climbing, instead of descending to Afers. The tarmac road goes to Kreuztal, 2000m (the same as the Hotel Kreuztal, 2016m), then forks. Ignore the sign 'Plose' to the L (this is for walkers), and take the R fork. The tarmac soon ends, and an unsurfaced road leads to the summit. It is just rideable (at any rate if you are lightly loaded), but the ride is bumpy, unpleasant and strenuous. From Kreuztal to the summit takes just over an hour. In good weather the summit should be a good viewpoint.

According to the map, a path (no. 4) starts from the most easterly hairpin of the rough road and descends gradually SE-wards to the Passo d'Eores. (We have no report of this path.)

(F. Wright, 8.8.95)

R51 PASSO DI LUSON (LÜSENER JOCH) — 2008M — E ++

F&B map S3, fold A3, and S4, fold H4 (Mair (Südtirol), 11B & 12B)

From Luson (Lüsen), 9km ENE of Bressanone (Brixen), to Antermoia (Untermoi), 9km to the SE, on the E side of the Würzjoch; 4km r/s, 3km rough road. There is a rough road from Luson to about 1600m, then a reasonably easy graded path (no. 13) over the top, to meet the Passo delle Erbe (Würzjoch) road at about 1650m. Starting at Luson, you could make an easy circuit by crossing first the Passo di Luson, then the Würzjoch, and returning from the W side of the latter, by the rough road down the upper Val di Luson (Lüsener Tal).

PASSO DI POMA (KREUZKOFELJOCH) 2340M

E SIDE D. W SIDE E +++

F&B map S5, fold C1 (Mair (Südtirol) 11C)

From Longiarù (Campill), 18km SSW of Brunico (Bruneck) or 19km NNE of Canazei, to Pizzago (Pitzach) in the Val di Funes (Villnösstal). From Longiarù (food shop, post office) follow the road up-valley past the church. The road soon crosses to the R (SE) bank of the stream. At a junction turn R (sign 'Speckstube Tlisörahof' – this is a Ladin name – there are no signs for Misci). The tarmac road crosses to the L bank of the stream at the bottom end of Misci, and ends at its top end. Here there is a sign 'Roda, Rundwanderung, Itinerario–2' (Ladin, German and Italian). The route is now a broad gravel track. Just after the last haybarns ignore a track to the L, which crosses the stream. Soon after this the track crosses to the R bank, and a few hundred metres later a path goes off uphill to the L, at a sign 'Naturpark Puez–Geisler', with a green disc. There is nothing to indicate that this is the path you want, but a little higher up there is a sign 'Schlüterhütte, Rifugio di Genova' (this is the hut just on the other side of the pass). The path is steep, among conifers, but towards the top it is over grass, and the slope is easier. There is an intermediate pass, after crossing which you bear R towards the true pass. From the latter there are good views of the Val Badia (Gadertal) on one side and the Villnösstal (Val di Funes) on the other. From the Schlüterhütte a broad and not too steep, but rough, track leads down to another hut at the Gampenalm (2062m). Here there is a path to the R, which may lead to the Villnösstal; our correspondent stayed on the track, which does lead there, but which he left shortly to return to Longiarù over the Kreuzjoch **R57**.

Allow 3 hours from Misci to the pass; ½ hour from the pass to the Gampenalm.

(F. Wright 10.8.95)

R57 **KREUZJOCH** (FORCIA DI MEDALGHES) 2293M

W SIDE D. E SIDE E +++

F&B map S5, fold C1 (Mair (Südtirol) 11C)

From Pizzago (Pitzach) in the Val di Funes (Villnösstal), 9km SSE of Bressanone (Brixen), to Longiarù (Campill), 14km to the E. We have no report of the first part of this route, but it should be straightforward, mostly a tarmac road up the valley to the Rifugio Zannes (Zanser Alm Hütte). The view of the Geisler Gruppe, a line of rocky peaks at the head of the valley, was thought good enough, in the late 1980s, to be reproduced on muesli packets in England; it has also been seen on a jigsaw and most recently (August 1999) in an advertisement for Renault cars. From the *rifugio* a fairly good track leads up to the Gampenalm and, above that, the Schlüterhütte (Rifugio di Genova). At 1878m on this track, turn R off it to follow another track, which is easy going but only lasts for ½km before giving way to a steep path with many steps in it, over which the bike has to be lifted. The scene is dominated by the rocky masses of the Geisler Gruppe. From the pass there are even better views than from

the Kreuzkofeljoch.

The path down to the E is quite different – gently sloping and grassy, later becoming a track, which at 2000m joins a gravel jeep track at some farm buildings. The path later separates from the jeep track again, but it may be easier to stay on the jeep track.

Times: from the point at 1878m to the pass, 1½ hours; from the pass to Longiarù, 2½ hours.

(F. Wright, for the bit above 1878m only, 10.8.95)

R60 **JUVEL (OR JUEL) PASS** 1725M

E ++

F&B map S5, fold D1 (Mair (Südtirol) 12C)

From Longiarù, 18km SSW of Brunico (Bruneck) or 19km NNE of Canazei, to Pedratsches in the Val Badia (Gadertal), 4km to the SE. This is an unsurfaced but fairly smooth and not very steep road which saves a journey down to St Martin. It can be combined with the Kreuzjoch **R57** by turning R off the track descending from the latter, before you reach Longiarù. There is a good view of the Val Badia from the top. When descending, you soon reach tarmac at the hamlet of Pescol. Here ignore the sign 'Pedraces': this is for walkers. The track is possible, but there is a good tarmac road, which you may as well use.

Times: Longiarù to the pass, 1½ hours; from the pass to Pescol, ½ hour.

(F. Wright, 10.8.95)

R63 **PASSO DI LIMO** (LIMOJOCH) 2172M

E +++

F&B map S5, fold F1 bottom (Mair (Südtirol) 13C)

This pass can form part of a loop, starting on the main road (the SS51), 7km NNW of Cortina, taking in the Rifugio Pederù, the Fodara Vedla Hütte and optionally the Senneshütte, and finishing on the SS51 1½km N of the start: this involves 16km rough road from the SS51 to the Rifugio Pederù, and 8km rough road from there back to the SS51. Alternatively you can approach the pass from San Vigilio (Sankt Vigil), 11km S of Brunico (Bruneck), but then you must choose between the Limojoch route and that past the Fodara Vedla Hütte.

A tarmac road leaves the SS51 and after perhaps 2km ends at a traffic barrier. There is then a rough road of loose stones, which a jeep might just be able to climb. After about 1½km you come to a spectacular bridge, the Ponte Alto, over a gorge which is perhaps 60m deep and so narrow that 6m below the bridge you could lean across and touch the other side. The bottom cannot be seen from the bridge because of the rock walls. Just beyond the bridge a track leads off to the R, which should be ignored; two chamois were seen here in 1984 (this area was at that time a game reserve). At some point near here, according to the map, the slope reaches 30%. You come to a waterfall, then to some fairly level ground where there are one or two small lakes and a memorial carved in a boulder to some German soldiers who fell 'for the Kaiser and the Fatherland' in the First World War. Above the lakes, in 1984, the river, or stream, ran over the road, and had to be forded. Then the road goes over a green alp and re-enters the pines. Above the treeline you come to a hut, the Grosse Faneshütte, which may be privately owned (it was deserted, but apparently in good repair, in 1984). Soon after this there is a small lake, the Lago di Limo, which marks the top of the pass.

After the pass the track descends steeply (28% according to the map) to the Faneshütte/Rifugio Fanes, where food and accommodation are available. Below this there is some fairly level going, then 300m (vertically) of steep descent (24% according to the map) on a road of 'deep shingle' (1956) to the Rifugio Pederù, or Pederuhütte (1545m).

From the Pederuhütte you climb what is, according to Denzel, the steepest road in the Alps (the slope is estimated to be 37%). The surface (concrete, with some loose stones) is much better than on the road over the Limojoch; the road is used by certain specially licensed taxis. At the top you come, after a short sandy track, to the Fodara Vedla Hütte (1980m according to the sign). The main track, a continuation of the concrete road, goes L before this hut and leads to the Senneshütte at the head of the Val Salata, which it then descends to the SS51. Our correspondent turned R (E) at the Fodara Vedla Hütte and took a much rougher track over a nameless pass at 2018m; this was steep and completely unrideable, but at about 1750m it reached the main valley track, which was rideable. Tarmac recommences at the Malga Ra Stua and continues down to the SS51.

Times: from the SS51 to the Pederuhütte, 5–6 hours; from the Pederuhütte to the Malga Ra Stua, 3 hours.

(For the bit from the SS51 to the Limojoch, R. Perrodin, c. 1970; for Limojoch–Pederuhütte, E. D. Clements, 1956; for Pederuhütte–Malga Ra Stua, J. A. Woodings, 1985; for the whole loop, F. Wright, 4.7.84)

R66 PASSO TADEGA
2157M

W SIDE D. E SIDE E ++

F&B map S5, fold F2 (Mair (Südtirol) 12C, 13C)

From a point on the road on the NW side of the Passo di Valparola (which is 10km ESE of Corvara) to a point on the track over the Limojoch **R63**, just E of the latter: 5km r/s, 3km rough road. It is not advisable to do the route in the opposite direction; see below. Leave the road over the Passo di Valparola at about 1650m by the rough road marked on the TCI map 1km SE of Armentarola (where there is an albergo – there are several hereabouts). The nearby Albergo Valparola was very good in 1956. About 1½km from the road, at a *rifugio* (Capanna Alpina), a mule path (no. 11) climbs through the woods and later becomes very steep up a scree slope in a cirque of cliffs. A double carry is needed, and doing this bit in the other direction is not recommended. Once on Col Loggia (not a true col), the path becomes very good, climbing gradually past a remote alpine pasture to the Passo Tadega. From this pass, it is (or was in 1956) possible to ride most of the way to the jeep track over the Limojoch.

(E. D. Clements, August 1956)

R69 PASSO POSPORCORA
1711M

M +++

F&B map S5, fold G2 (Mair (Südtirol) 13C)

From the Ponte Alto on the track over the Limojoch **R63**, to Cortina; 4km r/s, 5km rough road. The map shows a mule path on the W side, and a steep cart road on the E side (path no. 408), passing between Col Rosà, 2166m (which is a hill, not a pass—in this part of Italy 'colle' or 'col' sometimes seems to mean a subsidiary summit on a ridge), and the Tofana group. In this general area, the main road (the SS51) from Cortina to Carbonin is paralleled by a path along an old railway (path no. 208, then 201).

R70 PASSO VALPAROLA, OLD ROAD
2168M

E ++

F&B map S5

From Armentarola, 20km south of Bruneck to the Passo Valparola along the old road constructed by Austrian troops in the First World War. Leave Armentarola and go R at the crossroads, signposted 'Malga Valparola'. After 1km the metalled road ends; continue straight, still signposted 'Malga Valparola', on 15% gravel ramps alternating with flatter sections. At the *malga*, the gravel road climbs the meadow to the left, 10-12% gradient all the way to the pass. At one point you rejoin the new road (which was re-routed to avoid avalanches in the winter); follow it for 300m and the take a track L again. It's worth stopping here and hiking 5 minutes to visit the Austro-Hungarian military chapel.

(I. Tavella)

R71 PRALONGIÀ TRAVERSE
E +++

F&B map S5

From Armentarola to the Passo Campolongo, one of the most scenic roads in the Dolomites, so worth some suffering. Start as with **R70**, but when the tarmac ends turn R and follow the sign to 'Stores'. 4km in a forest of tall pines follows, at a steady gradient, with steep sections towards the end. The track emerges into open meadows and heads straight for a crucifix at the highest point. Our correspondent suggests the steep track to the L here, which takes you to a singletrack along the ridge, also eventually to the crucifix – the highest point at 2156m, with 360° views across the Dolomites. Continue to the Pralongià hut (open from mid June to mid September) then descend steeply on gravel to the Rifugio Marmotta. Facing the rifugio, the trail to the left (no. 3) descends all the way to the Passo Campolongo.

(I. Tavella)

R72 FORCOLA COL DE BOS
2331M

N SIDE D. S SIDE M +++

F&B map S5, fold F2 (Mair (Südtirol) 13C)

From a point on the road on the E side of the Passo di Falzarego, to the Ponte Alto on the track over the

Limojoch **R63**; 10km r/s, 8km rough road. A rough road leaves the Falzarego road 5km E of the pass and climbs the N side of the valley to Rozes (c. 2180m). There follows a steep path to the col and down to the Malga Travenanzes (1950m), then a mule path down the Val Travenanzes to the Ponte Alto, whence a rough road (tarmac after about 1½km) leads to near the big bend in the main road (the SS51); it joins the road well S of the point shown on the TCI map. (The Forcola Travenanzes, 2507m, the direct path from the Passo di Falzarego, may be possible, but much harder than the Forcola Col de Bos.)

R75 PRATO PIAZZA (PLÄTZWIESEN) 1993M
E ++

F&B map S3, fold E4, or map S10, fold B2 (Mair (Südtirol) 14C top)

From Carbonin (Schluderbach), 11km NE of Cortina or 12km S of Dobbiaco (Toblach), to Vallone (Pflung), 6km WSW of Dobbiaco; 14km rough road. The rough road from the SS51, just W of Carbonin, is mostly very rough gravel (there was about 1½km of tarmac in 1992); no cars or motorbikes were seen in 1992, only a few mountain bikes. From the long flat col there are fine views of the jagged mountains to the S and E. Here there is at least one restaurant, perhaps two. The metalled road starts at the N end of the flat stretch at the top, as shown on the TCI map. Down to a car park at about 1600m, there is supposed to be a nature park, with no cars allowed, but in fact some cars were seen in 1992.

(F. Wright, 27.7.92, and others)

R78 SOM FORCA 2130M
N SIDE E. S SIDE M +++

F&B map S10, fold B3 (Mair (Südtirol) 14C)

From the Passo Tre Croci, 6km ENE of Cortina, via the Val Grande to a point on the main road (the SS51) between Cortina and Carbonin, 3km E of the big hairpin which lies 7km NNW of Cortina (and which is the end of the loop described at **R63**): 1½km r/s, 8km rough road. Leave a rough road after 100m, and follow a mule path (no. 203); there is a steep climb of about 300m to the col. From the col, a rough road heads NW down the Val Grande to the SS51.

R81 MONTE PIANO 2324M
E ++++

Mair (Südtirol) 14C; F&B map S10, fold C2; Kompass map 55

The peak (which is called Monte Piana on the TCI map, perhaps by mistake) lies 14km S of Dobbiaco (Toblach), just E of the road which runs SE from Carbonin; there are 1½km r/s, 5km rough road. There is a rough road from Misurina, near the Col Sant'Angelo, to the Rifugio Bosi (2205m), then a mule path to the top. The flat top is covered with preserved trenches, lookout posts and foxholes from the First World War.

R84 FORCOLA DI LAVAREDO 2454M
N SIDE M. S SIDE E ++++

F&B map S3, fold G4, or map S10, fold D2 (Mair (Südtirol) 14C)

From the Lago di Landro, on the SS51 12km S of Dobbiaco (and just N of Carbonin/Schluderbach), to Misurina, near the Col Sant'Angelo, 6km SE of Carbonin: 6km r/s (on a path of loose gravel, which requires hardly any carrying) and 6km rough road. A very fine circular tour around the Tre Cime di Lavaredo (Drei Zinnen), in typical Dolomite scenery. It can be combined with the Passo Fiscalino **R87** to make a day trip from the Lago di Landro to near Sesto (this omits the tarmac road down to Misurina); or you could spend a night at the Auronzo or Lavaredo hut (a dormitory bed at the former cost 27,000 lire in June 2000), and descend into the Val Marzon towards Auronzo, as described below.

One kilometre N of the Lago di Landro on the SS51, a rough road, which later becomes a very stony (1995) mule path, turns off to the E and follows the stream up the Valle di Rimbon (Rienztal), which is hemmed in by tall rock faces. After a mostly not too steep climb of nearly 6km, the path comes to a pleasant grassy alp among the pines, at 1952m, where a bivouac is possible. Soon after this the valley ends in a rock wall. Two paths continue: take the one which goes R and makes two traverses up the scree; this is longer but much easier. Fill your water bottles here; water is hard to come by higher up. After the traverses you emerge onto an extensive rolling grassy alp, which reaches to the foot of the Drei Zinnen. Keep up L towards the Locatelli (Drei Zinnen) hut, and along a path about 100m below it. After contouring the western slopes of Monte Paterno for over 1km, on a rough path across the grassy rock-strewn slopes, you have a steep pull up to the Forcola di Lavaredo. Snow was met here in June 1994. A rough road starts from the col, and goes past the Lavaredo hut and on to the Rifugio Auronzo, from where a metalled road descends to Misurina on the Col Sant'Angelo (SS48 bis).

As mentioned above, instead of descending to Misurina you can descend into the Val Marzon, to the road leading to Auronzo (see F&B map S10, folds C2 and D2). This involves two short difficult stretches; otherwise the route is easy, and a good example of how a well-designed and well-constructed path can overcome difficulties. The path (no. 104) starts from a point on the level track between the Rifugio Auronzo and the Rifugio Lavaredo, about half way along the track. As becomes clear lower down from the stone revetments, the path was carefully constructed some time in the past. It maintains a steady and gradual slope by zigzagging and traversing across the steep hillside. The surface is fairly smooth, and very little carrying is needed, though the bumps make you go fairly slowly. With a mountain bike most of the path could be ridden. In places the path crosses, or has been crossed by, landslides; here care may be needed. About 2 hours from the start (if you are pushing), you come to the first difficulty – the path has been undermined for about 15m by a stream, and you may have to carry your bike and luggage across separately. Not long afterwards there is a similar, but more serious, difficulty; a landslide has carried the path away, and you have to carry everything up a steep and narrow path for about 30m (vertically), then down again. Soon after this, at 1506m, you meet a path coming down from the R, and the combined path deteriorates, becoming mixed up with the bed of a stream, stony, and sometimes hard to see. Finally, at a bridge over a stream (1360m), you come to the start of a road, which is unsurfaced for about 300m, then tarmac (lower down, overrun at one point by an avalanche in 2000).

Allow 5 hours to the col, 1 hour down (if descending to Misurina), or 4 hours (if pushing) down to the beginning of tarmac (if descending into the Val Marzon).

(Anon., 1967; A. E. Matthews, 1975, reported in RSJ March/April 1976, p. 39; E. & S. Wagstaff, 21.6.94; F. Wright 6.8.95; for the descent into the Val Marzon, F. Wright, 1.7.00)

R87 PASSO FISCALINO (OBERBACHERNJOCH) 2528M
S ++++

F&B map S3, fold G4, or map S10, fold D2 (Mair (Südtirol) 14C, 15C)

This route can, like **R84**, be started from Misurina near the Col Sant'Angelo; or it can be combined with **R84** to make a day trip from the Lago di Landro to near Sesto (a two-day trip if you stay the night at the Lavaredo or Auronzo hut).

The whole of this route is on what was the Austro-Italian front in the First World War, and there are many relics. At the Büllelejoch there is a cliff-face gun pit, also trenches, tunnels and dugouts in the cliffs. Strong nerves are needed in places. The best examples are on the rock ridges due S of the Büllelejoch.

If you are coming from Misurina, pass the Lavaredo hut and about 600m afterwards turn R off the road on a mule path, soon passing the little Lago di Lavaredo. If you are coming from the Lago di Landro, turn L on the mule path soon after the Forcola di Lavaredo. Keep to the main path (loose gravel, marked 104 or Rifugio Pian di Cengia, which is the same as the Büllelejoch Hütte), contouring around the Croda del Passaporto (2704m). The country soon opens out; the path drops gently, then climbs over a large step to a hanging valley with two small lakes (the Laghi di Cengia, 2324m) and a 1918 war memorial. Near here is the lowest point, 2229m, between the Forcola di Lavaredo and the Büllelejoch. The superb Croda dei Toni (Zwölferkofel), 3094m, is in front. From the Laghi (one of which had dried up in 1995) the path zigzags up a rock-strewn slope, finally heading to the L and reaching the crest of a ridge at the Büllelejoch (Forcola Pian di Cengia). Here, without crossing the ridge, you turn R along a level path which keeps below the top of the ridge on your L. At one point the path is supported on planks. Rounding a corner, you have a short descent to the small Büllelejoch Hütte. The path then continues, still level and still with the ridge (now only slightly higher than the path) on the L, for about 400m to the Passo Fiscalino; for this stretch the path is cut in the cliff face. At the Passo Fiscalino you finally cross the ridge, and begin descending to the R down a path which is

mostly steep, rocky and irregular. There is a good view of the impressive rock face of the Elfer Kofel (Cima di Undici). More carrying than pushing is required. At 2224m you pass the (large) Rifugio Comici. The difficult descent continues to about 1700m; then it is easier, and at 1548m you reach the Talschlusshütte, from where a smooth and easily rideable, though not tarmac, road leads down to the Dolomitenhof (hotel). Here tarmac recommences.

Allow 5 hours from the Forcola di Lavaredo to the Talschlusshütte, more if you spend time inspecting the relics of the war.

(A. J. Howarth 1963, F. Wright 6.8.95)

R90 FORCOLA COL DURO 2293M
N SIDE D. S SIDE M +

F&B map S10, fold A4 (Mair (Südtirol) 13D)

From Cortina into the hills to the S, then either SW to the road (SS251) over the Forcella Staulanza, or SE to Borca di Cadore on the main road (SS51) SE of Cortina: 8km r/s, 8km rough road. It is a rough road, mostly unrideable, to the Rifugio Croda da Lago (2046m), then a mule path slanting diagonally up a steep hillside to the Forcola da Lago (2277m), from where a path, steep in places, descends to the SS251 E of Toffol. Alternatively, from the Forcola da Lago, you can continue to the Forcola Col Duro (2293m); in this case, 1½km after the latter pass, you come to a fork; the path to the R, no. 467, soon becomes a mule path to the Rifugio Città di Fiume, whence a rough road leads to the SS251; and the path to the L, no. 458, also soon becomess a mule path to the head of the Val Orsolina, then a rough road to Borca di Cadore.

R92 FORCOLA FORADA 1977M
W SIDE E. E SIDE D ++

F&B map S10, fold A4, or S15 (Mair (Südtirol) 13D)

From a point on the road (SS251) over the Forcella Staulanza, just NE of the pass, to Borca di Cadore, 8km to the E; 3km r/s, 8km rough road. The pleasure is mostly on the W side; the E side is steep and stony, with no view to speak of.

Descending on the road from the Staulanza pass, go through a few bends, and at 1663m, where the road bends L, turn off to the R (yellow signs for the Malga Fiorentina and the Rifugio Città di Fiume). You have to get round a metal barrier, then push up a stony and sometimes steep dirt road. On the R are the towering cliffs of Monte Pelmo, and from time to time there are fine views of other Dolomite peaks near and far. At 1799m you pass a large farm, the Malga Fiorentina, and at 1918m you come to the Rifugio Città di Fiume. There is then a mostly easy path to the pass (muddy in places after rain), which is 20 minutes away.

On the other side, there is a stone bothy not far below the pass, where you could bivouac. The main path, however, does not go to the bothy but goes straight down. It is awkward, being steep and full of loose and fixed rocks.

Much carrying is needed, and care must be taken not to slip. Occasionally there are soft boggy patches. Progress is slow and tiring. About an hour from the pass the path improves, but only briefly. A track is reached 1½ hours from the pass, and carrying is no longer necessary, but the track, following the course of a stream, is very steep and full of loose rocks, so progress is still difficult. Finally, 2 hours from the pass, at a bridge over a stream, you reach a decent unsurfaced road, smooth and level at first, later stonier as it descends but still mostly rideable. This road goes through trees, and there are no views; it leads down to Borca.

Times: from Staulanza road to pass, 1¼ hours; from pass to unsurfaced road, 2 hours.

(Anon., undated; F. Wright, 29.6.00)

R95 RIFUGIO VENEZIA   1947M

W SIDE E. N SIDE M +

F&B map S10, fold B4, or S15 (Mair (Südtirol) 13D, 14D)

The route can be started either from a point on the road (SS251) over the Forcella Staulanza, just N of Pecol (1338m) and 2km S of the pass, or from Zoppè di Cadore, 18km SSE of Cortina; it ends at Borca di Cadore, 12km SE of Cortina; in the former case there is 8km r/s, 5km rough road, and in the latter case there is 3km r/s, 10km rough road. From the SS251 there is a mule path, steep at first but later contouring, to the Rifugio, which is situated on a col. From Zoppè di Cadore it is a rough road all the way to the Rifugio. From the Rifugio the descent is on a mule path, mostly steep, into the Val Orsolina. (If you are coming from Zoppè di Cadore, there is an alternative; 2km from Zoppè di Cadore, fork R over the Forcola Chiandolada, 1565m, on path no. 456, and descend to Vodo Cadore. Near the top about 1km is shown as a footpath; the distance from Zoppè di Cadore to Vodo is 8km.)

R98 PANORAMICA DELLE VETTE   1967M

E ++

F&B map 182, folds F4 and G4

From the Sella Valcalda (959m), 6km W of Paluzza (which is 14km N of Tolmezzo), to Comeglians (548m), 5km to the W. This is a high-level unsurfaced road which neither crosses a pass nor reaches a summit. It provides access to several *malghe* (hill farms for cattle, occupied in summer).

From the Sella Valcalda, on the main road from Paluzza to Comeglians, take a narrow, well-surfaced, steep, tarmac road which climbs through trees. Higher up the trees thin out and then give way to grassy slopes, and at about 1800m the tarmac ends at a hairpin bend. The road climbs for a short way, then goes over the shoulder of a hill and becomes almost level and smooth enough to ride slowly. It remains at between about 1800 and 1900m for some distance, passing several *malghe*. After 6½km of unsurfaced road tarmac recommences, just before the Malga Chiadinis (1934m). There is a short climb at about 15% which brings you to the highest point of the road (1967m), above the Malga

Chiadinis, 1½km after the beginning of tarmac. A long descent, on tarmac, with many hairpins, brings you first to Tualis, then to Comeglians.

(F. Wright 4.7.00, supplemented from map)

AFTERWORD: A Q&A WITH FRED WRIGHT

Fred Wright used the computers at Ashford public library to write the original version of this book, and he still goes to the library to do his emails. Initially, we had discussed his writing an introduction to the new edition. Eventually, after many emails and a short visit, we settled on a written Q&A, in which he explained his love of the mountains and his motivations for making the original rough-stuff guide.

WHAT GOT ME INTERESTED IN THE ALPS?

I mostly lived in India (before partition in 1947) for the first seven years of my life (1935-1942), and since my father, who was in the Indian army, got TB, for which there was then no cure, he was sent to Kashmir because it was thought the climate might alleviate his TB. So my mother and I went there with him, and I have happy memories of the mountains. We lived, in summer, in tents on the banks of the Sind River, near the Zoji La, a pass leading to Ladakh, and also spent some time at a place called Gulmarg, a settlement with a golf course and, in winter, snow. My father died in early 1942, and my mother and I went back to Britain, where I was sent to a school at Crieff in Scotland, at the foot of the Grampian mountains. We used to go picnicking in the mountains in summer. In the winters I twice had a fortnight's holiday in the French Alps, at St-Véran near the Italian frontier. I suppose this was what started my liking for mountains.

WHAT SORT OF BIKE?

I was taught to ride a bike on a lawn of my father's house at Peshawar, at the foot of the Khyber Pass, at the age of 5 or 6. My teacher was one of our Indian (Pakistani if you like) servants called Sadiq (which in Urdu, or as we called it Hindustani, I think means 'righteous'). It must have been a child's bike. Later, at Crieff in Scotland, my school headmaster, Mr Smythe (pronounced Smith), a kind old man in whose hands you could see bits of shrapnel from the First World War, gave me a Norman bike (made at Ashford in Kent, where I have ended up living). Mr Smythe was an angler and a cricket player, and he taught us Latin and cricket, and according to his obituary he was known to his Army colleagues as 'the Smith who fishes in shell-holes'. Then at the age of 17 I was given a 4-speed Raleigh, on which I did my first cycling tour in the Alps, with a school friend. That was in April 1953. We didn't know anything about the Alps in April, and had some difficulty, but we got over the San Bernardino in a blizzard. I still can't say I am very knowledgeable about bikes, but I did get a light Raleigh 15-speed, on which I did a good many Alpine passes, unpaved and smooth.

DID I ALWAYS CYCLE ALONE?

Yes, except for a tour in the Alps in, I think, 1981, and the trip in 1953, mentioned above. Did I ever feel intimidated or out of my depth? I don't remember feeling that, but I tried to avoid danger (once, on the Col Collon, q.v. in our book, I nearly failed).

WHAT LED ME TO PUBLISH A BOOK?

I had worked as a proofreader at a publishing house, and I suppose I thought there might be a market for a book on rough-stuff cycling. The writing wasn't too difficult, the publishing took quite a long time to read about, in a book I found in the library.

APPENDIX I: SOME TIPS

GENERAL

The average rough-stuff route in the Alps is shorter and steeper than some of the Scottish routes, e.g. Lairig Ghru and Glen Affric, but the surface is usually better. Perhaps because of the thin and stony soil, mud is very rarely encountered. Paths are nearly always clear to see and free from obstacles such as gates (stiles are unknown). They also tend to be quite well waymarked. Some of the routes in the guide are simply minor roads which have not been surfaced but which may be surfaced some time; some are jeep tracks, smoothed out of the hillside in connection with winter skiing or to give access to farms or other buildings; some, especially in Italy, are military roads, often built early in the 20th century or late in the 19th; some were constructed hundreds of years ago as mule tracks and roughly paved; some, especially in the higher parts, are mere footpaths, which can be steep, narrow, rutted, stony and twisting, and can impose on the cyclist a slow and strenuous progress, which can often be made easier by removing the pedals. Some of the paths are well used by walkers, and one of the pleasures of this pursuit is stopping to pass the time of day with walkers, who are sometimes surprised to see someone with a bike on a high footpath.

FEASIBILITY OF ROUTES

Snow can be encountered on many routes. It is difficult to say, with confidence, when and where it can be avoided – it depends on how much has fallen in the previous winter and how hot the present summer has been, also on the lie of the land – but, as a rough guide, routes over 2000m should be clear by late June, those over 2400m by mid-July and those over 2700m by August. A certain amount of snow is no problem, and it can be easier to walk over firm, i.e. not fresh-fallen, snow than over rocks. Ask about the weather forecast (see below), choose a fine day if possible and do not try a high route after a fresh snowfall. Remember that after heavy rain rivers may become impassable. Any route over 2000m may prove dangerous if attempted in bad weather. Beginners are advised to start with one or two easy or moderate routes.

STIFFNESS

You may find, after your first long descent on foot, that the muscles on the front of your thighs are painfully stiff. The stiffness will wear off after a few days, but it is possible to avoid the pain by getting it over before you start, as follows. Find a hill, the steeper the better, near where you live, and about ten days or a fortnight before the start of your holiday go up and down it enough times to make a total descent of, say, 750m. After three or four days, when the stiffness has worn off, repeat the exercise, and you should find you are less stiff afterwards. Repeat the exercise at intervals until your holiday.

WEATHER FORECASTS

Can usually be obtained at tourist information offices; in Switzerland, you can also dial 162 on a telephone.

GLACIERS

Some are safe, in some places. As a rule, if you are on your own it is advisable not to go on a glacier except where you can see it is frequented by walkers and/or skiers. The reason is hidden crevasses; what looks like a smooth field of snow may, in places, be only some centimetres thick, so that you go through into a crevasse. The following routes in this guide involve glaciers: the Col Collon E49; the Theodul Pass E54; the Col de Riedmatten and the Pas de Chèvres (F22 and F26) if approached from the W; the Lötschenpass F93; the Pitztalerjöchl M80; the Niederjoch M85: and the Livriohütte N06.

DISTRESS SIGNALS

Use a whistle, torch or flashes of sun on a mirror. Alternatively, shout or wave bright clothing: six regular flashes/notes in a minute, repeated at intervals of a minute. The reply is three signals a minute. To attract a helicopter, stand still, both arms raised above your head; to show you don't need help, stand with one arm up and one down, both at 45° to the horizon.

APPENDIX II: EQUIPMENT

Touring bike or mountain bike? Both are possible. There are rough roads and jeep tracks which ought to be rideable with a mountain bike but not with a touring bike, but on many paths riding is out of the question, and a touring bike, with its smaller tyres, may be lighter and easier to lift and carry than a mountain bike. Most of the reports in this guide are from people using touring bikes, but this may change as more and more people use mountain bikes. But note that in 1991 a cyclist reported that mountain bikes were banned in the Parc National de la Vanoise (northern French Alps); park rangers, he said, had stopped him, but on returning to Val d'Isère and complaining to the tourist office he had received (by telephone from the park management) permission to proceed, on the understanding that (a) he was not using a mountain bike, and (b) he had removed his pedals. The same ban applies in the Parc National du Mercantour: see the description of route **A69**. (An arrêté – decree – published by the Director of the Vanoise National Park on 22 June 1989 refers only to mountain bikes – VTT – and in particular the damage they cause to paths and vegetation, and the effect on wildlife.) On the face of it, a Moulton bike, with its small wheels and low weight, would offer some advantages on a difficult route; but we have no reports.

Except on an easy and fairly level route, or on a day trip without much luggage, you will probably need a rucksack. On any steep path it may be difficult or even impossible to proceed without putting most of your heavy belongings in a rucksack, because a bike heavily loaded with panniers is difficult to lift, carry and manoeuvre.

Camping equipment has its pros and cons. It relieves you of the need to find established accommodation, but it adds to the weight. Some saving in weight, at the expense of comfort, can be made by using a bivvy bag instead of a tent.

The most important quality of footwear is that it should be comfortable. Trainers have often been used with success; some may prefer boots or strong shoes. If you think you may have to travel over snow, especially steep snow, you may find a pair of short crampons (about six points, strapped on over the shoes or trainers) useful; these are light, cost little and take up little room.

Some of the routes in the guide, e.g. the Pas de Chèvres **F26** and the Col Collon **E49**, involve climbing ladders. Also, on the Pitztaler Jöchl **M80** you may find it better, at one point, to have both hands free. On the Trüttlisberg **G32**, there may be a handrail. For the first two it is necessary (and on the last two advisable) to take straps (of webbing or similar) in order to carry the bike on your back. You will need to fasten the front wheel so that it does not swing about. It is advisable to practise using the straps before going on your holiday.

GPS receivers and mobile phones may find a use in this activity, but we await reports. For whistles, etc., see Distress signals in Appendix I.

APPENDIX III: MAPS

PAPER MAPS IN 2018

Since the original edition of this guide, many map series have been modified and updated, and some discontinued. For the new Isola Press edition, current map references, where possible, are included on individual route entries in bold.

However, since Fred often talks about particular maps, and because readers might already have older maps, this edition retains all the original map references, even when doubtfully available. It is worth checking eBay and internet retailers for old maps, but those that are no longer being printed are listed in brackets and not bolded.

Below is a summary of what is believed to be on current sale.

D&R	Still available, but coverage seems sparse and scales vary, so these references are of doubtful help.
F&B	1:50K: some still current, some not, and seem to be now prefaced 'WK' – *Wanderkarten*. Freytag & Berndt have a very useful website, but nonetheless use references with caution.
IGN	1:100K: still available, but renumbered. 1:50K & 1:25K: appear still current.
IGC	1:50K: still current.
LK	1:100K & 1:50K: all available, and now called 'Swisstopo'. However, the usage of the

'tourist' designation seems to have changed. The current maps titled 'T' have walking routes highlighted, but do not cover quite the same areas. Follow the numbers in the map titles given here, ignoring Fred's 'tourist' designation, and the references within seem good

Kompass   Still current.

Mair   Mair still make maps, but under many brand names, and these references seem of doubtful help.

Michelin   1:200K, 1:150K: both available, but renumbered.

ÖK   still current.

PAPER MAPS: ADVICE FROM THE 2002 EDITION

Road maps include two series of Michelin 1:200K maps, the 200 series (£3.85 1999) covering more than twice the area of the original series (£2.35 1999). The Italian Touring Club Italiano 1:200K maps Piemonte, Valle d'Aosta; Lombardia; Trentino, Alto Adige are less detailed than the corresponding Michelin maps; in particular they show no footpaths. For Switzerland, Kümmerly & Frey publish a 1:250K map, and for Austria the AA publish several 1:200K maps; there are also Michelin maps.

For r/s routes, local maps are often on display, and sometimes handed out free, at tourist information offices; they are also often on display outside newsagents' shops. For some useful websites, in particular www.swissgeo. ch, see Introduction, p. iii. For those who prefer to obtain maps in this country beforehand, the following are recommended (they will also supply, free, key maps for the French and Swiss series mentioned below): Edward Stanford, 12-14 Long Acre, London WC2E 9LH, and The Map Shop, 15 High Street, Upton-upon-Severn, Worcs, WR8 0HJ. (Maps are also of course often obtainable in bookshops in any large town.)

WESTERN ALPS (SECTIONS A–G)

The French Institut Géographique National (IGN) 1:100K maps (£4.99 1999), and the superb but expensive Swiss Landeskarten der Schweiz (LK), at the same scale, are adequate for many of the routes, especially the easier ones. They show the main footpaths, cart and jeep roads, etc. Most metalled roads are coloured on all the series given below, except for the 1:50K series of the French Alps by Didier & Richard (£8.95 1999); this is based on the discontinued IGN series at this scale, on which roads were uncoloured. The Swiss Landeskarten also cover parts of neighbouring France and Italy, notably the several routes on the Italian side of Monte Rosa. The discontinued IGN 1:50K series has been replaced, in a tourist edition for areas such as the Alps, by a series at 1:25K, and from 1999 a GPS-compatible grid of 1km squares is printed on these maps in addition to margin ticks for the French national grid. For a very few routes in NW Italy, not covered by the French or Swiss maps, there is a 1:50K series by the Istituto Geografico Centrale (IGC) of Turin.

The following table gives some details of the above maps.

		APPROX. AREA COVERED (KM)	CONTOUR INTERVAL (M)	NAT. GRID LINES	OVERLAPS
FRANCE	IGN 1:25K	29 × 22	10	GPS (1 km)	some
	D&R 1:50K	60 × 50	20	none	some
	IGN 1:100K	120 × 89	40	none	some
NW ITALY	IGC 1:50K	50 × 37	100	none	some
SWITZERLAND	LK 1:25K	17·5 × 12	10	1 km apart	none
	LK 1:50K	35 × 24	20	1 km apart	none
	LK 1:100K	70 × 48	50	10 km apart	none
	LK (tourist) 1:50K	50 × 36	20	1 km apart	some
	1:100K	107 × 70	50	10 km apart	some

EASTERN ALPS (SECTIONS H–R)

For the western part of the area, the Swiss Landeskarten der Schweiz are superb, but expensive. For Austria and the Dolomites, the Freytag & Berndt 1:50K maps are probably best; there used to be a 1:100K series too, but it has been discontinued. For Austria, the government's Österreichische Karten are very good, but cover a relatively small area. Their 1:25K series is apparently a direct enlargement of the original 1:50K series. This makes it much clearer; these maps cost little more despite the fourfold increase in size. If still available, Touring Club Italiano maps of the Dolomites are good, though roads were still uncoloured in 1980 editions. Tabacco (of Udine) do 1:25K and 1:50K series of the Dolomites, while Kompass do a 1:50K series of Austria and northern Italy, useful for areas not covered by Freytag & Berndt.

The following table gives some details of the above maps (the six-figure grid references are to 1km, not 100m as in the U.K.).

	APPROX. AREA COVERED	CONTOUR (KM)	NAT. GRID INTERVAL (M)	LINES	OVERLAPS
SWITZERLAND	LK 1:25K	17·5 × 12	10	1 km apart	none
	LK 1:50K	35 × 24	20	1 km apart	none
	LK 1:100K	70 × 48	50	10 km apart	none
	Tourist LK 1:50K	50 × 36	20	1 km apart	some
	1:100K	107 × 70	50	10 km apart	some
AUSTRIA	ÖK 1:25K	18 × 27	20	2 km apart	none
	ÖK 1:50K	18 × 27	20	2 km apart	none
	F&B 1:50K	40–60 × 38	100	none	lots
	Kompass 1:50K	48 × 43	100	none	lots
ITALY	TCI 1:50K	38 × 29	25	none	none/tiny
	F&B 1:50K	46 × 38	100	none	lots
	Tabacco 1:25K	26 × 20?	?	none?	lots?
	Tabacco 1:50K	52 × 40	50	none	lots
	Kompass 1:50K	47 × 32	100	none	lots

INDEX

KICKSTARTER THANKS

Isola Press would like to thank all the Kickstarter backers, but in particular:

Adam Aldum
Andi Gschleier
Andrew Rumble
Andy Matthews
Andy Wray
Anton Blackie
Antton Miettinen
Arnaud Jousset
Ben Mills
Brent Harrell
Bruce Davey
Caitlyn KC
Chad McWhinnie
Chris Lansley
Christoph Laska
Claus Nielsen
Damien Cebulski
Dan Heywood
David Parnell
David Prusa
Dominic Frinzi
Doomy the Froomy
Douglas Weare
Duncan Bell
Edward Summerton
Emil Holt
George Huxford
George Plumbly
Graeme Morgan
Graham Ashton
Graham Lane
Grant Hill
Guy Townsend
Heather Dawe
Hugo Gladstone
Ian Harrison

Indrek Narusk
Ives Hedderich — The Hunt Cycling
Jakob Whitfield
James Beaumont
James Covert
James Cowan
James Fairbank
James Forder
James Higgs
James Olsen
James Spackman
Janice Yang
Jo Wright
Joachim Leitenmeier
Joe Lewis
John Stocker
John W. Baker
John White
Jonathan McGarry
Jonathan Struck
Jonty Tacon
Justin Koke
Kev Willers
Martin Junghans
Mark Weldon
Mathew Grove
Matt Wenham
Matthew Toms
Mauricio Ordonez
Max Burgess
Meredith Lloyd-Evans
Mike Edwards
Mike Weyerhaeuser
Miki Vukovich
Neil Dunn
Niall Porter

Nic Clarke
Nicholas Dey
Nick Dorey
Nick Newton
Nick Purnell
Nigel Emery
Noah Collins
Oliver Wright
Ollie Butterwick
Patrik Lundberg
Paul Barnes
Paul Errington
Paul Pullinger
Phil Judge
Philip Reilly
Philipp Doms
Ray Giddins
Remon Lemmens
Robert Fargo
Ross Hallard
Scotty McMorrin
Sean Lybrand
Sebastian Bönner
Seth D. Von Gretlein
Simon Muir
Sophie Gateau
Stephen Dodson
Steve Makin
Tilo Knott
Tim Clairs
Tino Ehrich
Todd Elmer
Tony Blake
Will Armitage
William George Goddard

British Library Cataloguing-in-Publication Data:
a catalogue record for this book is available from
the British Library

The publisher welcomes any information to
correct future reprints.

978-0-9954886-2-5

First edition © Ibex Press, 2002
Second edition published by Isola Press
© Isola Press, 2018

Adventures in illustrated books: IsolaPress.com

Photographs courtesy of and © Fred Wright
Design and layout: ©Andrew Edwards

FSC
www.fsc.org
FSC® C14767

Printing and binding: Graphius
Paper: Munken Lynx

Printed in the E.U.